37 – large-scale conversion to Xtianity became as
    so low cost
49 – e.g. of Anglican shift in worship style in face of
    ~~indigena~~ capability for indigenous groups

Hegemony and Culture

*Politics and
Religious Change
among the Yoruba*

David D. Laitin

The University of Chicago Press / *Chicago & London*

The University of Chicago Press, Chicago 60637
The University of Chicago Press, Ltd., London
© 1986 by The University of Chicago
All rights reserved. Published 1986
Printed in the United States of America
95   5 4 3

Library of Congress Cataloging-in-Publication Data

Laitin, David D.
  Hegemony and culture.

  Includes index.
  1. Yorubas—Politics and government. 2. Yorubas—
Religion. I. Title.
DT515.45.Y67L35   1986   306'.089963   85-28871
ISBN 0-226-46789-9
ISBN 0-226-46790-2 (pbk.)

Chapter 3 of this book was previously published in a slightly different form as
"Conversion and Political Change: A Study of (Anglican) Christianity and
Islam among the Yorubas in Ile-Ife," in Political Anthropology Yearbook, vol.
2, ed. M. J. Aronoff, © 1983 by Transaction, Inc. Published by permission of
Transaction, Inc. Chapters 5, 6, and 7 are an expansion and development of
David D. Laitin's article "Hegemony and Religious Conflict" published in
Bringing the State Back In, ed. P. Evans, D. Rueschemeyer, and T. Skocpol
(Cambridge: Cambridge University Press, 1985).

To Marc and Anna, who cheerfully came home singing:
Ọpẹ mi koito o
Ojojumọ ni o ma dupẹ
Ọpẹ mi koito o
Ojojumọ ni o ma yọ
and of course to Delia.

Contents

Preface

The moral or ideological goal of my fifteen-year career as a student of African politics is to dispel two invidious but widely held notions about the politics of independent Africa. The first is the belief that virtually all the new states of Africa are afflicted by premodern sorts of conflicts. Political toleration and consensus, basic to democratic survival, are seen to be absent from African politics and "primordial" conflict to be rampant.[1]

The second notion that I have found repugnant was intended to be a refutation of the first, but it has its own problems. This notion has portrayed present-day tribal conflict in Africa as merely another form of instrumental action by interest groups. Any tribal group on the African political stage is seen to be performing the same function as are labor unions or chambers of commerce in the industrialized states, using whatever means possible to enhance power and wealth. Conflict in Africa is not premodern; rather, it is isomorphic with political conflict in the advanced industrial states of the West.[2]

The first view demeans the political battles that take place in Africa and ignores serious indigenous discourse about power, legitimacy, and policy. Political battles are seen as symptoms of an affliction but not important in themselves. The second view ignores the cultural milieus of Africa. When we try to interpret politics in Africa in terms of our own structures of preference and our own categories of action, we learn less about either Africans or ourselves than we do by recognizing that our political understanding is not universal but is contingent on our sociological and historical experience.

In this book I hope to demonstrate, theoretically and empirically, the limits of both of these approaches. I portray the relationship between African culture and politics as Janus-faced, and suggest that these two approaches view politics and culture from opposite directions—both thereby missing half of reality. I have tried to demonstrate that African society can be understood neither as a Hobbesian war between premodern corporate groups nor as yet another exemplification of the workings of interest group politics.

With a goal of providing a better theory of politics and culture, I aim my study primarily to the social science community. I demonstrate that, although there was a social basis for internecine religious conflict among the Yoruba of southwestern Nigeria, there has been a remarkable and long-standing toleration in Yorubaland. (So much for the disease of endless primordial conflict.) I further demonstrate that different cultural attachments entail different commonsensical approaches toward political thought and action. Instrumental action implies goal-oriented behavior; but only a theory of culture can tell us what goals are being pursued. One cannot understand Yoruba political action until one understands the cultural cues that give substance to abstract goals. (So much for primordial groups being merely interest groups.) I hope to impress on social scientists the need for new sorts of theorizing concerning the relationship between cultural membership and political action.

As a contribution to Yoruba studies, already a rich and well-documented field, this book can provide some new ideas and data. In fifteen months of field research, I have participated in and observed Anglican and Muslim worship in the city of Ile-Ife, enabling me to describe religious observance in these two Yoruba subcultures. I also meld together some oral and documentary accounts of early Christian and Muslim history in Ile-Ife. Finally, I report the results of a small sample-survey on the demographics and political ideas of local Anglicans and Muslims. My major finding, that the sociocultural division between Christian and Muslim Yorubas is far wider than most Yorubas believe, goes against the grain of the standard treatises on the topic. The more I observed the *sociocultural* divide between religious groups, the more it served for me as a testimony to the *political* toleration among the Yoruba. In light of the centuries of religious conflict in Europe and millennia of such conflict in the Middle East, Yoruba politics force the social scientist to think again about "primordial" politics and which nations practice it.

But since my primary audience is the social scientist and not the student of Yoruba society, I have tried to make Yoruba politics accessible to the generalist. This means that I had to drive over turf well known to the area specialists, and to finesse many issues that remain unsettled among experts. I cannot in any way claim to have probed the depths of Yoruba culture, which is far too extensive for me to have explored. I hope that my summaries of the secondary literature do no disservice to the field.

It might clarify matters to compare *Hegemony and Culture* with J. D. Y. Peel's exemplary *Ijeshas and Nigerians*,[3] which was published when my book was in its final stages of preparation. Peel's fieldwork was in Ilesha, which, with modern roads, is about a half-hour by car from Ile-Ife, my field site. In his study of Ilesha, Peel provides a rich and detailed account of the development of Ijesha, Yoruba, and Nigerian identities and the way those identities were shaped by wider political structures. In his chapter on party politics he reveals the fluidity of identities, given changing political opportunities. Peel brilliantly uses sociological theory to elucidate Yoruba politics.

For my purposes, there is an interesting puzzle embedded in Peel's study. Peel has for a long time been a keen student of religious adherence and change among the Yoruba. His first book, *Aladura*, focused on a modern religious movement in Yorubaland. In *Ijeshas and Nigerians*, he goes into considerable detail about conversion to Christianity and Islam and the establishment of new Christian and Muslim identities among the Ijeshas. In the description of political conflict in Ilesha, however, religion disappears. Peel shows the relative importance of town membership, lineage, and occupational group in party divisions. Nowhere in his account does the fact that Ijeshas are divided on the basis of religious attachment serve even as a hypothesis about the social basis of political divisions. The explanation for this omission is not that Peel was unaware of the religious division but, rather, that he is a sensitive student of Yoruba society. He knew that religious adherence did not play a significant role in Ilesha political battles, and that there would be nothing to observe if he hypothesized such a basis for party division!

Students of Yoruba politics have not required a serious explanation for the nonpoliticization of religious differentiation; and it is therefore not surprising that Yoruba specialists have failed to provide one.[4] But for students of culture and politics in general, the Yoruba case provides an important anomaly which, if properly researched, could advance social theory. My book does not claim to answer questions about Yoruba culture to specialists in Yoruba studies (although I hope I have provided a fresh perspective); it seeks to explain the significance of Yoruba culture and politics to a wider array of social scientists interested in the development of a comparative social theory.

I have incurred many debts in the course of writing this book. First, I have been generously supported by two different grants from the National Endowment for the Humanities, one for a summer site visit to Yorubaland in 1977, and one supporting a full year of field research in 1979–80. The University of California, San Diego, through its Committee on Research, has provided a number of very helpful grants for language training, for travel, and for manuscript preparation. The University of Ife generously provided me with an on-campus house, greatly facilitating my research.

Second, I have relied on the support of many people to develop even a rudimentary understanding of Yoruba society. I want to thank Tomi Johnson and Toyin Oloyede for teaching me my first words of Yoruba. In Nigerian universities, R. G. Armstrong, A. O. Sanda, P. Ekeh, L. Dare, A. I. Asiwaju, E. D. Adelowo, B. Hallen, R. Abiodun, and A. Oyewole, all of them with much deeper knowledge of Nigerian cultures than I can ever hope to attain, were generous in the time and critical perspective they gave me. In Ile-Ife itself, members of the church and mosque that I regularly attended were generous and welcoming. I would especially like to thank S. A. Mayowa, J. Adedire, and Alhaji Ake for guiding me through the town with such humor, even though my run-down VW beetle hardly gave them comfort.

Finally, I needed the support and stimulation of fellow social scientists in the United States, few of them specialists in Yoruba society, who helped me to think through the the theoretical issues and criticized me at every turn. Myron Aronoff, Henry Bienen, Aaron Cicourel, Ellen Comisso, Peter Cowhey, Henry Ehrmann, David Friedman, Peter Gourevitch, Davydd Greenwood, Ernst Haas, Richard Joseph, Mary Katzenstein, Peter Katzenstein, Sanford Lakoff, Arend Lijphart, Samuel Popkin, Richard Sklar, Tracy Strong, and Crawford Young all read and commented on this manuscript at many different stages. Special mention must be made of the intellectual environment of my home department at UCSD, where my colleagues are willing to learn something about societies in which they have little research interest, because they are committed to a comparative politics that is sensitive to the particularities of each society, yet asks broad and general questions about all societies.

Technical Note

Yoruba orthography. For Yoruba words I use the full Yoruba alphabet, which includes the letters ẹ (as in net), ọ (as in hot), and ṣ (corresponding to the English "sh" in most Yoruba dialects). These letters, even with the omission of tone markers, convey sufficient semantic information for Yoruba specialists' needs.

Names. Since it is not necessary, for my purposes, to convey the semantic information contained in Yoruba personal and place names, I have anglicized these. Thus Ilẹ-Ifẹ becomes Ile-Ife; Oṣogbo becomes Oshogbo; and Ọyọ becomes Oyo.

For all translations and transliterations I have relied on R. C. Abraham's incomparable *Dictionary of Modern Yoruba* (London: University of London Press, 1958). Embedded in that dictionary is an invaluable ethnography.

Money. The Nigerian naira is made up of 100 kobos. At the time of my field research (1977; 1979–80), one naira fluctuated around $1.65 for official exchanges. In purchasing power, one naira was approximately equal to one dollar.

1 | The Two Faces of Culture

In 1976, with a new draft constitution submitted to the people, Nigeria was on the road to democracy. In the previous decade the country had undergone three coups d'etat (the first of which brought down a democratically elected civilian regime), one attempted coup whose perpetrators managed to assassinate the head of state, and a bloody three-year civil war in which the federal government staved off a secession attempt by one of its regions. Using the draft constitution serving as a blueprint, a constituent assembly met in Lagos to debate, amend, and approve a final document to restore democracy to Nigeria.

These were exciting days, in large part because Nigerians themselves were writing their own constitution without having to pay obeisance to the political values of a metropole. Nigeria's first independence constitution had been written with British colonial oversight. Now Nigerians alone debated the relative merits of a "presidential" versus a "cabinet" government. They also argued over the proper constitutional role of the military, for a number of Nigerians felt that a "union" government that would give a formal role to the military might help preserve democracy. The issue that generated the most heat, however, both in the press and in the Constituent Assembly, concerned the role of the Federal Sharia Court of Appeal (FSCA) in the Second Republic.[1] Many of Nigeria's Muslims, who constitute about 50 percent of the population, saw the Sharia courts—which are the principle avenue for justice in the Muslim world—as the symbol of political freedom. Yet these same courts were seen by many Nigerian Christians as the symbol of potential Muslim domination in Nigeria. Historical experience and social science theory have taught us that religious conflicts of this sort inevitably have bloody endings. Consequently many observers feared that the religious wars that have so bedeviled Lebanon, India, and Ireland could send Nigeria once again into civil war. It was therefore a surprise to many that the vitriolic language in the halls of the Constitutent Assembly and in the Nigerian press did not lead to a religious holocaust; rather, the issue was settled amicably, with compromise, and (for what turned out to be a short, five-year period) the hope of a Nigerian democracy was preserved.

The particular issue that consumed so much time in the debate was simple. The British, following the dictates of "indirect rule," had supported and helped rationalize the Islamic court system in the Northern provinces of Nigeria from 1933 onward. Certain appeal procedures were permitted, and eventually a Muslim Court of Appeal was created. Just before independence in 1960, it was renamed the Sharia Court of Appeal by the Northern House of Assembly. Alhaji Ahmadu Bello, the Sardauna of Sokoto, leader of the Northern Peoples' Congress (NPC), and first premier of the Northern Region, subsequently sent a group of experts in Islamic law on an international mission to rethink the relationship between the Sharia and the modern state. Their report led the Sardauna to replace the entire Sharia criminal law with a secular and comprehensive criminal code, and the Sharia Court of Appeal became limited to civil cases between Muslim litigants.[2]

In 1967, however, a legal anomaly developed. As part of the federal strategy to ward off a civil war, General Yakabu Gowon, head of the federal military government, divided Nigeria into twelve states. (The strategy was not successful. The entire Eastern Region, under a single military governor, seceded from the federation and declared itself the independent republic of Biafra, thus provoking the war.) Gowon held that regional conflict would be less threatening to Nigerian unity if the states were smaller in size. The old Northern Region was split up into six different states, and some of them set up their own Sharia Courts of Appeal. But there was no longer in Nigeria, as there had been when the north was legally united, a final Court of Appeal for matters relating to Sharia law. To have created an appeals court for the states of the former Northern Region alone would have been to acknowledge the continued political existence of a Northern Region, an idea the military rulers attempted to dispel. Thus, from 1967 onward, Nigerian litigants from different states who used the Sharia courts had no centralized court of appeal. It was in reaction to this legal anomaly, and to the northern wish for a formal acknowledgement of the role of the Sharia in the Second Republic, that the Constitutional Drafting Committee recommended a Federal Sharia Court of Appeal.

The Draft Constitution of 1976 included the recommendation of the Sub-Committee on the Judicial System that "There shall be a Federal Sharia Court of Appeal which shall be an intermediate court of appeal between the States' Sharia Courts of Appeal and the Supreme Court of Nigeria."[3] Although some members of the Constitutional Drafting Committee attempted to persuade the Nigerian public that the issue was only of minor significance, the requirements of technical procedures meant that the FSCA was referred to in forty-six different paragraphs of the Draft Constitution, which, while attempting to limit the scope of the new court, gave the appearance of enlarging it.[4]

The issue had all the ingredients of a cultural clash in which political compromise is impossible.[5] Although religious issues had not previously dominated the agenda of Nigeria-wide politics, this looked like an issue which would divide all Nigerians on the basis of their religious affiliations. The political climate was hot. Many commentators of the Nigerian scene foresaw bloody religious conflict in Nigeria that would rival the Biafran war in its devastation.

The rhetoric of the debate within Nigeria were certainly ominous. A Christian scholar from the old North reflected the feelings of many non-Muslims when he criticized the "religious fanatics" in the Constitutent Assembly who were engaged in "a neo-*jihad* in disguise."[6] An equally prominent scholar from the north defended the inclusion of the Sharia appeals procedure at a national seminar on Islam and the Draft Constitution held at Bayero University, Kano, where pro-Sharia interests planned their political strategy. He argued that "Christianity had influenced the thinking, mentality and belief of our constitution makers at present and in the past," and concluded that "any guarantee of religious freedom to a Muslim will never have any degree of authenticity unless he is governed by the Sharia Law."[7] This language—"neo-*jihad*" versus "Christianization"—is the stuff for crusades which have led to blood baths elsewhere in the world.

Symbolic rhetoric rested on socioeconomic realities. Socioeconomic development is at a far higher level in the south than in the north. Although the north, due to its large estimated population, had captured political power in the center, it had less influence in the economy and the bureaucracy. Northern Muslims saw the political attempt to discredit the FSCA as an attempt by Christian southerners to expand their power in Nigeria beyond the economy and bureaucracy.

The issue was fundamentally ambiguous. The Sharia law is based on a set of particularized rules of the Islamic tradition. For example, there are taboos against charging interest in gold, rubber, and other specified items, but there is no general admonition against such charges for all traded goods. With a particularistic law, appeal courts—which normally thrive on more general rules—were often considered inappropriate in the Muslim context. Islamic legal scholars have elsewhere been comfortable with the nonuniform application of the same law in different courts. Since different strands of rules can operate simultaneously, it was usually felt, the judgment of a *kadi* determined which rule was relevant. Appeal is less crucial in a system where uniform general rules are not felt to be necessary.

To be sure, the reason there have not been appeal courts in the Islamic tradition may well be because judicial appeal procedures correlate with political and administrative centralization, rarely experienced by Islamic states.[8] The Ottoman Empire, far more centralized than earlier Islamic states, entertained appeals in the deliverance of Islamic justice. Nonetheless, institutionalized procedures were an exception rather than the rule for the application of Muslim law in the Muslim world. As mentioned earlier, in northern Nigeria it was the British and not the *kadis* who first promoted appeal procedures for the Muslim courts.

Hence the ambiguity. On one hand, non-Muslims in Nigeria could reasonably ask why northern Muslims were pushing for an institution which was hardly central to the Islamic experience. Undoubtedly, this made many non-Muslims suspicious that the FSCA question was the tip of the iceberg and should be circumvented before Muslim claims for an ever expanding role for Sharia law penetrated the whole ship of state. On the other hand, Muslims could equally ask why unsympathetic members of the Constituent Assembly (MCAs) should object to a court which would redress an administrative anomaly and not encroach upon the rights of any Nigerian who did not wish his case to be heard by a Sharia court. The ambiguity of the issue helped feed the suspicions of both sides.

In the debate of the Constituent Assembly, the Sharia issue easily overshadowed questions concerning the applicability of the presidential system to Nigeria or methods of electing representatives. The Reverend Joseph Agbowuro (Ondo) ruefully noted that the chairman of the Constitutional Drafting Committee had "spent 45 percent of his time on the explosive issue of Sharia which unfortunately has engulfed the nation"(c. 55). Dr. I. Abubaker, who later would serve on the Adebo subcommittee that worked out a final compromise—claimed he would "have just a word on the Sharia. We are all witnesses to the fact that since the debate started in this House about four days ago, the question of Sharia has dominated the discussions" (c. 274–77). Despite his promise of a "word," the Sharia controversy dominated his presentation as well. The next speaker, Mohammed Buba Ahmed (Bauchi), felt that the real problems facing Nigeria were economic, and claimed to be astonished when he "woke up this morning to find that religion is trying to divide us":

> Mr. Chairman, Sir, I was in London two weeks ago and the *Financial Times* . . . came out with an article grouping Nigeria as one of the countries that is bound to go into bloodshed because of religious differences. Last Sunday, Mr. Chairman, Sir, I also read in the *Observer* of London that religion is bound to divide us in this country. Now I am imploring the Members of this House, our Reverend Fathers, our Mallams, and our Imams, . . . please prove these foreigners wrong. (c. 278–83)

Speakers in the debate were not considered finished unless they had addressed themselves to the FSCA. When one particularly long-winded and incoherent speaker was testing the audience's patience, an MCA, trying to get him to finish, urged him to "go to Sharia" (c. 1022). Exasperated over the protracted wrangling another member, Alhaji Umaru Muhammed Bab (Gongola), admitted: "I certainly wonder, if after all, the Army should just continue" (c. 1477).

The political divide on this issue pitted the Muslims of the far north against the Christians of the region between the far north and the south, today constituting Benue, Plateau, and Gongola states. I shall refer to these states as constituting the Middle Belt, even though its boundaries, in Nigerian discourse, are somewhat more extensive.[9] The Middle Belt is religiously diverse, having many adherents to Christianity, Islam, and traditional religions. Nonetheless, these states were part of the Northern Region until its breakup amid the Civil War in 1967. The obvious political strategy for both pro-and anti-FSCA forces was to increase support for their positions by recruiting from the south. In the old Eastern Region (now Anambra, Imo, Rivers, and Cross River states), where Islam had never penetrated, delegates viewed the Sharia issue with insouciant contempt. In Yorubaland, however, delegates took a keen interest in the debate. The Yorubas—those delegates from Lagos, Oyo, Ogun, and Ondo states, with significant representation in Kwara State—represented a population evenly divided between Christians and Muslims. Some fifteen million Yorubas constitute abut <u>20 percent</u> of Nigeria's population[10] and were thus a political force to be reckoned with. Northern and Middle Belt delegates actively sought Yoruba support for their different positions.

The swing potentiality of Yorubaland (known as the Western Region in Nigeria's First Republic) was clearly understood by the northern delegates. Consider this analysis by Alhaji Yinusa Paiko (Niger) in his presentation to the Constituent Assembly:

> This is the position [to deny the FSCA] of my brothers and sisters who happen to represent the four Western States of this country . . . I would insist that anything up to 40 percent of that population is indeed Muslim. Unfortunately, what is the nature of the representation which that population has received in this House? I do not believe that out of about 30 or more members here there are more than five Muslims representing that area.
> *An Hon. Member*: That is a lie.
> *Alhaji Paiko*: But why? Simply because the Muslim population for so long in these areas have gone to Missionary Schools . . . The representatives who by default have returned to this Assembly being Christians, are now afraid that this 40 percent of Muslim population as soon as they see any mention of Sharia Court of Appeal in the Constitution, will go back and say they want an *alkali*

court. That, to my mind, is the secret, the bottom of their fear about this issue . . . Simply because they have dominated a significant portion of their population for so long and terrorised them into accepting their system of justice for so long, is no reason for you to oppose the correction of that evil. You should not be afraid to have the Sharia Court of Appeal simply because you own . . . [cut off by the Chairman].

From the material I shall present in chapter 6, it will become clear that Alhaji Paiko was not substantially wrong in his numbers. What was wrong was his social and political analysis. He mistakenly assumed that the religious divide was the deepest cleavage throughout Nigerian society and that Christian oppression had prevented the politicization of religion in Yorubaland.

CULTURAL DIVISIONS WITHIN NIGERIA

Despite Alhaji Paiko's assumption that religion is the major divide in Nigerian society, a variety of sociocultural cleavages have cut the Nigerian population in diverse ways. To illustrate this point, let us look at two different cuts in Nigerian society—one based on tribe, the other on religion. At the time of independence, each of Nigeria's three regions was led by a major tribal group: in the north, the Hausa-Fulanis; in the east, the Igbos; and in the west, the Yorubas (see map 1-1). Each of the regions had different interests, and national politics involved bargaining among the three "majority" tribes. In the late colonial period, the association between tribe and party (the AG for the Yorubas; the NPC for the Hausa-Fulanis; and the NCNC for the Igbos) became progressively more solid, leading may observers to interpret Nigerian politics solely in terms of tribal divisions.

Religious attachment cut Nigerian society in a slightly different way (see map 1-1). The religious cleavage divided Nigeria's Muslims from its Christians, a cleavage that only imperfectly coincided with tribe. Southerners were most subject to Christian evangelization and education, and many were literate in English. They therefore became dominant in the colonial civil service, much to the chagrin of the Muslim leaders in the north, who feared, as independence approached, that they would be ruled by Christian Nigerians from the south. Meanwhile, southerners feared that the Muslims would form a demographic majority, which would permit the (Muslim, backward) northerners to rule over the (Christian, progressive) southerners. Nigeria divided by tribe contained three regions; divided by religion, two regions. Tribe and religion each cut the Nigerian population into different slices.

Both the Nigeria of three tribes and the Nigeria of two religions repre-

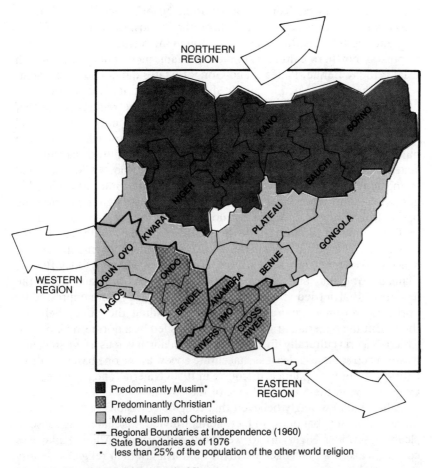

NORTHERN
REGION

WESTERN
REGION

EASTERN
REGION

■ Predominantly Muslim*
▨ Predominantly Christian*
☐ Mixed Muslim and Christian
— Regional Boundaries at Independence (1960)
— State Boundaries as of 1976
* less than 25% of the population of the other world religion

Map 1.1 The World Religions in Nigeria

sented only partial sociocultural truths and inadequately describe the cultural reality of Nigeria. The three major tribes were themselves of recent historical vintage. The idea that there was a single Hausa-Fulani tribe, for example, was largely a political claim by the leadership of the NPC in their battle against the south. Similarly the notions of "Yoruba" and "Igbo" were created from nineteenth-century political experience. Many elders intimately involved in rural Yoruba society today recall that, as late as the 1930s, "Yoruba" was not a common form of political identification.[11] Nigerian tribes are not well-defined, closed corporate groups. Nnamdi Azikiwe, an Igbo, achieved great popularity in the Yoruba city of Lagos, where he edited his nationalist paper, the *West African Pilot*. It was only subsequent political maneuverings that led him to be defined in Nigeria as an *Igbo* leader. Furthermore, the three tribes constitute perhaps no more than two-thirds of the Nigerian population.[12] In the south, minority tribes include the Efiks, the Ibibios, the Edos, the Urhobos, and the Itsekiris. In the north, although the reigning NPC attempted to portray northern culture as unified in Islam, many minority groups in what is today Benue, Plateau, and Gongola states did not consider themselves either Hausas or Fulanis. In the 1950s, minority leaders appealed unsuccessfully to the British for the break-up of the regions, since that would allow members of the minority tribes opportunities for political leadership in smaller units. As the 1967–70 civil war approached, it was the minorities who most feared the break-up of Nigeria into three separate states, and they saw in Gowon (from a minority tribe, a Christian, and from the north) someone who would represent their interests. Thus Nigeria divided by allegiances to three major tribes, though it did form the basis of party alignments, did not do justice to the socio-culture reality.

The notion of the Muslim north and the Christian south has its own anomalies. The Yorubas are in the south, yet about 40 percent of them are Muslim. And many northern groups, especially in what are today Benue, Plateau, Gongola, and Kwara states, are largely Christian. When the leaders of Biafra tried to convince the world that they were oppressed by northern Muslims, ignorant foreigners (including the pope) believed them. But the Nigerian army, as we saw, was led by a northern Christian. Thus a Nigeria culturally divided by a Muslim north versus a Christian and westernized south is at least as inaccurate a view as the one based on three tribes; yet it infused political discourse in 1950s Nigeria[13] and reemerged, as we just saw, in the Sharia debates of the 1970s.

Alhaji Paiko wrongly believed that religious divisions in Nigeria were more real than tribal ones. In fact, neither divide was real in the sense of cleanly ascribing Nigerians to well-bounded groups. Alhaji Paiko was correct in his view that Nigerians in the far north saw their religious identity as a central component of their overall identity. But that view was incorrect for the Yorubas. In the Constituent Assembly and in the context of Nigerian politics of the late 1970s, they saw themselves primarily in terms of their "tribe." His error raises a crucial issue for sociological analysis. Under what conditions does a single cultural divide in a society come to be seen as deep, while other cultural divides come to be seen as shallow and unimportant for collective political action? Yorubas were members of a tribe as well as a world religion; why was the former but not the latter a key element in their personal identities? To answer this important sociological question is a central purpose of this book.

POLITICAL ANALYSIS OF THE SHARIA ISSUE

Alhaji Paiko's political claim was that the Christian Yorubas, economically but not demographically dominant in Yorubaland, opposed the recognition of an FSCA for fear that it might plant the seed for a Muslim political awakening in the Yoruba states. His view, that of a political strategist seeking to advise Muslim Yorubas on how to enhance their bargaining power in the electoral politics, showed a complete misunderstanding of Yoruba politics, as we shall now see as we observe how Yoruba MCAs handled the Sharia issue.

To analyze the Sharia debate systematically, each MCA can be coded based on whether he took a "moderate" or an "extreme" position. Moderates included both pro-FSCA members who acknowledged the difficulties involved yet supported the FSCA as the best companies and anti-FSCA members who emphasized the technical problems involved in the proposal but did not rule out some accommodation. Extremists took heavily ideological positions, sometimes threatening the opposition. Eighty percent of the solid Muslim north (Kano, Niger, Sokoto, Borno, Kaduna, and Bauchi states) and 77.8 percent of the Middle Belt delegates took extreme positions. Between the Muslims of the north (including those in the Middle Belt) and the Christians of the Middle Belt, the battle lines were drawn.

Yorubas, however, were the least extreme on this religious issue. Seventy-six percent of them took moderate positions. Furthermore, more Yoruba delegates suggested new compromises and more took renegade positions (that is, support of the FSCA, though they were Christians, opposition though Muslims) than any other group in the Constituent Assembly. Among the Yoruba members nominated by the Supreme Military Council (and not voted in by the people), 40 percent suggested new compromises and 20 percent were renegades. The chairman of the Constitutional Drafting Committee, Rotimi Williams, who had defended the original compromise, is a Yoruba; so also is Simeon Adebo, the chairman of the subcommittee which proposed the final compromise, as well as three members—one Muslim, two Christians—who had all taken "moderate" positions on the Sharia issue in the general debate. In other words, the Yoruba delegates created the ideological underpinning that permitted the Second Republic to become established without bipolar religious conflict. In the final compromise, appeals from the state Sharia courts could be heard by a panel of judges who were "versed in Islamic law," and chosen from the (secular) Federal Court of Appeal.[14]

The Yoruba people are divided religiously. As Alhaji Paiko intimated, Muslim Yorubas had done far less well economically than their Christian counterparts. Here was an opportunity for the Muslim Yorubas to join in an alliance with northern Muslims to counter, in Paiko's terminology, Christian domination. Yet the Christian-Muslim divide in Yorubaland, far from fanning the flames of religious conflict in Nigeria, actually built the foundation for compromise. From the outside, this looks to be a case of unnatural toleration.

To be sure, there was never a Sharia court system in existence in most of Yorubaland in the colonial period. Therefore it could be argued that the Muslim Yorubas had no interest in consolidating the system nationally and that Christian Yorubas had no real fear of being subjected to the system's dictates. But this acknowledgment does not fully explain Yoruba moderation on the Sharia issue, because the Yoruba delegates from Kwara State (the old Ilorin emirate), which was also (as was the Middle Belt) administrated as part of the Northern Region, were equally moderate. The emirs of Ilorin were Fulani; the people were Yoruba. By the logic of the Middle Belt, one would expect Kwara Christians to perceive the Nigerian Federation as a mechanism to avoid the oppressive rule of the Muslim north. Although only seven members of the Kwara delegation spoke, making statistical analysis unreliable, the following presentation gives the flavor of religious politics among Kwara Yorubas:

> A. B. Awoniyi: . . . Suffice it to say that I am a Christian, and it is significant that of the nine of us from the State I come from, there are only two of us here who are Christians. The rest [are] Muslims . . . I attended a Secondary School in which in my last year among 360 students only 26 of us were Christians . . . as House Captain I had to go and wake up my Muslim boys to go and take their morning meals during the Ramadan. I have no problem with religion whatsoever, and I beg us not to introduce religious controversy in anything we do. (c. 440)

Although Awoniyi praised the local Sharia courts as efficient and used by Christians, he asked for a new committee to fashion another compromise on the FSCA. Other Kwara delegates followed suit. In Kwara State, as in the Middle Belt, many Christians perceived Hausa-Fulani rule as foreign, and there is a long history of Kwara Yorubas seeking autonomy from the North. Christian Yorubas from Kwara might well have seen the FSCA in the same light as the Christians from the Middle Belt. But they did not. Certainly they showed no fear of Yoruba Muslims, as Alhaji Paiko had suggested.

Yorubas, then, were not recruited by agents of either side to further polarize Nigeria on the religious dimension. Furthermore, they took compromise positions gratuitously, taking no political advantage of their insouciance on the issue. Some cynics have suggested that certain Yoruba individuals were "bought off" on the issue; but that can hardly explain away the many Christian Yorubas who were moderate or even renegades, and who then went into the electoral arena in bitter opposition to the National Party of Nigeria (NPN), the party built from a base of far northern interests.

The Yorubas are well known in Nigeria for playing politics with keen strategy. Yet on this issue, they performed a mighty service and exacted no price for it. A political analyst might ask why the Yorubas did not press leading northerners for a commitment to universal free education (a key plank of the Unity Party of Nigeria, the UPN, whose center was in Yorubaland) as a price for Yoruba support of an FSCA; or even for the recruitment of a prominent northern politician into the UPN, which failed to win the presidency in the Second Republic in large part because of lack of support in the northern states. In the case of the FSCA, Yorubas were given the historical opportunity to realign their identities according to their religious affiliations. It was not for lack of opportunity that religion failed to become politicized in Yorubaland.

CULTURE'S TWO FACES

The Yoruba role in the historic Sharia debate compels us to consider the two faces of culture. First, we must ask how *culture orders political priorities*. Do people who share a culture also share a set of values about what goals are most important to pursue? What does it mean for someone to see himself as a "Yoruba" or "Muslim"? Do Muslims mean something different from Christians when they call for justice? Will Christian and Muslim Yorubas develop different sets of values and beliefs based on their religious difference? When arguing about Sharia courts, were Nigerians debating ideas of justice? What sort of justice would those courts promote, and how would it be different from that provided by the secular courts? These questions concerning values address culture's first face.

But culture is Janus-faced. The Sharia debate makes us recognize that *shared cultural identities facilitate collective action*, for people who share a culture can communicate with each other more easily. The persistence of cultural politics in Nigeria—with Yorubas, Hausas, Igbos, and other nationality groups providing the fundamental basis for membership in party politics—demonstrates the organizational potential of groups whose members share a culture. Cultural identity becomes a political resource. Political entrepreneurs recognize that through appeals to culture they can easily attract mass followings. Individuals learn that by modifying their cultural identities they can improve their life chances. The political power inherent in shared cultural symbols is what lies behind the machiavellian smile of culture's second face.

Present-day social scientists have adopted a division of labor in order to theorize about culture. Social systems theorists focus on culture's first face. Believing that culture is deeply influential and that its embedded values affect political and economic behavior, these theorists attempt to specify the links between cultural meanings (embedded in symbols) and political or economic behavior. To demonstrate the tenacity of culture, these theorists hold that cultural identities are primordial and self-reinforcing and that they provide ideological guidelines for collective action. Emphasis on the effects of cultural "meanings" on behavior is the hallmark of the social systems theorists' approach.

Rational choice theorists have examined culture's second face. They postulate that individuals are utility maximizers and will therefore manipulate their cultural identities in order to enhance their power and wealth. The study of the political use of shared cultural symbols is the rational choice theorists' approach.

These two schools offer only partial analyses of the role of culture in politics. When only one face of culture is addressed, the other gets lost. For example, in analyzing the success of the Ayatollah Khomeini in his revolution overthrowing the Pahlavi dynasty in Iran, students of the first face of culture have emphasized the tenacity of Shi'ite Islam and its calls for religious purification. These students conclude that culture has great influence over mass behavior. Students of the second face, however, have contended that the basis of the Ayatollah's mass following, the entrepreneurs of the *bazaar*, followed and acted as true believers not because they believed deeply in Islam but rather because they were threatened economically by the shah's policies, and thought Khomeini would permit them to trade freely. For them, cultural symbols were an instrument to fight a class war. Can both views be right? How does one reconcile the opposite interpretations of these two schools?

AN ANTHROPOLOGICAL DIALOGUE: GEERTZ VERSUS COHEN

It is principally the anthropologists who have attempted to apprehend Janus-faced culture in both its guises, but without great success. The two schools of culture continue to face each other in bewilderment, in large part because the two traditions have such different theoretical and methodological commitments. Social systems theory builds upon the sociological foundations laid by Max Weber, while rational choice theory extends the economic paradigm of Jeremy Bentham. In Chapters 2 and 5 I shall discuss the Weberian and the Benthamite frameworks; but for introductory purposes the epistemological bases of the social systems and rational choice perspectives are best highlighted through a comparison of the work of two current anthropologists, Clifford Geertz and Abner Cohen.[15]

In his definition of culture, Geertz, relying on Weber, sees it as those "webs of significance" that man has spun and in which we are all suspended. (*IC*, p. 5). What we (or a Balinese cockfighter or a Jewish shopkeeper) mean by justice, by power, by authority, by love, by change, is unavoidably symbolic. Ultimately, symbols are important because they provide to individuals a sense of meaning. For Geertz, these symbols or, better, the various systems of symbols constitute "culture."

Culture is therefore divided into a set of "subsystems." Although

Geertz is not himself explicit about the components of a cultural subsystem, it is possible to elicit from his essays a sense of what they are. Cultural subsystems are those aspects of collective life which (a) are shared across classes; (b) differentiate a collectivity from other collectivities; (c) are not necessary for species survival; (d) have continuity amid economic change; (e) provide significance to events, and goals for collective action; (f) rely on the production and use of symbols; and (g) become institutionalized into "systems" of patterned activity. Religion and language, as well as kinship and art, are examples of cultural subsystems.[16]

For Abner Cohen, a culture group simply has a "special style of life or a special combination of a variety of symbolic formations, that distinguish it from the rest of the society." (*TDM*, p. 91). Culture is important largely because a great number of people *share* a set of symbolic forms. Not symbolic meaning but symbolic sharing is the key to Cohen's analysis. This sharing makes them a natural group for social and political action.

Not only do Geertz and Cohen disagree about what constitutes culture, they disagree as well about its significance. For Geertz, culture is both a constraint and an opportunity, for it not only (remember the Weberian web) locks man into a certain approach to life but also provides answers to the deepest questions about the meaning of life (why, for instance, less rain falls on the unjust, and how that "unjust fella" was able to procure the just man's umbrella) (*IC*, p. 106). In other words, it tackles the problem of theodicy. For Cohen, although symbols do provide meaning, or at least a sense of what ought to be done, the significance of symbols lies in their ambiguity and hence, their manipulatability by groups to enhance their political and economic power. Symbols, then, are resources for groups to help them to solve a variety of political problems (*TDM*, p. 85).

The methodological implications of these differences for anthropological research are considerable. Geertz advocates the "interpretation" of cultures, which is sometimes portrayed as an activity similar to the interpretation of great literature or art (*IC*, p. 213, and the discussion of metaphor) and sometimes as a kind of medical diagnosis, involving a detailed description of a situation from an actor orientation, followed by specification (identifying the meaning of the observations for a particular society and for social life generally).

Cohen will not settle for interpretation or even diagnosis, but seeks instead "to probe into the nature of politico-symbolic causation" (*TDM*, p. 39). With a statement that most positivists would agree to, Cohen seeks to separate analytically abstract variables—namely, the "power order" and the "symbolic order"—so that he can discern the social conditions under which each of these variables influences the other. He is concerned less with interpretation than with causal relationships among abstract variables.

Other methodological differences follow. Whereas Cohen seeks the articulation of abstract categories to make generalizations across cultures possible (for example, the cousinhood or the long-distance trader), Geertz avoids abstraction and even generality by drawing "delicate distinctions" (*IC*, p. 25). Geertz derives methodological delight from distinguishing the variety of themes of violence—"animal savagery, male narcissism, opponent gambling, status rivalry, mass excitement, blood sacrifice" (*IC*, p. 449)—that can be spun together in a single cockfight. For Cohen, each distinction reduces the possibility of verifiable causal laws: the more the categories, the fewer the cases. For Geertz, causal laws are chimeras (*IC*, p. 14) and abstract categories hide rather than elucidate meaning.

How, then, can Geertz verify his interpretations? Cohen criticizes Geertz's methodology because its "formulations have often been conjectural, non-verifiable, non-cumulative, 'meanings' attributed to symbols and are mostly arrived at by sheer intuition and individual guesswork" (*TDM*, p. 5). Cohen seeks verifiability in his own formulations so that future scholars may know what evidence must be adduced in order to disconfirm his casual statements. It should be clear to any reader of Geertz that while one can ignore, ridicule, savor, or reject his interpretations, one would not know how to invalidate them. Geertz would certainly agree to this: he prefers the "appraisal" (*IC*, p. 16) of interpretations to their verification, and instead of the cumulative development of theory he seeks the "refinement of debate. What gets better is the precision with which we [anthropologists] vex each other." For Cohen, good theory can be verified or disconfirmed; for Geertz, good theory enables us to write about social life with more penetration.

"The essential vocation of interpretive anthropology," Geertz concludes in his essay "Thick Description," "is not to answer our deepest questions, but to make available to us answers that others, guarding other sheep in other valleys, have given" (*IC*, p. 30). And the reason we want to hear their answers is "to enlarge the universe of human discourse" (*IC*, p. 14). When we think about "pride" in social life, we can no longer avoid the case of the Jewish shopkeeper (named Cohen) in Morocco who demanded his payment for a wrong done to him by a Berber group. He was insured by another Berber group and went with his agents to collect sheep as payment. "The two armed Berber groups then lined up on their horses at opposite ends of the plain," Geertz records, "with the sheep herded between them, and Cohen, in his black gown, pillbox hat, and flapping slippers, went out alone among the sheep, picking out, one by one and at his own good speed, the best ones for his payment" (*IC*, p. 8). Nor, in thinking about "ideology," can we omit the case of Sukarno, who vainly tried to recreate the image of the *nagara*, the "exemplary center" of the Javanese state, for the purpose of giving direction to (1964) Indonesia (*IC*, pp. 222–24). We have no causal theory about pride or ideology from these cases; but they enlarge our repertoire as we try to enrich our understanding of "Pride" and "Ideology."

Cohen's purposes (now those of the social anthropologist but equally those of the trader) are of course very different from Geertz's. "The challenge to social anthropology today," Cohen concludes in his study of Hausa migrants, "is the study of sociocultural change, of the involvement of custom in the change of social relations . . . We seek to answer the broad question: Under what structural conditions, what customs, will perform what political functions, within which political unit?"[17] Cohen asks us to see secret masonic orders in Sierra Leone not as a reflection of Creole values about information but as a Creole response to a difficult dilemma. These Creoles required hierarchical organization to further their political and economic aims, but they also, because they were a cultural minority in a newly formed democratic polity, needed to maintain a low profile. Secret masonic orders were a rational response to this structural dilemma (*TDM*, pp. 106–10). Similarly, in considering antiwar demonstrations in the United States of the 1960s, when apparently well-educated people blindly chanted "Ho! Ho! Ho Chi Minh," Cohen describes these chants not as childish nonsense but as a ritual that enabled leaders of the antiwar movement to create organizational solidarity (*TDM*, p. 135). Once we see that Sierra Leone Creoles, Hausa migrants in Yoruba towns, and American antiwar demonstrators face similar organizational problems, and respond to these problems in similar ways, we can begin to construct a general, and causally informed, theory about the role of symbolic manipulation for the attainment of social, political, and economic ends. This is Cohen's vision.

Geertz and Cohen are anthropological virtuosos. Each has developed his own methodology to examine culture. Cohen has been able to address culture's "second face" through his examination of the strategic manipulation of symbols by political actors in order to enhance their political power. Culture is a resource for political entrepreneurs; it provides a plethora of shared symbols. Among a large number of people who are otherwise divided among themselves, these symbols serve to create cohesion as well as to sustain political communication. Political entrepreneurs in all societies are rational when they use these shared symbols to enhance group cohesion. Through this modified rational-choice approach,[18] Cohen is able to get a grip on the mechanisms through which people identify with a group in order to take collective action—the second face of culture.

But Cohen's methodology is less successful in addressing the first face of culture. How does he find out what the preference functions of a cultural group will be, given the fact that they share a set of symbols? All people may want wealth and power; but they may also want security, participation, love, and community. To assume that all people will act rationally to maximize their goals cannot tell us what goals are more important for an individual, or for a cultural group. How can students with Cohen's orientation discern the nature of group values?

Rational choice theory has no easy answer to this question. As Graham Allison has pointed out in another context, any set of actions can be made to appear rational if the investigator is permitted to define the goal. Allison demonstrated that virtually any set of actions by Soviet leaders could prove to American deterrence thinkers that their adversaries had been brilliant maximizers.[19] Without access to independently derived data about actor preferences, rational choice theorists cannot verify the rationality of political actors.

Here is where Geertz's thick descriptions of symbolic systems become methodologically useful. Anthropological description is, if anything, the result of a careful examination of the deeply held values of a cultural group. The data base consists in symbolic structures. Only with a keen understanding of the meanings embedded in shared symbols—the first face of culture—can one adduce cultural preferences without tautologically claiming that preferences can be derived from the behavior of actors who are assumed to be rational.

Meaning, values, and preferences are embedded in symbolic structures. To understand how symbolic structures guide political preferences is to appreciate the first face of culture. The fact that people share these symbolic structures (whatever the meaning inherent in them) is itself a political resource. People who share symbols tend to be influenced by political entrepreneurs who employ them and find themselves better able to communicate with others who are equally responsive to them. Furthermore, the sharing of symbols creates an aura of political trust. To understand the political implications for collective action of the sharing of symbols is to appreciate the second face of culture.

In the course of this book, it will be shown in what ways Geertz's premises about social systems are inadequate to appreciate fully the dynamics of meaning that engage his attention. It will also be shown why Cohen's rational actor approach is not fully equipped to study the role of symbol sharing for collective action that is his particular focus. Yet both these anthropologists have made significant inroads in clarifying the problematics associated with culture. It is the goal of this book not only to amend Geertz's and Cohen's theories but also to develop an appreciation of both faces of culture from a single theoretical viewpoint.

The Two Yoruba Problematics

Yorubas can be categorized on the basis of their tribe or their adherence to one of the world religions. Their symbolic attachments to "ancestral cities" (often referred to as subtribes), remains powerful. The largest of the ancestral cities are those urban kingdoms that were, in Yoruba traditions, conquered by different sons of Oduduwa, the mythical progenitor of the Yoruba peoples. The peoples of the various city-kingdoms have distinct dialects, political institutions, facial markings, and religious practices. Although all of these city-kingdoms were part of a common culture zone, cultural differences among them are marked, and virtually all Yorubas see their attachment to an ancestral city as a key aspect of their identity. In reality, many Yoruba families and even whole lineages have not lived in "their" ancestral cities for generations, but the symbolic attachment to them remains strong.1 In Yoruba social life and politics, an individual's connection to an ancestral city provides an important clue to his political leanings.[20]

Over the past century the Yorubas have become divided on the basis of their religious attachment. About half have converted to Christianity, half to Islam. Devout adherents of both religions order their private lives within the symbolic frameworks of these two world religions. Nonetheless, as we have seen, members of neither group are led to organize politically on the basis of their religious affiliation. The symbolic messages inherent in each of the two religions have virtually no role in Yoruba political discourse and have led to no political conflict between adherents of the two religions (see map 1.2)

The Yoruba context allows us to pose two interrelated problematics, which will form the empirical foundation for this book. First, in what ways, after a century of differential religious experience, have Christian and Muslim Yorubas become different in the way they think about politics, and in the meaning they give to political concepts? Second, why, after a century of religious differentiation, when opportunities for success were clearly different for members of each of the two world religions, has religion not become a basis for collective political action in Yorubaland?

The Search for Explanation

The initial theoretical focus for addressing the question of the *meaning* of religious change—my first problematic—was on the "social systems" approach exemplified by Geertz. Talcott Parsons and his collaborators envisioned society as a complex web of social subsystems and suggested that exogenous change on any subsystem would yield concomitant changes in other subsystems so that equilibrium would be achieved. Subsystems have to be "congruent" in order for there to be a healthy social system.[21]

Research cumulated when a change was identified in one social subsystem, allowing the ramifying effects of that change to be observed on other subsystems. The model study was Weber's *Protestant Ethic and the Spirit of Capitalism*; changes in religion had an "elective affinity" with a different approach toward work and accumulation. The economic subsystem ad-

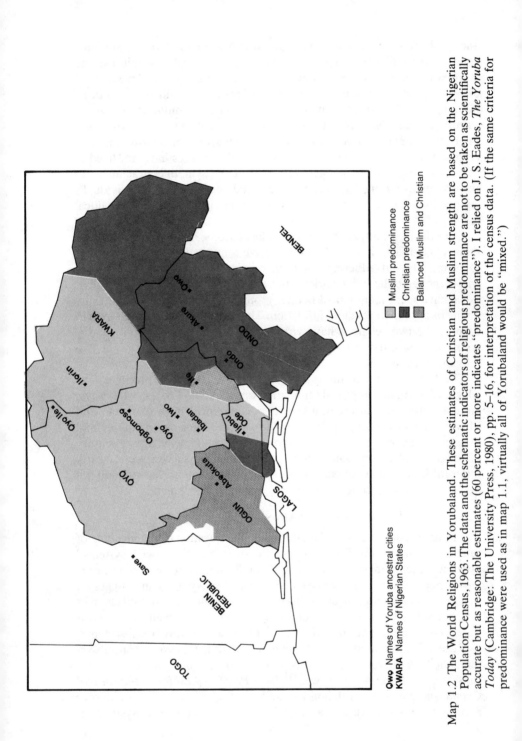

Map 1.2 The World Religions in Yorubaland. These estimates of Christian and Muslim strength are based on the Nigerian Population Census, 1963. The data and the schematic indicators of religious predominance are not to be taken as scientifically accurate but as reasonable estimates (60 percent or more indicates "predominance"). I relied on J. S. Eades, *The Yoruba Today* (Cambridge: The University Press, 1980), pp. 5–16, for interpretation of the census data. (If the same criteria for predominance were used as in map 1.1, virtually all of Yorubaland would be "mixed.")

justed, or became congruent with, the changed religious subsystem. This same research tradition guided my research in *Politics, Language, and Thought: The Somali Experience*,[22] where I found that a change in the official language of political discourse could be associated with parallel changes in the way Somalis thought and acted politically. Those seeking to study "political culture" have therefore attempted to trace the impact of changes in a cultural subsystem on the political system.

Social systems theory and its application to religious change in Yorubaland will be elaborated in chapter 2, the theoretical introduction to part 1 of this study. For present purposes, it is enough to point out that some basic suppositions of social systems theory are put in question. Instead of finding adjustment of the political framework in the face of vast religious change, I found that the symbols generated by the mosque and the church were thoroughly contained within the religious subsystems. Subsystems did not automatically adjust to each other. Instead of finding any move toward congruence, I found that in Yorubaland religious symbols were constrained, while another cultural division—that based on membership of different ancestral cities—clearly informed practical life. In Marshall Sahlins's terms, there was "a privileged institutional locus of the symbolic process, whence emanates a classificatory grid imposed upon the total culture."[23]

To understand how one arena of symbolic production gets its privileged position, I began to explore the concept of "hegemony." Borrowing from the work of Antonio Gramsci, I define hegemony as *the political forging— whether through coercion or elite bargaining—and institutionalization of a pattern of group activity in a state and the concurrent idealization of that schema into a dominant symbolic framework that reigns as common sense.*[24] The research findings in part 1 demonstrate, consistent with social systems theory, that cultural subsystems *do* contain symbolic repertoires that provide social meaning. Inconsistent with social systems theory, however, these repertoires do not automatically create readjustment in other subsystems. To understand the basis for meaning in a society, one must seek the values embedded in the dominant or hegemonic subsystem.

If social systems theory requires adjustment to address the first face of culture, rational choice theory requires adjustment as well to address culture's second face. Rational choice theory and its relevance to the Yoruba case will be examined in chapter 5, the theoretical introduction to part 2. There we will see that the persuasive and dominant "rational choice" theory exemplified by Cohen's work proves inadequate to explain the second problematic of the nonpoliticization of religion in Yorubaland. If one assumes, as rational choice theorists do, that individuals will reformulate their identities, given their cultural resources, to maximize their opportunities for power and wealth, then the nonpoliticization of the

Yoruba Muslims as *Muslims* becomes an intriguing anomaly. As we saw in the Sharia debate, there was less manipulation of cultural identity than a rational choice perspective might have led us to expect. I found that Muslim Yorubas refused to calculate the potential gains possible that might be attained through the creative readjustment of their identities. Why should this be so?

To address this question, I reinterpret British colonization (in chapter 7) as a form of external hegemony that reinvested "ancestral city" with political reality. The imposition of a system of stratification by a hegemon gave the resulting set of group indentifications a sense of being real or obvious. Under certain conditions, hegemons are capable of reifying certain patterns of social stratification; they can use their power to manipulate and petrify individual identities. The reification of "ancestral city" at the expense of "religion," as the data in part 2 demonstrate, helps explain the long-term nonpoliticization of religion among the Yoruba.

A successful explanation for the pattern of political culture that exists in Yorubaland would have to account for the features associated with both faces of culture. Social systems theories that could explain religious differentiation between Christian and Muslim Yorubas but wrongly predicted the politicization of religious differentiation would be inadequate. Similarly, rational choice theories that could explain the nonpoliticization of religious cleavages but not the different political meanings associated with conversion to Christianity and Islam in Yorubaland would also be inadequate. In my case study, I found that neither theory made correct predictions in its preferred realm. It was the need for a general theory of culture and politics, as well as the inadequacy of the two theoretical traditions on their own turf, that led me to develop the model of hegemony and culture.

I | The First Face of Culture

2 | The Weberian Tradition

> It is a great sight, for a Muslim, to see a Christian town for the
> first time. I am not talking about the things which strike every-
> one straight away, such as the differences in architecture, or
> clothes, or way of life. Even in the slightest trivialities there is
> something curious, which I feel and cannot express.
>
> Letter from Usbek to Ibben
> in Montesquieu's *Persian Letters*.

Montesquieu believed that religion, as one aspect of culture, influenced
political and social life. He was therefore one of the earliest students of the
first face of culture. But Montesquieu's own formulations were hardly
better than Usbek's, who was Montesquieu's caricature of an itinerant
social scientist. For example, in his *Spirit of the Laws*, Montesquieu
wrongly reasoned that, "as [Christianity] forbids the plurality of wives, its
princes . . . have more humanity . . . and [this] has hindered despotic power
from being established in Ethiopia."[1] Good analysis of the political consequences of religious differentiation would require a stronger social
theory.

The goal of this chapter is to provide a theoretical base so that the
differential impact of Islam and Christianity in Yorubaland—that is, the
first face of culture—can be examined systematically. Although the work
of Clifford Geertz was cited in chapter 1 as highlighting this aspect of
culture, Geertz's methodological predilections have led him to shy away
from postulating that a world religion can have a systematic and generaliz-
able impact on politics and society. In fact, in his *Islam Observed*, Geertz
demonstrates that the same world religion can have nearly opposite impacts in two different countries.[2]

Without denying the cogency of Geertz's demonstration that Islam in
Indonesia and Morocco embody divergent values and transmit different
symbols, I still believe it worthwhile to posit that the various religious
communities that claim to follow a world religion such as Islam share
"family resemblances." These resemblances mean, inter alia, that discourse about authority, equality, and responsibility in different Islamic
communities will have similar patterns.[3]

In another context, Geertz acknowledges this point. In his "Religion as a Cultural System" he quotes approvingly Santayana's formulation that "every living and healthy religion has a marked idiosyncrasy. Its power consists in its special and surprising message and in the bias which that revelation gives to life."[4] In that essay, Geertz defines religion as a "system of symbols which acts to establish powerful, pervasive, and long-lasting moods and motivations in men by formulating conceptions of a general order of existence and clothing those conceptions with such an aura of factuality that the moods and motivations seem uniquely realistic."[5]

But this definition has some glaring problems. For present purposes, it is worthwhile to focus on Geertz's notion that a religion "acts to establish . . . a general order of existence." By implying that there is a coherent religious interpretation of what is "really real," Geertz's definition misses the social reality that any religion encompasses a number of traditions that are in some degree in conflict. His definition ignores the historical dimension of religious dissemination, and the fact that religions pick up different baggage in different eras and areas. World religions constitute complex social realities; and adherents to these religions are not limited in their repertoires for action by a single system of symbols. Religious adherents have available to them the original books and founding ideology, the various traditions of the priests, and the contemporary developments of the religion elsewhere in the world. These traditions are rarely isomorphic. Of course, Geertz saw this in his *Islam Observed*. But he never reconciles his view of family resemblances within a religion (as set forth in "Religion as a Cultural System") with his view that the same religion can take on very different faces (in *Islam Observed*). History and semiotics must be better integrated.

For a firmer methodological base, I go back to the work of Max Weber.[6] In his work, Weber provided a richer sociological definition of religion, one that accommodated historical and symbolic factors. Weaving these strands into a complex tapestry, Weber provided an "ideal typical" approach to religion that is useful for sociological comparison.

WEBER'S DEFINITION OF RELIGION

Although Weber shied away from an explicit definition of religion (*SR*, p. 1), his work suggests that its impact can be understood in terms of the confluence of three different levels: theological doctrine, practical religion, and the practical religion of the converted. I propose to specify more fully Weber's definition of religion, so that the independent variable of the first face of culture—religion as a cultural subsystem—will be more amenable to comparative analysis.

1. *Theological doctrine.* The substantive or theological approach toward religion focuses attention on the doctrine, in its purest and most consistent forms, of the charismatic founder of the religion. For Judaism,

the Pentateuch of the lawgiver, Moses, is the source for understanding the essence of the religion. For Christianity, it is the teachings of Jesus. Even when, as in Buddhism, no single book acts as an ultimate reference for all its adherents as to the meaning of the religion, an original doctrine usually not only announces the faith but also provides guidance for living a moral life consistent with the religious conceptualization. That this guidance has consequences for the organization of political life and for political values is intuitively obvious; it is the first source of hypotheses on the effects of religion on politics.

Too often, analysis of religion as an independent variable stops there. When religion is defined solely in terms of founding doctrines, scholars, in the tradition of Usbek, tend to make broad comparisons between religions that cannot be sustained empirically. Some are arresting and contain kernels of truth. Usbek himself, twenty-four letters after he admitted inability to express the differences between Christianity and Islam, bravely suggested that, whereas the Bible contains the ideas of God written in the words of men, with the Qur'an it was "as if, by a remarkable act of caprice, God had dictated the words, while mankind provided the thoughts."[7] Other symmetrical comparisons abound:[8] In Christianity believers are called *children* of God; in Islam, *servants* of God. Jesus warned that wealth was a barrier to the kingdom of heaven; Muhammad, by requiring the pilgrimage, gave a strategic advantage to the rich. While the Christian believes in using peaceful means to spread the Gospel, the Muslim does not rule out military invasion as a means of winning converts. The Bible abounds in analytical reasoning; the Qur'an supports a more poetic or analogical mode of reasoning.[9]

Maxime Rodinson, who tried to emphasize the similarity of the two religions rather than their differences, relied as Montesquieu did primarily on the substantive definition of religion. In order to challenge Weber's finding that, in opposition to other religions, protestantism encourages rational calculation and bookkeeping, Rodinson pointed out that the Qur'an emphasized rational behavior (*'aqala*) and that the Islamic traditions glorified profits. But there is a flaw in Rodinson's argument, since Weber's sociological conceptualization of religion would invite us to consider those (Muslim) texts not as attributing divine grace to capitalists but rather as attempts by the Prophet to acknowledge the right to commercial profits if certain moral principles were observed.[10] Whether one's purpose is to elucidate differences or similarities, the overall effect of limiting one's view of religion to this level of analysis is to petrify religion—to give the impression that, while economic and political categories are fluid, religious categories are unchanging. The caricatures of religion that emerge from a concentration on the theological essence of a religious community have been well elucidated in Edward Said's polemic against them. He argues that orientalism is an ideology of the West to promote and sustain a self-conception in the Islamic world that is a caricature of itself.[11]

2. *Practical religion*. The essence of Weber's contribution was to see religion itself as a product of its times, and often of a particular class with its own social needs. A new religion may emerge from a doctrinal schism which, while the debate centers on theological niceties, is really a class or caste conflict in disguise. If the original doctrine is really a product of a larger (or smaller) social, economic, or political milieu, in what sense can the religious doctrine itself be considered an independent variable explaining certain political predispositions? Consider a religious movement among intellectual classes, where a charismatic leader arises who can attract a large following. Suppose he imparts a message that certain esoteric practices, requiring an intellectual elite, are necessary for salvation. How are we to explain the phenomenon? Is the religion itself the cause of the emergence of a self-contained intellectual elite, or has an intellectual elite developed an ideology with which to achieve and maintain power?

The interaction between the founding doctrine and the social, political, and economic conditions of the time yields what might be called "the practical religion." That in itself can have an independent effect on political life, often quite different from the political or economic intentions of the original propagating group. Indeed, that is the level of analysis at which Weber worked (*PE*, p. 187). Jesus' doctrine, recoded to suit the politics of Pauline propagation, yields a social message that has had an independent effect on the course of history. This message should be analyzed separately from the actual doctrine, the hopes of Jesus, or the visions of Paul, for it is something different from all of these. Similarly with Judaism: the social fact that the Jews were a pariah people interacts with the Mosaic message and yields a practical Judaism. This level of analysis is more abstract than the level of the charismatic founder's doctrine, since there is nothing to which all students can ultimately refer for guidance as to its real nature; it is nevertheless the crucial level for sociological study.

3. *The practical religion of the converted*. The "social fact"[12] of the practical religion is transformed still further as the Christianity of Galilee becomes the Christianity of Rome, or of its empire, or of Africa. Or again, the social fact of Islam, the interaction of the sacred message with the social position of the Quraysh lineage in Mecca, itself is transformed as the Muslim religion moves on to Basra, Java, and North Africa. As the religion spreads, both in form of original doctrine and in its practical form, it must interact with the cultural life of the new community. To what extent, then, do the social, political, economic, and cultural conditions of that place transform the religion to meet the needs and demands of the people? And to what extent will the demands of the people put pressure on

the religion? These counterpressures will create a new sociological fact, a new practical religion different from the one from which the original doctrine emanated, and different again from the wishes of the converted peoples who try to shape the new message in their own image. One might call this new social fact "the practical religion of the converted"; it is constantly being influenced by contemporary social conditions. Cultural systems may offer some resistance to socioeconomic forces, but they are nonetheless dynamic and changing.

In any society outside the birthplace of a religion, three religious elements may influence political life: first, the pure doctrine as it would be analyzed by theologians; second, the practical religion which emerges out of the interaction of doctrine and the social origins of the ideas; and, third, the interaction of the practical religion with the cultural conditions of the community of converts from a different culture, which yields a practical religion of the converted. Figure 2.1 illustrates these elements. Each level represents a different era—with all the historically unique aspects of that era attached, as it were, to the symbols created in the birthplace of that religion. But in each period the symbols created take on a life of their own, even if the original social, economic, and political factors are gone. Thus, the effects of all three levels can exist simultaneously, and it is a strategic question for research which of the levels should receive primary attention.

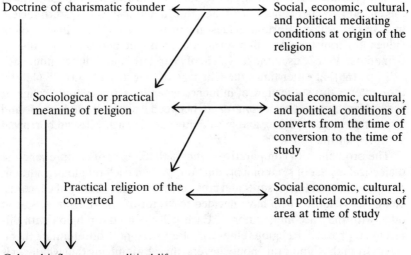

Figure 2.1 The Three Levels of Analysis in Studying the Cultural Influence of
    Religion on Political Life

Weber's work, despite a tide of empirical refutations[13] made a lasting methodological contribution. Weber combined the historical and symbolic approaches to the definition of religion and was therefore able to identify different levels of religious impact. For him, religion constituted a web of significance: in that web are caught a set of theological ideas (especially those concerning salvation and sin) that have been mediated by the social, economic, and political realities of the various eras and areas in which those ideas have spread.

THE WEBERIAN FRAMEWORK AMENDED

Before analyzing the three levels of religious influence on society from a Weberian perspective, it is imperative to amend two aspects of Weber's paradigm. First, although he insisted throughout his work that social groups make use of cultural symbols in order to further their political goals, Weber did not integrate that insight into the analysis of the religious ethics he studied. In a study of Islamic debates concerning capitalism, socialism, and industrial development, Rodinson concludes that if there were a vibrant elite in Islam espousing capitalism or socialism, nothing in the doctrine or history of Islam could not be molded to support that elite's position.[14] Hence the first amendment to Weber: a theory concerning the impact of religious meaning on society must be integrated with a theory concerning strategic molding of religious meaning.

The second amendment has more direct application for the concerns of this chapter. Weber conceived of the Protestant impact on Western society in a static fashion. Certain values are promoted by the religion; these values are transferred in like form into economic and political milieus. Sometimes Weber used the language of "support" and "direct influence" (*PE*, p. 166), at other times the language of "elective affinity."[15] Geertz, too, accepts this static view of influence when he assumes that "religious symbols formulate a basic *congruence* between a particular style of life and a specific . . . metaphysic, and in so doing sustain each with the borrowed authority of the other."[16]

The problem with comparative statics is that it cannot comprehend the dialectical aspect of symbolic production. Within each religious tradition, there are inevitable pressures and cross-pressures on a variety of concerns. Religious virtuosos who have decided to "reform" the religion will be at odds with the "accommodators." Each will define the religion with different emphases.[17] Religious elites will often attempt to differentiate themselves from the "immoral" nonbelievers, thereby implying that whatever is bad about society forms no part of their religion. An example: Catholicism had coopted Roman magic; practical puritanism in England defined itself in terms of a strong rejection of magic. This stance set the puritans against professional astrologers.[18] In a study of a religious profanation, James Scott concludes "that any moral order is bound to engender its own antithesis, at least ritually, within folk culture."[19] The notions of "elective affinity" or "congruence" miss the social reality of an ideological dialectic within any cultural system.

How then, should we speak of religious influence on society when the religion itself reflects certain values *and* their opposites? Thomas Metzger, in a brilliant essay on Neoconfucian values, suggests an answer. He sees culture not as values which are upheld but, rather, as "points of concern" which are debated. Rather than examine Confucian bureaucrats' preferred answers to questions of value, Metzger examines the questions generally considered worth asking and the cliches implicitly accepted. "We can understand" the Neoconfucians, Metzger suggests, "by understanding what they worried about . . . what their shared points of uncertainty and concern were . . . Therefore I suggest looking at Neo-Confucianism as a widely shared 'grammar' defining the problems of intellectual struggle by positing a discrepancy between the goal of life and the given world. Sharing this grammar, Neo-Confucians differed in terms of their solutions for these problems."[20] Focusing on points of concern rather than congruent values allows one better to appreciate the dialectical nature of symbol systems.

Consider this example: Fazlur Rahman analyzes the Qur'anic verse, "God it is who has made for you all that is in the earth." This, he tells us, was once interpreted as a liberal belief in men having their right to control the earth. Today, socialists interpret the "you" to mean all men equally. While Rodinson would use this example to demonstrate that the Qur'anic verse can be used for any ideological purpose, Rahman uses this doctrinal modification to illuminate a common Muslim point of concern, namely, the recognition that Muhammad's life has relevance as a model for proper behavior in the modern world.[21] Similarly, in a recent discussion of the tremendous range of equality and inequality in different Muslim environments in Nigeria, Henry Bienen points out one overriding similarity: everywhere Islam provided a languge in which equality demands were legitimately expressed.[22]

Applying the Weberian framework for the remainder of part 1, I shall attempt to incorporate the dialectical nature of the religious impact on society. With this important amendment, I am now ready to give some substance to the three levels of religious impact on society.

THE WEBERIAN FRAMEWORK APPLIED:
COMPARING CHRISTIANITY AND ISLAM

Although both Christianity and Islam are outgrowths of Judaism, neither has been directly associated with a single tribal, national, or racial group—

both have sought converts worldwide and have thus become world religions. But the differences between them, on each of three levels of analysis, concern us here.

Founding Doctrines

The heart of the Christian message is that God, through love, saved mankind in a corrupted world through the ultimate sacrifice of his son. If a believer acts according to the moral principals set forth in Christ's Sermon on the Mount, and if he understands that even though he may sin, God's redemptive love will allow him to be saved, he can lead a life of joy. In contrast, the central Muslim message is that God has provided a model for proper living, and each believer, as a vicegerent for God, has a personal responsibility for the maintenance of that moral ordering. Not Adam's corruption but his turning to God for moral guidance is the Qur'anic interpretation of the Garden of Eden. Not his unlimited love but the perfect exposition of how to live (written in the perfect Book) is the sign of God's greatness. And not joy but human dignity coming from submission to harsh yet just standards of conduct marks a virtuous Muslim life.[23]

If the central messages differ, so do the textures of the respective theologies. Emerging from the complexities of Jewish theology, and spreading through a sophisticated Rome, the Pauline message was complex, urbane, and (like a legal presentation) subject to multifarious interpretations. Emerging from a more straightforward desert environment— where the laws of nomadic and trading relations were unambiguous— Islamic theology was, from its initial stages, starker and less ambiguous than the Christian.

This difference can be felt in a number of places. While Christian claims that the Trinity represents one God requires a whole literature of exposition and defense, in Islam each believer chants the phrase, "There is no god but God" repeatedly. In early Christianity, those lost to the faith are held to be corrupted but susceptible of being brought into the fold. In Islam, apostasy is a sin, to be dealt with on the harshest terms—again the starkness of Islam: either you are a believer or you are not. Christianity, although holding all believers to be equal in the eyes of God, has permitted hierarchies to develop within its formal organization. In Islam, inequality can rarely be overlooked or justified. The Islamic starkness is also clear in the mode of prayer (simple recitations regularly repeated; austere dress with emphasis on cleanliness during prayer; prostration on mats while praying on the floor). This can be contrasted with the variable and complex development of Christian prayer.

Islamic starkness is, in M.G.S. Hodgson's words, "a single-minded sophistication which integrates all the diversity of experience through a few potent and comprehensive conceptions."[24] Christian ambiguity, on the other hand, reflects an intellectualist attempt to incorporate diverse notions into a single theological mold.

Practical Religion

The interaction of theological and sociological factors in the early periods of a religion's development forms the practical religion. The institutional outgrowth of this interaction will in itself have a profound impact on future social, economic and political life of the society which has come to adopt the religion. Let me take as an initial example the idea of equality. The early Christian communities were exemplars of egalitarian communism. In his letter to the Galatians, Paul wrote that "there is no such thing as Jew and Greek, slave and freeman, male and female; for you are all one person in the Christian message." But the practical problems faced by Paul as he attempted to create self-sustaining Christian organizations in Cyprus, Asia Minor, Macedonia, Greece, and Rome led him to create church organizations. Ecclesiastical hierarchy, by becoming a central attribute of medieval Christianity, implied that on earth not all Christians were equal. Church hierarchy modulated early Christian claims for secular equality. Equality in Christianity became something that would occur in heaven; on earth, inequality became an institutional fact of life.

In contrast, the issue of inequality on earth continued to be a point of concern in Islam. Muhammad's great-grandfather, Hashim, had enhanced Mecca's trade position in Arabia. To help maintain solidarity in Mecca, Hashim introduced a transfer tax. By Muhammad's time, however, wealth began to go to a few Meccan merchants in a disproportionate manner, and the losers were attempting to disrupt Meccan control of the trade network. The core of Muhammad's message was based on a belief that "the salvaton of his fellow Qurayshites was to consist in taking care of their poor relatives . . . This cooperation between rich and poor is the basic tenet of all Muhammad's preaching just as Love is for that of Jesus Christ."[25] In subsequent Islam, the question of alms to the poor (*zakat*) and that of inheritance to a wide range of relatives in order to thwart intergenerational accumulations of wealth became central issues. Equality was valued in the founding doctrines of both Christianity and Islam, but only in the practical religion of Islam has radical egalitarianism become a persistent point of concern.

The practical religions of Islam and Christianity can perhaps best be compared in the context of the twelfth and thirteenth centuries. At that time both religious traditions were, in many places of the world, hegemonic in their societies in the sense that their moral frameworks infused many domains of practical life. We may contrast, relying on Hodgson, Christian "corporatism" to Islamic "contractualism."[26]

In Christian institutional development in the West, legitimate authority was ascribed to "autonomous corporative offices" (kings, bishops, burghers) which fit into hierarchical relations within a fixed social body. Legitimate incumbents to these offices were those people who fit into a predetermined procedural pattern of election. In Occidental history, the Christian *church* and its "autonomous corporate unity and hierarchical structure,"[27] was therefore decisive. In Islam, by contrast, authority was invested in anyone who took personal responsibility for the maintenance of standards. Authority, conferred in egalitarian individual contracts, led to improvisation or what Hodgson calls an institutional "occasionalism."[28]

This contrast—between Occidental Christian corporatism and Islamic contractualism—manifested itself in a number of ways. Occidental Christianity developed a strict hierarchy leading up to a pope, and the whole question of hierarchy versus individual witness became a point of concern which tested Christianity to its limits over the centuries. Current concern in the church for "shared testimony" demonstrates that the conflict between hierarchy and individual participation has indeed remained a point of concern.[29] Islam never developed an institutional hierarchy. When Muhammad died, the choice of Abu Bakr as the Khalif was "an ad hoc decision taken by the community in a moment of supreme crisis . . . This decision should never be thought of as founding the Khalifate as a permanent institution." For the subsequent half-year, Abu Bakr continued his commerical dealings, and even moonlighted by milking his neighbors' sheep to supplement his income. When the Islamic empire reached Egypt, the conquered peoples appeared more accustomed to authoritarian rule than their conquerors did. The early problems that the Islamic community faced in succession to office were in large part due to the fact that the incumbents thought their own positions unnecessary.[30] Muslim armies were indeed created; and Muslim garrison cities were well organized. But, in the Muslim tradition, urban military organizations rarely outlasted their original purposes—they existed only to serve the occasion for which they were formed. We have then in practical religion a differentiation between institutional hierarchy and institutional occasionalism.

Christian corporatism led naturally to a vision of law that accorded greater legitimacy to procedures than to matters of substance; a vision of office that demanded fixed rules for succession; a vision of society that clearly differentiated private from public. In contrast, Islamic law focused more on the intent of actors and equity than on correct procedure. Succession was seen not as a procedure but as a contest "where a personal responsibility was to be undertaken by the best man."[31] The distinction between public and private, so crucial in the Occidental Christian tradition, has had little meaning in Islamic thought.

Finally, given the multilayered hierarchy of the Christian church, there were many levels at which individuals could press for reform—at the parish level, the diocese, or as high as the offices of archbishop or pope. Small reforms could filter up or down the hierarchy. It took centuries for a new form of rebellion to become available—that of leaving the hierarchy in order to form a parallel institution. Once Luther made that breakthrough, institutional separation became a central part of practical Christianity. [32] In Islam, on the other hand, there was no hierarchy through which to filter new ideas. Reformers were compelled to make moralistic appeals to the whole Islamic community, and "military venture with wholesale revolt continued to pose an ideal for reformers."[33] Not institutional separation but geographical escape, modeled on the Prophet's escape to Medina (*hijra*), became a way to challenge authority.[34]

To be sure, this contrast should be muted. The Shi'ite tradition in Islam had a very different and certainly more hierarchical view of the Khalifate than did the Sunni. Similarly, the Presbyterian tradition in Christianity forthrightly rejected the church hierarchy. But these examples testify to the dialectical nature of culture discussed earlier. The essential point remains that hierarchical organizations became the norm in the Christian tradition, and from that norm many adherents rebelled. Since hierarchy was never a point of concern within the Muslim tradition, a Presbyterian-like movement within it would have been irrelevant. Muslim sects or orders emphasized ritual cleanliness and a personal responsibility to uphold the Qur'anic law.

Corporatism and contractualism are not intended to provide descriptions of all Christian and Muslim communities; rather, these concepts are meant to emphasize different cultural concerns. Christian corporatism and Islamic contractualism do, however, have links to the founding theological principles. The Christian promise of salvation takes the burden off of individuals and allows them to accept the authority of the church. Asking God's forgiveness in a proper manner prescribed by the church implies support for those procedures that exemplify corporatism. The view of the church as a "redemptive fellowship, a special sacramental society,"[35] is consistent with a social idea of fixed institutions hierarchically arranged. In Islam, the rigid moralistic appeals of the Qur'an were translated in both the Arabian and Persian core areas as invocations to take personal responsibility for their fulfillment. The moral certitude of both the Qur'an and the traditions were consistent with the development of a moral community rather than an institutional hierarchy. The Prophet's use of mercantile metaphors as well supported the idea of an individual contract with God.

The Practical Religion of the Converted

Christianity was a dubious sect for the Jews in Jerusalem; an Eastern cult for the Latins of the later Roman Empire; a "Latin" product for northern European subjects of Rome; but for nineteenth-century Nigeria it was a

Western European import. Islam to the Persians was a symbol of Arab overrule; to the North Africans it was a mechanism for political control; and to the Yorubas, it had elements of Fulani control, but also, since many conversions took place in Lagos and the Yoruba converts proselytized to other Yorubas as they traveled north, it had an image of being a local product.

To say simply that Yoruba social life was influenced by Christian "love" or Muslim "responsibility," or by Christian "corporatism" or Muslim "contractualism," would be to ignore many intervening social processes within the religious subsystems. To identify religious differences as they manifest themselves in African social life, we must therefore begin with a careful scrutiny of the cultural milieus into which these world religions came.

THE CULTURAL CONTEXT OF THE CONVERTS IN YORUBALAND
Traditional Religion

The indigenous cultural subsystem most strongly affected by the two world religions was the traditional religion; so it is worthwhile to examine some of its attributes.[36] Yoruba traditional religion, like Christianity and Islam, has a conception of a god—Olodumare—who is abstract and unknowable. Since the religion claims 401 deities in its pantheon, however, it can hardly be described as monotheistic, or even, as Idowu has, as "diffused monotheism."[37] But such issues are never clear-cut. Muslims and Christians, claiming to be monotheist, worship saints who, though once mortals or revered ancestors, have taken on significance far beyond their temporal roles. To contrast the monotheistic religions of Judaism, Christianity, and Islam to the polytheist religions of Africa therefore obscures more than it illuminates. Yoruba religion shares with Christianity and Islam an understanding of an ineffable, abstract, and deeply symbolic high power.

The Yorubas have developed a sophisticated theology and a priestly class. Their theology contains notions of predestination and the transmigration of souls. Much careful collective thought has gone into the idea of "life" or "breath" (emi), and how it exists independently of the body.[38] A rich poetic literature has contributed to Yoruba theology with its complex system of divination (ifa). Those priests who lead divination prayers (baba'lawo) and healers (oniṣẹgun), who are well versed in theological matters, have had high status in Yoruba society.[39] Yoruba theologians have zealously attempted to recharge the tradition by incorporating ideas learned amid vast sociological and technological change.

An important difference between the two world religions and Yoruba traditional religion is that Christianity and Islam are confessional religions. In the confessional religions, each individual (not group) adheres to a set of beliefs that are held to have universal validity. Yoruba traditional religion, where political membership—or nationality—was commensurate with religious affiliation,[40] was challenged by the world religions' demand that an individual make a *personal* confession of faith to a systematic corpus of beliefs.

Second, Yoruba religion is multilocal, not universal. Within the common pantheon, each Yoruba city has shrines and a relationship with a set of deities which is unique to it. In Yoruba tradition, children are taken to Ifa diviners to be assigned a personal god. The diviners in different towns and different lineages specialize in different gods, and festivals to gods differ from one ancestral city to the next. (In Ile-Ife, hardly a day passes without a festival for one of the gods.) To be sure, some cult societies (e.g. *Egungun*, *Oro*) cut across descent groups and sometimes recruit outsiders.[41] Willingness to recruit selected outsiders, however, can hardly be compared with the proselytism of Christianity and Islam. In the world religions, while localities do have special customs, outsiders are made welcome and are treated as honored guests. In the Yoruba religion, strangers to a city often find themselves unwelcome at local religious festivals.

Third, participation in Yoruba worship is restricted. Although some festivals attract exuberant public participation, many of the "deep" religious rituals take place in private. Some like the *oro*, take place late at night, and women are not permitted to participate. Important religious organizations such as the *ogboni* have secret memberships. Shrines in each town have groundskeepers who also restrict entry. Central to the Yoruba traditional religion is the idea that religious expression is fundamentally private. One sensitive commentator to an anthropological description of a Yoruba festival noted that only the anthropologist "might appropriately be called a spectator to it."[42]

The *ogboni* help to illustrate the dialectical nature of practical religion. Yoruba Christians, who chafed at European control of church organizations (yet did not wish to break away to form a new church) confounded the missionaries by forming fraternal associations, the "Christian *ogboni*." That these were modeled on traditional secret societies bothered the Europeans; but the Yorubas pointed out that freemasonry (analogous to *ogboni*) was an acceptable Christian outgrowth in Europe and therefore could not be criticized in Africa. While the practical meaning of Christianity in Yorubaland encompassed the idea of public ceremonies, the Christian *ogboni* expressed the value of private societies.[43] The public nature of prayer in the orthodox Christian and Muslim traditions represented a challenge to the Yoruba tradition.

Fourth, the idea that theological truths should be relevant and available to all peoples of the world is alien to Yoruba traditional religion. Should an outsider inquire into the meaning of an Ifa verse, he or she is likely to be told that the meaning of that verse is "deep," indeed too deep for a non-Yoruba to understand properly. Different from Christian and Muslim proselytizers who simplify their messages so that all can understand them, Yoruba theologians hold that their message is so deep that only those who have made a thorough study of the esoteric knowledge embodied in the religion have the capacity to receive it.[44]

Reasons for Conversion

With a sophisticated and complex religious corpus of their own, why did so many Yorubas convert to Christianity and Islam in the late nineteenth and early twentieth centuries? The dominant "intellectualist" theory of conversion claims that the new religions provided an answer to the problem of meaning on an issue in which the former religion was silent.[45] Some intellectualists point out that with changing social conditions and a wider world of relevant activity, a religion whose gods serve only a locality becomes empty.[46] There is, however, both a theoretical and an empirical problem with this approach. Theoretically, intellectualists must demonstrate that the new religion covers more ground than the old one. That is difficult to do, since traditional Yoruba religious concepts are rich, varied, and open to change (and, as we shall see in chapter 7, the Christians were able to build on these Yoruba religious concepts with great ease). Empirically, intellectualists must demonstrate that people converted because the theology of the new religion had more scope or better answers than the old one. In the Yoruba case, as we shall see, no evidence can be adduced to demonstrate such a contention. In fact, Yoruba theology was changing to meet the new circumstances created by wider geographical relevance. Local deities were becoming regional ones; and the Yoruba pantheon was becoming more hierarchical in the direction of monotheism.[47]

From a sociological (rather than an intellectualist) perspective, massive Yoruba conversions to both world religions can be attributed in part to great social change. Internal warfare rocked Yorubaland for much of the nineteenth century. Whole cities were razed, and refugee camps became large urban centers. Modern Oyo, Ibadan, and Abeokuta, among the largest cities in Yorubaland today, were all built up from small villages by nineteenth century refugees. In Ile-Ife, a major section of town, Modakeke, was settled by refugees from Oyo, a "foreign" city-kingdom. Many Yorubas were subject to no local authority.

Also, many Yorubas in the nineteenth century became directly involved in the Atlantic trade, selling palm oil, palm kernels, cotton, and wild rubber. By the early twentieth century, increasing numbers of Yoruba traders were establishing commercial relations with people from other towns.[48] These Yorubas—traders and refugees—were far removed from the priests, shrines, and local festivals of their ancestral cities. This distance was at once liberating and alienating. Many such Yorubas became the early converts to the world religions,[49] not because these religions offered new answers to the problem of meaning but because they offered strangers a new basis for community identification.

The sociological approach tends to trivialize conversion as utilitarian. When interviewed, early converts often remember that the religion they joined had power and prestige. The literacy of the Christian missionaries, the trade linkages of the Muslim mallams, and the arsenal of remedies for illness offered by both groups provided potential converts with useful skills and remedies. As Gbadamosi notes for Victorian Lagos—which, due to its economic growth as a colonial outpost, had become a city of considerable prestige—"it became fashionable and respectable to be a Muslim or a Christian.[50] Also important was that these skills and remedies, as well as the appearance of fashion, were available at extraordinarily low cost. Potential converts were asked (initially) to give up virtually nothing to associate with the new religions. It is no wonder that both Peel and I, in our different studies, elicited only the shallowest answers to the "why" question of conversion: "Everyone was joining, so I joined," or "I wanted to move with them."[51]

The most interesting answer we both received, and this from a number of informants from Islam and Christianity, was "Because of civilization" (*nitori ọlaju*), which means literally, "Because our eyes were opened." This concept is associated with progress, health, and development, but not with answers to the problem of meaning.[52] What informants "saw" was new opportunities at low cost in affiliation with a world religion.

The utilitarian approach to conversion is consistent with Fisher's and Nock's analyses.[53] Fisher delineates three stages of religious development in a new community: quarantine, mixing, and reform. In the quarantine stage, only outsiders or strangers to the community associate with the new religion. These strangers, perhaps because of their contacts with the outside world, derive wealth, skills, or status from the association and begin to attract some of the more progressive young indigenes; this is the mixing stage. The indigenes at this stage rarely renounce their former beliefs but hold both systems to be complementary; Nock argues that the indigenes are now demonstrating not conversion but only "adhesion." Generations later, there is often a return to the original set of beliefs or practices of the new religion with an ideological commitment to expunge from religious practice all preadhesion atavisms; this is "reform" according to Fisher, and true "conversion" according to Nock. This approach to conversion—as opposed to that of the intellectualists—explains why, though the sources for conversion may be instrumental, the consequences of adherence by individuals are ideological for the community. To use Weberian imagery, the decision to adhere may begin to spin the individual and his surrounding community into a web of significance out of which it is not easy to escape. The implications of conversion may go far beyond the expectations of the early converts.

In nineteenth-century Yorubaland both Christianity and Islam had a supply of evangelists and an incorporative ideology which allowed the creation of communities of strangers, as well as an arsenal of skills and powers of some use to a socially mobilized population. Both religions were remarkably successful in winning converts. But the secondary consequences of conversion to each of these religions were not the same, in part because of the differential social contexts of conversion. These contexts form the basis of the practical religion of the converted. It is therefore to a detailed description of Yoruba conversion to the two world religions that I now turn.

Islam in Yorubaland

Islam came within striking distance of Yorubaland as far back as the eleventh century, when Borno (a state some 500 miles northeast of old Oyo) and Songhai welcomed Islamic refugees from the Middle East, and the local people began to convert.[54] Over the next few centuries, the Madinka and Nupe traders brought Islam even closer to the Yorubas. In Hausaland, north of Oyo, Islam was introduced in the fourteenth century. Through war and trade, the Yorubas had contact with these peoples, and in the seventeenth century there is already some record of Muslim converts in Yoruba cities. By the early nineteenth century, Islam was well known in Yorubaland, as it was the religion of Hausa slaves, of higher-status Hausas engaged in interregional trade, of learned scholars who set up schools in Yorubaland, and of a few Yorubas (mostly in Ilorin) who themselves began to convert. Yet most observers in Yoruba cities in the early nineteenth century, while seeing some Hausa clerics engaged in missionary work, found very few Muslims among the local population. At this time the Oyo Empire, which ruled over much of what is today Yorubaland, promoted the observance of the traditional gods and gave support to Ile-Ife as its theological center.

In 1817, the provincial military commander of the Oyo Empire, Afonja, stationed at Ilorin, embarked on a rebellion to challenge the king of Oyo; by the 1830s, Oyo city was destroyed. Afonja enlisted foreign military aid from a Muslim Fulani general who had designs of initiating a jihad in Yorubaland. The Fulani general turned the tables on Afonja and had him murdered. In control of Ilorin, he then sought to conquer other Yoruba cities. (This effort failed, but Ilorin remains a city with a Fulani emir.) Ironically, Afonja's defeat gave to many Yorubas an appreciation of Islamic power and possibilities. Among the war refugees, who were unhooked from the rituals of control in their ancestral cities, Islam was seen in a new light—as a religion of power. Indeed, Oyo also received Muslim foreign aid from Borgu, whose people were trade rivals of the Fulanis and had established themselves in Oyo well before Afonja's rebellion. Also important for the success of Islam was the "dignity" and self-worth of Islamic converts, which deeply impressed many Yorubas.[55]

Islam penetrated into southern Yorubaland as well. In the early nineteenth century, the British navy began to blockade the West African coast in order to suppress the slave trade. Captured ships were directed to Freetown, Sierra Leone, where the slaves were freed. Many Yoruba "recaptives" became exposed to Islam in the environs of Sierra Leone, and ultimately made it back to Yorubaland. These "Aku" Muslims had learned modern skills in Sierra Leone, and had accumulated some capital. There was already a community of Muslim Hausa slaves in Lagos, and the Akus increased the critical mass. In 1861, they built their first mosque in Lagos. Their numbers increased to 14,300 over the next thirty years.[56]

After Afonja's rebellion in Ilorin and the establishment of a Yoruba Muslim community in Lagos, Islam established itself as an important social force in city after city from the mid-nineteenth century on. In the 1820s, Prince Atiba of Oyo traveled to Ilorin in order to become educated in Islam. But elements in Oyo hostile to change put pressure on the Alaafin to massacre members of the fledgling community. In the 1830s, when Ilorin's armies compelled evacuation of Oyo, Atiba—now Alaafin and a convert to Islam—led his people to "new Oyo," a small settlement about 100 miles south of the old imperial capital (called Oyo-Ile on map 1.2). He invited some learned Hausa Muslims to inaugurate an Islamic community in Oyo, permitted them to found their own quarter, and subsidized the building of a new mosque for them. To the present day, the chief imam of Oyo is from that line of Hausa mallams. Despite the immediacy of military defeat aided by a foreign Muslim commander, new Oyo's Muslim community grew, and by 1877 there were twelve mosques in Oyo.[57]

Ibadan, which became the largest refugee center during the nineteenth-century wars, was the most powerful city in Yorubaland until the British conquest of the 1890s. Although Islam was associated with the archrival city of Ilorin, Ibadan manifested little antipathy to the spread of Islam. To be sure, in the early years of Ibadan's consolidation, *Başorun* Oluyole ordered the Hausa mosque razed. But Opeagbe became the *Balę* of Ibadan in 1850, and he, a supporter of Islam, subsidized the building of a mosque in his (the king's) market place; by 1877, Ibadan boasted twenty-four sectional mosques.[58]

In the Ijebu city-kingdom, which had remained autonomous from the old Oyo Empire, neither Islam nor Christianity were given much support by the king (*Awujalę*), largely because the Ijebu, by maintaining some degree of order amid the breakup of the Oyo Empire, were able to control one important trade route to Lagos. High tariff barriers enriched Ijebu-Ode, a major entrepôt between the Sahara and the Atlantic coast. The closed walls of the city and its intense mercantilist policies militated against the spread of foreign religions. But many Ijebu traders had links with Hausas in other towns, especially in Ibadan and Lagos. And, since the palace contained an influential group of Muslim slaves, there was some contact between Ijebu authorities and Islam.

The British attempted, among other things, to destroy Ijebu mercantilism in 1892 when they conquered the town. By threatening the tax base, the British victory weakened the Awujalẹ and his military and strengthened the hand of itinerant Ijebu traders. It was in this period that the Awujalẹ, Aboki Tunwase, coopted the leading Ijebu traders, many of whom lived in Lagos and Ibadan and had converted to Islam. The Awujalẹ, recognizing his weak position, had already welcomed back Ali Akayinode, who had been exiled from the town for praying to Allah in public. Akayinode became chief imam and was given a piece of land for public prayers on the outskirts of town. In 1902, Balogun Kuku, one of the great men in Ijebu history, and enriched by his successes in the salt and ammunition trade, converted to Islam and opened up his modern residence to the public. He took the name Momodu Bello, and was joined in his conversion by scores of other prominent Ijebu men. The newly installed Awujalẹ in 1906 was a Muslim; and from that time on, Islam became the religion of the elite in Ijebu-Ode.[59]

We now see the pattern of Yoruba conversion to Islam. Despite economic and cultural contact with Muslims until the end of the eighteenth century, and despite conversions by Yorubas in Ilorin, Islam was quarantined. Then, in the wake of the Yoruba civil wars, many Yorubas were displaced from their ancestral cities. They saw the business opportunities, the dignity, and the claims to supernatural powers of Islamic preachers. Initially little was asked of them to join this attractive community, and, since they lived outside of their ancestral homes, they faced little pressure to resist. They were at the stage of accommodation or adhesion. Armed with amulets, a sense of dignity, and a source for business contacts, these refugees returned to their ancestral homes for purposes of trade or resettlement. That they had converted was attractive to the young men of their towns. Their dress alone signaled a new dignity and cosmopolitanism. Political authority, anxious to accommodate to the interests of the returned refugees who had become rich, could not easily deny these converts the right to engage in Islamic prayer. Instead, the traditional authorities tended to coopt the religion, regarding it as a new cult to be added to the traditional corpus. Thus the basis for an institutionalized Muslim community was laid.

In this period of accommodation, the organizational structure of the mosque took on elements which were quintessentially Yoruba. The initial leaders of Yoruba Muslim communities were often called *Parakoyi*, a Yoruba office conferred on the organizer of long-distance trade.[60] Mosques developed officer corps with traditional Yoruba chiefly titles, such as *Balogun* (commander of the old warriors), *Sẹriki* (commander of the young warriors), and *Sarumi* (commander of the cavalry). Not surprisingly, there has been a tension between the push for the "Yorubacization" of the religion and the pull toward the Islamicization of the Yoruba.

These new roles each represented a contract between the incumbent and the community. Throughout Yorubaland, new posts were created in an ad hoc manner: Head of Arabic Scholars, Imam's Deputy, Patron of the Religion, Leader of the Youth, Assistant leader of the Youth, and King of the Muslims.[61] Roles often disappeared with the death of an incumbent.

The lack of corporate structure in Yoruba Islam translated into a particular set of problems. First, nearly every city faced intense battles for succession to the chief imamship. As early as 1902–3 in Epe, Muslim factions fought for control of the central mosque. Such battles—common among Yoruba Muslim communities and usually lacking ideological or substantive content, were fought for control, not policy.[62] Second, Hausas and Yoruba "stranger" communities in host cities pressed for their own central mosques. Since the power over a central mosque gave considerable sources of revenue to distribute, these conflicts were intense.[63] Third, there has been a breakaway sect in Yoruba Islam, the Ahmadiyya movement, which came to West Africa in World War I. Claiming that its founder was a second prophet, this group had been banished by orthodox Islam. The Indian missionary who brought the movement to Nigeria tried to build on a split within the Lagos Muslim community, with minimal success. This group attempted to proselytize using European methods (formal organization, foreign missionary control). Only 7,000 Yorubas were Ahmadis in Nigeria in 1960.[64] Within Yoruba Islam there have been two sufi mystical orders, the Tijaniyya and Qadiriyya, as well as reforming societies—Ansar Ud-Deen and Nawir Ud-Deen—to encourage Muslims to push for the fruits of western education. But the mystical orders and reforming societies saw themselves as supportive of orthodox structures. The growth of Islam in Yorubaland was thus not without conflict, but the conflict was played out largely within orthodox confines.

Yoruba Islam has now gone beyond accommodation, and there are indications of Islamic reform.[65] Many Yorubas have become *alhajis* (i.e., made the pilgrimage to Mecca); most imams are literate in Arabic and go back to original sources, the *hadith* (the traditions of the Prophet) and the Qur'an, to provide guidance to their communities. Most Yoruba Muslims are confronted by principles and ideas from all three levels of religious impact. We may conclude, using Nock's expression, that true conversion to Islam has now occurred in Yorubaland.

Christianity in Yorubaland

By 1830, after nearly two centuries of sporadic contacts between Christianity and Yoruba society, contacts became systematic and socially significant.[66] European missionary churches saw great opportunity for conversion of those "recaptives" in Freetown, who were far more subject to Christian evangelization than to exposure to Islam. Many recaptives saw the Christians as the responsible agents for their freedom, and as allies in their attempts for personal enrichment. At the mission schools, Yorubas were given literacy and training for a variety of jobs (surveyors, carpenters, clerks) for which there were considerable employment opportunities. Away from most constraints and the ritual life of their ancestral cities, the recaptives were receptive to the community offered by the Christian missionaries.

In the late 1830s, some of the recaptives arranged for ships to return them to Yorubaland. Many of these "Saros"—Christian and Muslim recaptives had different sobriquets—found Abeokuta, the great refugee center for the Egbas, a pleasant place to resettle. Others went to Badagry and Lagos on the coast. Their literacy and their connections with powerful Europeans gave them considerable status, which made their religion attractive, even though it was still quarantined. In 1841, English evangelists fitted three ships to travel up the Niger River in order to win converts and induce trade. On the mission was Samuel Ajayi Crowther, a recaptive of extraordinary abilities. Although the mission was a disaster, as nearly a third of the members died of malaria, the social force of Christianity could not be contained. In 1842, the head of the Gold Coast (now Ghana) Methodist mission, Thomas Birch Freeman (himself part African), opened a station in Badagry. In that same year, the Abeokutan Saros made appeals to the Church Missionary Society (CMS) in Freetown to open a mission. The authorities in Abeokuta clearly saw the political advantages of an alliance with Europeans for purposes of fighting their own intercity battles. Their king, Sodeke, who had perceived the potential of a missionary alliance, died just as the CMS was about to send a missionary, and it was four years before Henry Townsend was permitted to open a CMS mission in Abeokuta.

The early Christian converts in Yorubaland—recaptives, traders, and war refugees—all converted outside of their ancestral cities. In these early years, Christianity remained in quarantine. In later decades, however, when Christians not only were seen to be progressive and powerful but offered literacy (hence the potential for good jobs) and free health care, they won converts more broadly. Also, they offered excellent trading contacts to a growing commercial class. These incentives must be coupled with the fact that few Christians gave up their connection with traditional religion, and few paid high costs for converting. Christianity was moving from quarantine to accommodation.

Consider how these forces were played out in Abeokuta and Ijebu, two of the leading centers of Yoruba Christianity today. In Abeokuta, ties with the missionaries led to British support in the face of an invasion from Dahomey in 1854. Missionaries even distributed British ammunition to Abeokuta's chiefs. Later, in a commercial battle with Lagos, Henry Townsend supported the trading interests of Abeokuta and got British-government support for his position. Finally, the Abeokuta-CMS alliance led to economic gains for Abeokuta, as the large trading firm of T. Hutton set up an office there, attempting to make cotton commercially viable.

But all was not sweetness between the missionaries and the Egba elites. There were African slave-trading interests who opposed British authority; many Saros wanted positions of authority in the church that were denied them by Europeans; and Lagos trading interests began to dominate those of Abeokuta. An Abeokuta request to set up a customs post on the trade route to Lagos was denied by the British Governor of Lagos, leading to an 1867 riot, when European traders and Christian missionaries alike fled the town. For the next twelve years, the CMS was effectively confined to the coast.

The missionaries returned, however, and restored their influence. In 1888, the CMS missionary in Abeokuta heard that Egba authorities were negotiating with French missionaries in order to play off the British against the French. CMS people tipped off the British authorities, who immediately signed a treaty with the French giving each a restricted sphere of influence. Incensed, the Egbas in 1891 again tried to expel the missionaries, this time unsuccessfully. Christianity had established a foothold in Abeokuta, and many Egbas found useful contacts and opportunities in their alliance with the missionaries.

In the Ijebu kingdom, as we have seen in regard to Islam, the local authorities were strongly opposed to the penetration of outside religions until British troops overran the capital city, Ijebu-Ode, in 1892. CMS missionaries, however, in contact with a number of Ijebu traders, saw the Ijebu people as the hardest nut to crack, blocking the successful penetration of all Yorubaland. Indeed the Ijebus reacted to the CMS gambits by closing their roads and turning back missionaries, threatening to kill them.

Once the invasion opened up Ijebu, both Islam and Christianity made great advances. Probably because most traders in Ijebu-Ode found Islam to be more useful in developing their trading networks, Islam expanded more rapidly than did Christianity. But in the small villages surrounding

Ijebu-Ode, where many people chafed at the authoritarian rule of the capital city, Christianity was seen as a connection which would help these people confront Ijebu-Ode's power. Local men who viewed themselves as progressives found Christianity especially attractive. Obafemi Awolowo, who has been one of the leading political forces in modern Nigeria, describes in his autobiography how his father was converted. This man, from a small village outside of Ijebu-Ode, hated "paganism," with its "innumerable rites, rituals and festivals . . . He had contempt for the medicine-men and he openly pooh-poohed belief in witchcraft and wizardry."[67] Awolowo's father became part of the wave of postinvasion converts, which helped solidify the religious differentiation between the capital and its environs. In 1952, Muslims made up 69 percent of Ijebu-Ode; in the wider Ijebu Division, however, Christians accounted for 46 percent.[68]

Between 1864 and 1877, Samuel Crowther, virtually alone in the upper Niger, was instrumental in setting up numerous missions. In Eastern Yoruba country (around Ondo), where much British trade was directed amid the civil wars in an effort to circumvent Ijebu-Ode's tolls, missionaries attained notable success.[69] By the turn of the century, most Yoruba towns had a CMS mission and a school or hospital, as well as an established connection with international Christianity. Christianity in Yorubaland was secure.

Organized Christianity in Yorubaland was hierarchical but dispersed. All missionary organizations had head offices in Europe or North America (or Lagos, headquarters for the African church). They had functionally specific tasks, annual budgets, and clearly defined goals for fieldworkers. Regular messages concerning budget, numbers of converts, book shop ledgers, and other bureaucratically defined matters passed between the central office and the field. In that sense Christianity presented a model of hierarchical—or corporate—organization. But Christianity came with multiple hierarchies. With no serious coordination (although there were some agreements among Protestant denominations concerning which church could specialize in which city) the Methodists, the Anglicans (organized as the CMS), the Baptists, and the Catholics, among others, all attempted to win converts.

Corporatism is also reflected in the functional specificity of roles in the Christian community. From the African point of view, the role differentiation among missionary, trader, government administrator, and warrior was novel and puzzling.[70] Consider the missionary relationship with European traders. The CMS agents saw the traders as natural allies in the creation of a Yoruba middle class—the necessary condition for a solid basis of Christianity. So merchants found themselves welcome guests at missionary stations up-country. Later, many missionaries served on the boards of multinational companies, and some were key shareholders.[71] Unlike the traders, however, most missionaries were repelled by Adam Smith's invisible hand. They did not want *any* trade; rather, they wanted trade that required hard work. Merely collecting wild rubber is not conducive to a Christian life; growing cocoa or cotton is.

Missionaries and merchants held very different views of profits. CMS Secretary Henry Venn, in order to encourage cash crop farming in Abeokuta, helped set up a model farm there. But he was appalled by the prospects that the CMS itself might be deriving profits from its cotton venture. The missionaries in the field had only "distaste for [the] role" of cotton entrepreneur.[72] The most profitable enterprise of the CMS was the selling of books; yet in the multitudinous correspondence between London and the field, honest accounting was of far more concern than maximization of profits.[73]

A similar pattern occurs in missionary relations with colonial officials. The two groups shared an interest in European penetration of Yoruba society. The CMS provided lobbying support in London for motions that helped advance the interests of British colonial officers in Nigeria, especially when members of Parliament raised motions to decrease expenditures in the colonies.[74] In the field, CMS personnel were only too glad to act as administrative envoys in the search for a lasting peace to the Yoruba civil wars.[75] In the British bombing and occupation of Oyo in 1895, Yoruba Christians in Oyo convinced the Alaafin that he would gain a substantial advantage over his rivals in Ibadan if he collaborated with the British. He nonetheless resisted, and the British shelled the town, but British officers had given advance warning to the Christian missionaries so that they could avoid injury. The CMS and the British government did appear to be in collusion in this engagement.[76] And in many Yoruba localities, when kings attempted to subvert the goals of Christian missions, the missionaries knew they could go to the local colonial Resident and get a "fair" hearing: the Resident would threaten the king with loss of salary if he continued to harass the missionaries.[77] In Lagos, ties between the CMS and the colonial administration were so close that CMS officials took pride in being called Sọṣi Ijọba, the State Church, in the high society of Victorian Lagos.[78]

There were also, however, certain tensions between missionaries and colonial officials. Colonial administrators often excluded religious observance from their personal lives, which distressed the missionaries. Furthermore, the administrators found that their less than compassionate methods of social control were best performed in secret. They saw the missionaries as whistle-blowers who would report each indiscretion to London society.[79] And even though the Residents were so willing to help the missionaries proselytize in peace, Yoruba chiefs learned how to play one off against the other. In Ile-Ife, for example, the king told the Reverend Phillips that, if Phillips did not show patience in his negotiations for a church, he would tell the Resident that the missionary would not be satisfied with moderation, and this "may cause future complications between you and the white man."[80]

There were ambivalent relations between the missionaries and the British army as well. Missionaries would never consider themselves soldiers, and kept a firm social distance from all but the officers. Missionaries preached peace. Yet after the British ransacked Ijebu, the *Foreign Mission Journal* editorialized that "thousands of slaves will rejoice to see the Union Jack waving . . . War is often a means of opening a door for the gospel to enter a country . . . The landing of troops here now may be part of the divine plan for answering our prayers and opening Ijebu and other interior countries to the gospel."[81] When the missionaries were secure in Abeokuta, they supplied their Egba allies with the latest military technology.[82]

It should be borne in mind that a Christian state conquered Yorubaland both politically and militarily. This is of overriding importance in our consideration of the practical religion of the converted. Christianity, though regarded as something that must be fought against to assure national survival and autonomy, was also a social force to be emulated and studied so that some of its power could be harnessed for nationalist purposes. The Ijebu Yorubas fought Christian evangelization as hard as any Yoruba group; but when the British overran them and their entrepôt monopoly was thereby destroyed, new social forces were unleashed. Young traders, many of whom had already converted to Christianity, became important to the town's well-being.[83] Quick to convert, Ijebus developed the language abilities and contacts with British traders which have served them well, and they have achieved success in the postindependence race for jobs and status. Missionaries came to be seen as resources for a town's development: cities competed against cities; within towns, quarters competed against quarters; those who had access to missionaries had access to literacy. While the advantages of literacy were not entirely clear to most people, there was justifiable fear that a competing group might get more of it and thus get ahead.[84] The construction of the railroad had "created an enormous and an increasing demand for clerks, accountants, commercial agents, dispensers, dressers, sanitary and other inspectors, guards, stationmasters, and others with a good knowledge of English and accounting." Those who had exposure to CMS education were eligible for fancy salaries in their new jobs.[85] The relationship between Christianity and economic resources under colonial rule could be even more direct. In the Lagos colony, the government gave outright grants of land to Christian repatriates from Sierra Leone; and these grants were parlayed into vast fortunes.[86]

Muslims, too, offered literacy; but while literacy in Arabic could enable some Yorubas to widen their trade with Hausa merchants, it could not promise jobs in the civil service or status in the new political center.[87] Hausa and Fulani missionaries would become local authorities; but they either assimilated by learning Yoruba and becoming permanent members of the town, or they gave way to locally elected imams. Muslims in Yorubaland, qua Muslims, did not experience overrule by an exogenous hegemonic elite and thus felt little of the hatred associated with colonial rule; but they had less opportunity to exploit their religious affiliation in order to expand their political power. Hegemonic (and foreign) political power was associated essentially with Christianity.

Christian church organization not only was connected with colonialism but was also progressively racist. To be sure, the missionaries cooperated in a collegial manner with Samuel Crowther. After the failure of the Niger Mission, European missionary societies became convinced that Europeans could not survive in the African interior, and that the gospel would have to be entrusted to Africans. Crowther soon became a bishop. But Henry Townsend, representing the first generation of European missionaries who served in the interior, saw African missionaries as a threat to his career development and to the integrity of the Christian message. By the end of the nineteenth century, the next generation of European missionaries, imbued with a Darwinist ideology, argued that the Africans were not yet at the stage in civilization where they could run their own church. These young men successfully demoted Crowther from his position in order to establish "undisputed European rule" of the church.[88]

Racism and the model of multiple hierarchies help to explain the rise of "Ethiopianism" in the last quarter of the nineteenth century. To the astonishment of the CMS authorities in London, Crowther, shortly before he died and deeply disturbed by the racism in the Church, gave his support to the Delta church in Lagos—a church which claimed to be independent and African. The CMS eventually brought the Delta church back into its fold, but a number of its leaders tried again to break away into the "Bethel" church. Churches with an African flavor began to spring up throughout Yorubaland. The model for rebellion had been fashioned: counterelites in a church upset with the mission would break away rather than fight for control.

While the CMS derided the independent churches for what today we would call "syncretism"—the merging of the new and the old—the move toward an Ethiopian church might better be viewed as initial "reform." African Christians, many of whom accepted the ideas of the church and were shocked by the hypocrisy of the missionaries, were attempting to "purify" Christianity by purging it of the racism and oppression inherent in the foreign-controlled church.

Rebellion persisted in Yorubaland. In the economic isolation of the

First World War, and in the face of some catastrophic epidemics of influenza, people sought new religious prophets. In southern Yorubaland, a variety of indigenous prayer groups (called *aladura*) were organized. From these groups grew many churches that have attracted copious memberships. The new churches—the Cherubim and Seriphim, the Christ Apostolic church, the Church of the Lord—offered more petitionary prayer than did the European-dominated churches, and engaged in curative medicine more in line with Yoruba traditional practices. But their doctrines are clearly in the Christian tradition.[89] Though they have themselves been subject to many breakaway movements from within, these are the fastest-growing churches in Yorubaland today.

PRACTICAL RELIGION OF THE CONVERTED: HISTORICAL AND SOCIOLOGICAL REFLECTIONS

Because the practical religion of the converted is really a mixture of social and religious forces, one must consider contextual factors and dialectical forces as independent variables. For example, in the Middle Belt of Nigeria (north of Yorubaland), the jihad of the early nineteenth century was particularly oppressive. When Christian missionaries appeared there in the early twentieth century, they were widely seen as potential protectors against the (Muslim) Fulani overlords. Local elites were perfectly willing to drop their support for the traditional pantheon as the price to be paid for missionary protection.[90] In Brazil, on the other hand, Christianity became a mechanism by which Yoruba slaves could surreptitiously worship traditional gods. Catholic feast days provided the opportunity for the slaves to dissimulate in order to subvert the Christian-controlled state.[91] In one colonial context Christians are saviors; in the other, tyrants.

The timing of evangelistic activities is an equally important variable. For example, nineteenth-century Christianity in England was a different religion from what exists there today. Anglicanism has lost much of its Victorian moralism in late twentieth-century England. Influenced by theologians such as J. A. T. Robinson in the early 1960s, as well as by social changes, Anglicanism has become more existential, and perhaps more bookish.[92] But these modern influences on English Anglicanism are only dimly felt in Africa today (although, as I will show, the vicar in Ile-Ife was aware of them); the social meaning of Christianity in Yorubaland is more closely attuned to the practical religion of Anglicanism in nineteenth-century England.

What aspect of the world religion was most easily adopted by the social groups that first converted? What did *they* see as essential to the religion? The elements that induced the early converts to adhere to Islam or Christianity shaped the entire social definition of the religion. In Indonesia, different social groups adapted different versions of Islam (some more mystical than others); so it would be possible to identify different practical religions for the same world religion in a single cultural environment.[93] In Yorubaland, one could distinguish the Islam brought down by Fulanis from Ilorin from the Islam that dominated Ile-Ife, which had been brought north from Lagosian Islam and transmitted by Yoruba coastal traders.

The practical religion of the converted has its own dialectic. While Victorian moralism is an essential part of Christianity in Yorubaland, so is its opposite. The Anglican church, to retain its "market share," was compelled to respond to the Aladura churches, which had very expressive and exciting ceremonies. In response, the CMS churches permitted the children in the choir to shake their hips in their procession to the altar to the beat of the "talking drum." So Anglicanism represents both "anti-African moralistic civilization" and its opposite, "exuberant and colorful rhythmic observance." Similarly with Yoruba Islam: the affront to Yoruba sensibilities of the *jihad* led many Yorubas to support doctrines of "peaceful jihad" and the spread of the Muslim faith through the professionalization of the missionary calling.[94]

The dialectic of the practical religion of the converted provides some support for James C. Scott's position that religious and political ideologies may have coherent messages for a few central elites; but the material deprivations of peasants, which are the same everywhere, determine their political action. To understand peasant action, Scott warns, it is futile to study the elite cultural codes. Once they become transmitted as "little traditions," these cultural codes become virtually meaningless.[95]

But it is sociologically wrong to ignore the ideological strands of the little traditions just because the great traditions do not influence them in a linear and unambiguous way. In Yorubaland, to be sure, the little traditions were not exact replicas of the religions in Europe and the Middle East. But the way in which Yoruba society incorporated the two religions was different, with some social impact. For example, Yoruba Muslims tended to associate Allah with Ṣọpọna, the member of the Yoruba pantheon who supposedly causes smallpox. Maintenance of one's dignity amid catastrophe is the accepted relationship with Ṣọpọna: "one who kills and is thanked for it" is what he is sometimes called. In contrast, Yoruba Christians often associated Jesus with Ẹla, a member of the Yoruba pantheon who did good deeds. He was nonetheless maligned by the people of the earth, and he escaped for safety by climbing a rope to the heavens. When disorder comes, Ẹla will restore order for he "rectifies unhappy destinies."[96]

Thus the two religions tap different roots of the same peasant culture. In an anthropological account of one Yoruba city, Aronson provides his reader with two biographies, one of a Muslim, the other of a Christian. The Muslim considered becoming a Christian but could not stomach the rules on polygyny. He had been a slave trader, but after the British conquest he enriched himself in the rubber trade, making contacts with the northern traders and converting to Islam. His devoutness and his wealth made him a model for future Muslim converts in his town. His forthright honesty and his unequivocal desire for political control were considered character traits of what Aronson calls the "northern" orientation of Yoruba culture.

The second man was from a poor family who built up capital by selling medicines. When the Christians came, he used his wealth to trade in palm oil and palm kernels. The missionaries taught him how to read and write and encouraged him to invest in some new economic enterprises. Although he had four wives (a fact he kept quiet about), he became a pillar of the Anglican church and a model for the town's Christian community. His administrative competence and humble birth leading to fortune were considered character traits of the "southern" orientation of Yoruba culture.[97] Peasant societies do not learn precisely as evangelists or ideologues might want them to. But different religious or ideological "great traditions" evoke different aspects of the peasant tradition.

CONCLUSION

Geertz's work has clearly identified the features of the first face of culture. Embedded in any religion are symbols that provide believers with a sense of the "really real" and, hence, with what economists call "preference functions." Rational action can only be properly understood when preferences are known; culture helps set those preferences.

But Geertz's work could not furnish a theoretical framework for comparing the differential impact of Christianity and Islam on social and political behavior. I have therefore adopted Weber's methodological approach even though his substantive findings have been put in question. Following Weber, I have distinguished among three levels of religious impact: the founding doctrines, the practical religion, and the practical religion of the converted. These levels sometimes conjoin and present a common impact on a community of converts; they sometimes influence society in different ways.

I have also attempted to sort out the mechanisms and the cross-pressures involved in the translation of religious values onto society. In so doing, I have focused on the dialectical processes within a religious tradition and the common points of concern rather than on the points of value congruence between religion and society. The differences between Christianity and Islam on each of the three levels form a set of expectations of how the two Yoruba subcultures—Muslim and Christian—may begin to differ in their political behavior after a century of different religious exposure. Finally I provided a sociological and historical basis for understanding the practical religion of the converted among Yoruba Christians and Muslims.

3| Christianity and Islam in Yorubaland: Differences in the Practical Religion

In this chapter I show how Christians and Muslims in Ile-Ife have developed different orientations toward authority, community, equality, and responsibility.[1] Many Yoruba intellectuals hold that there is no real difference between Christians and Muslims (for their views, see the Appendix). But in everyday behavior within their religious communities, I found that members of the two religious subsystems respond to very different political concerns.

This finding will allow me to demonstrate a serious shortcoming in social systems theory. To be sure, the fact that different subsystems promote different concerns does confirm one aspect of social systems theory. But the failure of these different concerns automatically to spill over into other domains of the social system (as we shall see in chapter 4) disconfirms the congruence hypothesis, a central component of social systems theory. It will therefore be necessary to propose an alternate theory of the first face of culture that can better account for cultural differentiation without concomitant differences in political outlook. The alternate theory—the hegemonic model of culture—will receive its initial statement in the conclusion to chapter 4.

HISTORY OF ISLAM AND CHRISTIANITY IN ILE-IFE
Islam in Ile-Ife

In the 1870s, an Ilorin man named Danielu—a traditional healer who incorporated Muslim prayers, incantations, and medical knowledge—had built up a clientele in Ife for his reputed healing powers and his ability to help women overcome infertility.[2] Civil warfare in 1882 caused the Ife people to scatter to huts on their farms. Danielu, however, through loyalty to his customers (along with good profits), followed them to the farms and thus enhanced his reputation among the Ife people. Although he won few converts to his religion, he was well respected.

During the civil war a young Ife boy from the Adeosun family was captured and sold into slavery to a Lagos businessman. In Lagos, Adeosun took lessons in Arabic on his own, unbeknownst to his master. His master learned of this, was impressed, and, being without male issue, adopted Kaseem (the boy's Muslim name). Kaseem became rich—mostly by selling ammunition from Lagos and buying rubber from the interior. After the return of the Ife people to their city, Kaseem's mother urged him too to return to the city of his father.

He did, only to find Danielu, then an old man, trying to establish the Muslim religion in Ife. They prayed together in the mosque at Modakeke, a section of town where Oyo refugees lived and there were already a few Muslims (Adeosun's mother was from Modakeke). After constant appeals to the Ife king (the Ọọni) Olubuse, they were permitted in 1903 to build a mosque at Itakogun, in Ife Town on the road toward Modakeke. Although a number of Ife men had become Muslims in the period of exile, Kaseem Adeosun was the only returnee who was versed in Arabic. He became *naibi* (second man to the imam) and succeeded Danielu as chief imam in 1922. To win converts, Adeosun threw large celebrations, rich with palm wine and cultic activities. He would then teach Muslim prayers and link the Islamic religion to progressive Lagosian trends. Only after he had won his converts (each of whom declared his faith individually) did he tell his followers that drink and idol worshiping were forbidden. His prestige based on his Lagos business associations (and the business associations of other Muslim returnees) certainly enhanced his evangelical cogency.

The returnees provided the critical mass to make for a real life Muslim community. Laani Akogun had returned from Lagos; Asani Ogbingbin from Ibadan; Jojolade from Modakeke; Mohammed Areago from Bida; Sanni Alegbe from Epe; Bakare Oloko from Ejinrin; and Bello from Ilorin. The Muslim refugees who returned, had adopted Islam in various towns and made some money. The prestige of Islam, as nearly all my informants emphasized, lay in its association with the esteemed trading community in Lagos. And, despite the useful service the mosque in Modakeke played in providing Danielu and Adeosun with a place for Friday prayers, it was not until the Modakeke people were temporarily driven from Ife in 1909 that the Muslim religion began to expand in Ife. In 1922, Adeosun began to appoint sectional chiefs throughout the town, paralleling Ife's authority structure. With Adeosun as chief imam, Islam had a true local base.

In the 1930s, the Hausas built their own Friday mosque at Sabo, their expatriate quarter in town. When the Modakeke people returned in 1921, they prayed on Friday at Itakogun and ultimately (though their request was initially rejected by the Ọọni and the District Officer) built their own Friday mosque.[3] Many local mosques were constructed, and the number of sectional mosques grew from three at Danielu's death to about seventeen in 1956. The Ahmadiyya mission came to Ife in 1930 but, as elsewhere in Yorubaland, never attracted many adherents. No more than twenty men pray at the Friday services in Ife's two Ahmadiyya mosques. The Tijaniyya sufi order also has a following in Ife, with about six teachers, but the leading Muslims in Ife's mosque are not themselves sufis.

Conflicts among Muslims in Ife, like those in other Muslim Yoruba communities, have concerned appeals by Hausas to get their own sectional mosque, political battles for succession to the chief imamship, and relations with the Ahmadiyyas. Despite these conflicts, and a more recent and bitter court case over the embezzlement of mosque funds, the Islamic community is strong and visible in Ife. As of 1967, there were in Ife twenty-five sectional mosques.[4] During my stay in Ile-Ife I came into contact with a vigorous society of Alhajis, and an active Ansar ud Deen society, which helps run a local school.

As other Muslim converts in Yorubaland, individuals in Ife were drawn to Islam in large part due to utilitarian benefits, such as remedies for illnesses and opportunities for trade with high-status Lagosian merchants. By the 1920s and 1930s, Islam had become an institutionalized community in Ife, and it attracted an ever wider circle of converts from within the town. Generations of Ife people have now been raised in Islam, and see their religious attachment as part of their personal identities.

Christianity in Ile-Ife

Christianity came to Ile-Ife directly from neighboring Ondo.[5] With the open trading route for Europeans in Eastern Yoruba country, the CMS made successful contacts in Ondo, a city just a few day's walk from Ife. In 1873 the governor of Lagos colony, Captain Glover, used his influence to help restore the deposed Ondo king to his throne. To reward the British, the restored king invited the CMS to his town. Two years later, the Reverend David Hinderer opened a mission there and quickly transferred authority to the Reverend Charles Phillips, the son of a Freetown recaptive.

In 1899, when Phillips had a thriving community of some 158 converts, a small delegation from Ile-Ife that had formed a Christian prayer group the previous year went to Ondo to appeal to Phillips for CMS support. The delegation was led by John Adelaja, an Ijebu rubber merchant, and Daniel Amodu Lawani Ologbenla, an Ife man who had gone to a CMS school in Lagos. Phillips had been to Ife in 1886 to act as an emissary of the British governor of Lagos in order to attempt a settlement between Ife and Modakeke.[6] Phillips returned to Ife, this time with a catechist, E. A. Kayode, to help organize the new church. Kayode's ancestral city was Ife. His father had been sold into slavery during the civil wars, and the young Kayode was born in Osiele, a small village near Abeokuta, and lived with a Christian family. When the Ibadan army was threatening to destroy Abeokuta, Kayode's parents took their son to the CMS mission for protection. Thus began his long association with the CMS.[7]

At this time, Ọọni Olubuse of Ife was unwilling to incur the wrath of the traditional religion's virtuosi, and refused to permit the fledgling Christian community use of his land for a church. His major objection was that the core group of Christians was mostly from other towns.[8] He was right: in a report of a small service in 1898, Phillips noted that the Christians were "mostly Ijebus who came to Modakeke for trade."[9] Indeed, it was not until 1904 that the CMS even regarded themselves as proselytizing in Ile-Ife. Their main targets were the Oyo refugees of Modakeke.[10]

Phillips, more ambitious, sought to capture Ile-Ife itself. This goal led him into a prolonged conflict with the Ọọni, who fended off all of Phillips's gambits. "I have been acquainted with [Phillips] for the past 80 years," the Ọọni claimed, with some exaggeration, "and I do not want him to be hurt by the gods who always parade the precincts of Ile-Ife."[11] Later, Phillips tried again, and could only report that the Ọọni "prevaricated as usual."[12] It took direct intervention and intimidation by the British Resident in Ibadan before the Christians could get land at Iyekere, a midpoint between central Ife and Modakeke.[13] At Iyekere a small church with a school was built. By 1899 the chapel was completed, and Kayode, now the local catechist and schoolmaster, had a constituency of 156 worshipers.[14]

The Ife-Modakeke conflict affected the church's development. When violence became particularly intense, Ọọni Olubuse tried to induce the Ife Christians to leave Iyekere, but Kayode refused. The ill-will between Kayode (who had served as the Ọọni's scribe) and the Ọọni had unfortunate consequences for all Ifes. Ibadan's leaders were able to get the British to cede some of Ife's land to them; but the Ọọni, now without a legal aide, could not frame a response. Angered by Kayode's disloyalty, the Ọọni induced a number of the Ife Christians to form a "Bethel" church in Ife.[15] Ife Christians who remained at Iyekere were harassed.[16]

In 1919, Ademuluyi succeeded Olubuse, and the new Ọọni was more receptive to the Christians. Although never baptized, he gave the CMS land in the four quarters of Ife, sent his children to the CMS school, went annually to the New Year's service, and insisted that the first CMS church to be built in Ife proper should be in his own quarter at Ayetoro. Christians in the other quarters soon started building churches; Iremo (the church of Ọọni Aderemi, who was reigning during my field research) and Aiyegbaju (the church I studied) in 1923, and Ilare in 1925. When the Modakekes returned to their section in 1921, their Christians sought land, and by 1923 began worshiping in a new church, St. Stephen's Modakeke.

With five thriving churches in the early 1920s, the CMS was on the threshold of growth. Fortunately for them the charismatic pastor J. S. Adejumo was assigned to the Ayetoro church in 1925. His influence was felt throughout the town. An Ibadan man himself, he had been to Ife before as a teacher at the CMS school at Iyekere. One of his wives was an Ife woman and his compound was one of the liveliest in town. His alleged polygynous activities were famous, and his children (one of whom married

Ọọni Aderemi) were omnipresent. He had been involved in a small monetary scandal earlier in his career but had absolved himself.[17] He was an accomplished traditional healer, and his clinics in Ife were popular in the entire region. The great irony of Christian expansion in Ife, then, was that it fed on Adejumo's supposed polygyny and traditional healing, both of which were scorned by the CMS authorities. Adejumo never became a bishop, however, probably because of rumors concerning irregular behavior—but he did more for the Anglican church in Ife than anyone else. Christianity spread in Ife without the "benefit" of any European missionary. It was propagated, in the eyes of the Ifes, in both CMS and independent churches, by Yorubas.

If Ife Christianity was not strongly associated with Victorian social norms, the practical religion of Ife's converted did entail a large dose of organizational hierarchy. Kayode and other members of the congregation corresponded regularly with outside higher authorities, and they were judged by bureaucratically set standards. Kayode, like all other African novices, had to write an essay on his views on polygyny before he could be ordained.[18] Like Adejumo he had been accused of scandalous behavior. When he was serving in Oyo, his wife had quarreled with a local woman, who, filled with revenge, accused the young pastor of "an immoral act." The church hierarchy demanded a full investigation of the allegations against Kayode, as it had done for Adejumo. Both were ultimately exonerated.[19]

Along with church hierarchy came multiplicity. Ife also had Methodist, Baptist, Seventh Day Adventist, and Catholic missions, all of which competed for Ife souls. In the 1920s and 30s, the *aladura* began to grow as well. Today, all the major prayer-oriented churches are represented in Ile-Ife, and they have large constituencies. I have no reports of fights for the control of any church; when there was conflict, churches of whatever denomination would split up and become separate units. Multiple and competing hierarchies was the normal pattern of Christian authority in Yorubaland.

Like Islam in Ife, Christianity gained its initial adherents from strangers in the town or from sons of the town who had returned from refugee status. Early adherents foresaw some utilitarian benefits and no extraordinary costs. Thus nonrefugees were encouraged to join forces with the returning converts. Unlike Islam, however, Christianity did not face deep rivalries within a single structure; rather, it faced segmentation of churches in the face of conflict. Again unlike Islam, Christianity (especially with the CMS) had an international hierarchy and a modern bureaucracy.

FIELD OBSERVATIONS OF PRACTICAL RELIGION

My field data show that Muslim and Christian Yorubas differ most significantly when concerned with questions of community vs. society; authority; equality; and responsibility.

Community and Society

The hierarchical nature of the Christian institution as compared with the occasionalist nature of Muslim organization suggests the distinction between Muslim *community* and Christian *society*.[20] The mosque in Ile-Ife is best described as a club or a fraternity. As in any club, entrance requires guidance. Entry into the mosque entails a personal commitment (indeed, as I recount in the Appendix, it required an act of courage for me to enter the first time). Since the doorway leading into the mosque is very narrow, participants in Friday prayers find themselves crowding together to enter. Every person who enters is thereby seen and noticed. Inside the mosque, behavior patterns alter. Men who have been joking and laughing in the street suddenly become austere and quiet. The Muslim requirement to perform ablutions before prayer further requires self-revelation to the group. Strangers cannot easily slip into the mosque unnoticed. By entering, one crosses a threshold which makes one part of the Muslim community.

St. Paul's Church is best described as a bureaucratic society. Any client can enter to seek grace. The doors are plentiful and wide, inviting all strangers. Many people can enter at once, and although some Christians cross themselves upon entering, most people do not noticeably change their behavior when inside the church. People can enter from a side door, sit down with their friends, and keep a private conversation going throughout the service. The church is a society of Christians.

On the platform in which mosque officials lead prayers there is apparent anarchy. The imam, the tafsir (charged with providing Qur'anic commentary; in Ile-Ife called *taosir*), the treasurer, and other officials all share one microphone and stand in a circle grabbing it from each other as each has something to contribute. This embodies the institutional occasionalism discussed in chapter 2. In contrast with the supposed authorities, the congregation is perfectly organized in symmetrical rows that run perfectly straight for thirty men in each row. If a colleague is out of line, someone on the line exhorts him to readjust himself to attain collective symmetry. The opposite applies in the church. There, only in the chancel is there perfect symmetry. The choir is evenly divided by sex, by size, and by robe color. Everything in the chancel represents balance. The institution revels in official symmetry. But in the congregation there is asymmetry. The women considerably outnumber the men, but they are allotted only half the space; so the church is overcrowded on one side and sparce on the other. People are free to sit anywhere (on their side), which often means large empty spaces, with friends from a particular club crowded into a small section. As in any bureaucratic society, the bureaucrats tend to be more organized than the clients. Nonofficials in the mosque share a community feeling; nonofficials in the church are individuals within a society.

And so, in the mosque, one does not stake out one's personal space. If a man sits alone, others will crowd around him on his left and right until the row is completed. In the church I have seen many men sitting alone, their personal space respected. Crowding into a bench is rare if there is space elsewhere. Many times when I appeared early for Sunday services and sat alone, I would remain so through the entire service. This never occurred in the mosque. An individual can be abandoned in a society; he will not be permitted to isolate himself in a community.

One explanation for this difference might be traced to the social conditions under which conversion took place. Victorian Englishmen held a deep concern for the protection of their personal space. Anglican seating patterns in Yoruba churches have more to do with nineteenth-century northern European views of the human body than with Christianity. (How this pattern got to Ile-Ife, which never had a European pastor, is unclear.) Another explanation lies in the way authority came to be established in Ife Christianity and Islam.

Authority

Christians in Ife belong to a hierarchical institution. They share a view of authority that emphasizes procedures over substance and grants legitimacy to leaders whose role definitions are specific. Muslims belong to an occasionalist institution. They share a view of authority that emphasizes substance over procedures and grants legitimacy to leaders whose role definitions are diffuse.

The Church Missionary Society forged a hierarchical institution. In London, the CMS Secretary wrote copious memos to the missionaries in the field emphasizing the organizational criteria for successful evangelization. A typical set of regulations concerned the constitution for Native Church Committees and Provisional Church Councils:

> The duties of the Church Committee shall be the election of Delegates to the Provisional Church Council (where qualified to send Delegates); the general supervision and management of the temporalities of the congregation; the collection of Church funds . . . The Chairman of a Church Committee shall have a veto upon all proceedings . . . No Church Committee shall be recognized as qualified to send Delegates unless raising £3 a year in aid of the Church Council Fund.[21]

After considerable minuting, the phrase "by bona-fide native contributions" was added to the last sentence.

Clear regulations were set for the performance of every job. The Reverend Kayode, for example, who did yeoman service for the CMS in Ile-Ife, was not ordained until all regulations had been scrupulously met. In 1903, Bishop Phillips of Ondo recommended him for ordination and wrote a letter to the Executive Committee on his behalf. As we have seen, he had first to be exonerated from an allegation of immoral conduct. Yet it was another year before the Executive Committee approved his ordination.[22] Bishop Phillips, too, was made constantly aware of his position on an institutional ladder. Once he had to make a series of formal requests for £5 so that he could purchase presents for local chiefs. Another time, when he raised money locally, his success was blunted by an admonition from the Executive Committee that "the Fund shall henceforth be known as the Ondo Native Pastorate Fund instead of 'Bishop Phillips Jubilee Memorial Fund.'"[23] The overall message was that the church required utmost attention to the successful application of hierarchically set rules and regulations.

Institutionalization and hierarchy necessitate bookkeeping. In St. Paul's Church, during my field work, the bursar was a key church officer. He kept records of contributions for every church member, for every church society (ẹgbẹ), for every Sunday, and for every major holiday. Each contribution was further categorized according to whether it was given for the regular fund (the first church collection) or the building fund (the second collection). Careful records were also kept for the contributions given during the children's service, which amounted to a few naira per week. As should be clear, the forging of the institution was translated into practice as the creation of rules of procedure.

Christian proceduralism was most noticeable in staffing. For the Anglican church in Ife, the vicar is chosen by the bishop of the Ibadan Diocese. The bishop heads a whole hierarchy of sextons, catechists, deacons, vicars, and archdeacons. He chooses incumbents on the basis of impersonal bureaucratic criteria. The wishes of particular functionaries within the bureaucracy or the wishes of particular congregations have no official worth. Institutionally set qualifications (plus ability to preach in the Yoruba language) determine placement and promotion. Early Yoruba preachers were very sensitive to the fact they were being asked by CMS authorities to serve in towns in which they were strangers. In 1904 in his Annual Letter to London, the Reverend R. S. Oyebode from Ilesha reported from his evangelical travels (of perhaps thirty miles) that "the Ifes seem to be intelligent as a race."[24] There was, in fact, much grumbling about postings in strange towns. In 1918, the Reverend Adeyemi, serving in the wider district of which Ife was a part, requested a transfer to Ondo, his ancestral city. His patron, the Reverend Oyebode, testified before the CMS Executive Committee in Lagos that the people too wished "to have an Ondo born Clergyman in their midst." He was told by the Secretary, however, that Mr. Adeyemi's appointment "implied his readiness to take any charge to which he might be appointed.[25] Five years later, the Reverend Akinyemi in Ife was relieved of his official duties with the Anglican Church because he would not accept transfer from his ancestral city.[26]

It is therefore not surprising that there has not been one son of Ife town itself who has ever been the vicar of St. Paul's, Aiyegbaju. Ekiti, Ijebu, and Ibadan men have served as vicars; these men were always considered "strangers" by the congregation. Even the Reverend Adejumo, whose exploits on behalf of Ife Christianity are famous, was an Ibadan man. To some extent, because so many of his children grew up in Ife and because he willed to be buried in Ife, he has been adopted by the town. But his initial legitimacy to rule an institution in Ife derived from sources outside his standing within the town. The present archdeacon of Ife is an Owo man. He registered his automobile plates in Ife in order to demonstrate solidarity with the people; but his authority too derived from the procedural dictates of the Anglican hierarchy. To be sure, that hierarchy is not blind. In the late 1970s, St. Paul's received a new vicar, the Reverend Akinyemi (an Egba), who could not establish rapport with the leading parishioners. Church officers successfully appealed to the bishop for his transfer. Akinyemi was reposted to his ancestral city; but St. Paul's paid a price. Months went by before a new vicar was appointed, and the church began to lose members fast. Bureaucratic procedures rather than any special qualities of the incumbent determine postings in the Anglican hierarchy.

Anglican proceduralism is also evident in the practice of inviting lecturers to the church. Visitors regularly preached on the St. Paul's pulput. While sometimes these lecturers were lay members of the church, more often they were colleagues of the vicar's in the local Christian council. In the case of outside visitors, few in the congregation knew who it was that was preaching to them. Twice the vicar from the nearby university lectured; his sermons were erudite, long, and over the heads of the peasant constituency. Church members would yawn, tell jokes, and divert themselves in other ways; they would not question the right of the visitor to lead them in prayer.[27] Because the visitors wore the proper garment and had been invited by the vicar, they received the respect due to their office.

The procedural basis of legitimation has implications for the way in which authority is exerted. Vicars tend to be modest, unassuming men, who make no great claims for themselves. They stand aloof from the more garish Yoruba institutions, like the spraying of money on foreheads. They are without that air of toughness and imminent anger that characterizes "big" men in Yoruba society. Most of the vicars I observed seemed to exert authority as progressive schoolteachers do: they exhorted and explained, but rarely screamed or threatened.

Legitimation through bureaucratic procedures breeds a rhetoric of legalisms. This became apparent to me when I interviewed Christians about where they would be buried. From the advent of Christianity in West Africa, missionaries put considerable stress on the importance of church burials. A true Christian, they argued, should not worry about proximity to his family after his death; heaven provided richer contacts. But the custom of compound burials was hard to change, and Yoruba churchyards were rarely used. At St. Paul's, however, the construction of a greatly expanded church structure severely limited graveyard space, and I was able to observe the clearing of a new burial ground on land donated by a church member. While participating in the service blessing the new grounds, I inquired about the choice of whether to be buried there or in the compound. Every answer I received had a legalist tint: "Don't you know, pagans and Muslims bury in their compounds; Christians bury in cemeteries," answered one of my informants. The archbishop gave the sermon and told the group that his wife had asked him, If a good Christian gets buried in his compound, is he still a Christian? The archbishop responded to that question by restating the law of the church on burials. The church rhetoric of legalisms was being transferred to the congregation.

Proceduralism of course requires the filling of *particular* offices. In this sense it leads toward role specificity in church life. Every church function has a role. The church requires both religious and secular authority, for example, and so there are two routes to power in the church. The vicar is the apex of religious authority and is nominally the head of the church in the meetings of the parochial church council. But the PCC also consists of twenty of the leaders of the church "societies" (ẹgbẹ), of which there are nearly one hundred. Also on the PCC are the church chiefs—the Baba Salẹ, the Balogun, the Ọtun Balogun, and the Alatunṣe—all of whom have titles modeled after those of Oyo, the political center of Yorubaland from the seventeenth through the early nineteenth century. Those individuals who contribute generously, who are successful in inducing others to give, and who keep a helping eye on church activities are favored in chiefly assignations, for service in the interests of the church is the understood criterion for chiefly status. Religious virtuosity is not a criterion. The vicar's role is to provide religious services; the chiefs' roles concern the organizational integrity of the church. Different roles have different incumbents.

But it is not only in the church hierarchy that roles abound. Roles proliferate in the church with a hierarchic pattern manifest in the size-placed procession of the choir as it moves up to the chancel. The church has specified roles for those who lead the choir, who collect the money as it passes down the aisles, who count the money once it has been blessed by the vicar, who police the aisles so that proper decorum is preserved, and who take precise attendance figures at every service. The bursar, a paid officer, himself, performs several roles, which are carefully enumerated and include the collection of rent on the fruit stalls that were constructed on the perimeter of the church compound. The vicar, too, performs different roles, kept spatially discrete. For instance, he uses the lectern to raise money, the pulpit to give a sermon.

The Sunday service was an apt time to celebrate the installation of new officers. One Sunday I observed the installation of the "father" of the women's societies along with the officer in charge of keeping the vicar informed about who is ill and requires a priestly visit. The archdeacon attended that service and congratulated the congregation for its good judgment in its choice of officers. He then went into a careful description of the tasks associated with each role. He pointed out, for example, that no one should blame the vicar if he did not visit a sick person, unless he had been informed by the proper official. The vicar, he stressed, had his own overwhelming administrative tasks, which the archdeacon proceeded to summarize. In this talk, and in regular participation in the church, Ife Anglicans were experiencing a procedurally based method of legitimating authority in which roles were specific and carefully circumscribed.

Authority in the mosque had very different attributes. The Muslim community in Ife is less interested in organizational roles, though there is some hierarchy and organization. The chief imam is the presiding officer of the mosque, and under him in most Yoruba mosques is a *naibi* (second in command); a *tafsir*; a council of imams from the sectional mosques in the town; and a *muezzin*, the person who calls the faithful to prayer. Most mosques have a set of secular offices as well, such as the *balogun* (a military officer in Secular Society), commensurate with the Oyo system of chiefly titles. There are also a great number of *ẹgbẹ* (societies) associated with the mosques. One scholar researched the development of these societies in a number of Yourba mosques in various towns in today's Oyo state and found many with inventive and unusual names: "the association of those who rejoice in Arabic"; "the association of those who have money to demand Arabic knowledge"; etc.[28] Most towns also have associations with societies that transcend their own mosque, such as the Ansar Ud-Deen Society, which has been responsible for encouraging Muslims to expose themselves to a modern education. Associationist tendencies, which are found in the churches, are no less prevalent in the mosques.

Association does not mean hierarchy and distinct organizational roles, however. In the central mosque of Ile-Ife, roles never were specific. Just as the Prophet found it normal to proselytize, trade, and lead armies in one and the same career, many Muslim teachers provide not only Qur'anic teaching but medicinal and oracular services as well.[29] In the weekly money collection at Enuwa Mosque (the central mosque of Ile-Ife, where all

Muslims are expected to congregate for Friday afternoon prayers), the tafsir also plays the role of exhorting the community for financial contributions. While he, microphone in hand, on center stage, solicits large donations from the wealthier members, a few others circle through the ranks collecting small change. This task usually went to the less prestigious adherents. But it surprised no one when one Friday one of the richest members of the Islamic community took the small collection box, crawled through the rows, and begged for coins. If a member of the society of *alhajis* (men who have made the pilgrimage to Mecca) wanted to collect small change, so be it. One Friday a young alhaji wanted to make a plea for greater efforts toward Arabic education in the town; he merely asked the imam a few moments before the prayers, and his request was granted. (In the church, many of the services have printed programs, making last-minute changes unlikely.)

Because roles are not specific, role substitutions are not easily made. Visiting authorities did not substitute for the chief imam as they did for the vicar at St. Pauls. In fact, there is no institutionalized procedure to cover for the imam should he be absent from Friday prayers. One Friday when the chief imam of Enuwa Mosque was late, a hush fell over the mosque. His absence could only mean illness. An argument erupted as someone had to substitute for the chief imam; but the rules for substitution were unclear. The imam appeared amid the debate, much to the relief of the community, so the question was not resolved. But the nature of authority in the Mosque was clearly revealed: *who* it is leading prayers is more important than the procedure by which he was chosen.

Even the apparently clear distinction between secular and sacred routes to power was not consistently maintained in the mosque. The officers of the mosque tend to exhibit, by local criteria, religious virtuosity. The society of alhajis bridges secular and sacred authority. Wealth makes possible the pilgrimage to Mecca, which in itself provides the opportunity for importing into Nigeria goods that will further enhance one's wealth. Religious fulfillment is therefore rarely the major motivation for making the pilgrimage. Nonetheless, preparations for the pilgrimage are extensive and require considerable religious instruction. So those who hold important offices have gone through special religious training. The blending of the sacred and secular is further demonstrated in seating patterns at the Mosque. In the church the religious and secular elites have their own groups with whom they sit. In the mosque, the leading Muslims, whether by age, wealth, or special religious qualities, all sit together, close to the imam. Minute role differentiations have little meaning in mosque authority structures.

Outside authority plays a less central role in mosque leadership. In the early years of Islamic penetration into Yorubaland, it was common for "strangers" to be chosen as chief imam. In some Yoruba cities, such as Oyo and Ilorin, the chief imamship has passed down a family line of outsiders. In these cases a new position, called *parakoyi*—which in secular politics meant the person having authority over long-distance trade, but in Islam's appropriation, the term is used to mean the political intermediary between town authority and the Mosque—went to a son of the town. In most Yoruba towns, however, locals eventually captured the chief imamship.[30] In Ile-Ife, ever since the death of Danielu (the Ilorin doctor who brought Islam to Ife), the chief imams have all been sons of Ife town.

Because mosque organization is role-diffuse and does not easily allow role substitutability, the institution runs on ad hoc judgments rather than standard operating procedures. This point was nowhere more evident than in the question of imam succession—probably the most difficult organizational problem faced universally in Islam. Ile-Ife's experience with succession exemplifies Islamic authority.

In the first generation, there was no problem. Kaseem Adeosun succeeded Danielu to the chief imamship in 1922. At his death in 1934, he was succeeded by Raji, who led the town in prayer until his death in 1949. In that year, a thirty-year battle for the chief imamship began. The two claimants for the imamship were Yusuf Adeosun, the son of Kaseem, and Oseni Odukuro, Raji's naibi. Oseni claimed that Kaseem had been naibi to Danielu and that Raji had been naibi to Kaseem; therefore the precedent had been set that the naibi succeeds the imam. Not so, said Adeosun's supporters, proclaiming Adeosun's better knowledge of the Qur'an and his greater popularity within the Muslim community.

Oseni, wrongly postulating that the procedures of the colonial judicial system would work to his advantage, brought suit against Adeosun. To Oseni's surprise, the judge in the Benin Judicial Division dismissed Oseni's plea because he did not demonstrate that he became "Chief Imam in accordance with the Muslim law practice. He must be elected by a gathering of the whole community."[31] The Ọọni of Ife brought a temporary settlement then by getting both parties to agree to lead prayers on alternating Fridays. This was only the first round in the courts, where the disputants focused primarily on their moral claims to the office while the common law judges were arguing about (their vague ideas of) Islamic procedure.

In 1956 Oseni died, and his naibi, Asani Bello, claimed the chief imamship. That year the Asani group sued Adeosun; and, in a separate action two yeas later, Adeosun's group sued Asani's. The decision at the Ife Magistrate's Court was in favor of Adeosun. The Asani Bello group then appealed to the Supreme Court of Nigeria in Lagos, where Justice Ayodole Coker wrote the opinion which overturned the Ife court's decision. He ruled that neither group had gotten the "vote, either unanimously or of the majority of the whole Muslim community."[32] The judge did not rule out a new hearing should a proper procedure be followed.

At this time the Asani group was gaining strength. Their candidate, unlike Oseni, was well versed in the Qur'an and had a strong following in Ife based on his exceptional character and his political activism. His group therefore attempted to stage a formal vote on 1 July 1966. The Adeosun group ignored this ploy, and Asani was elected. But on the following Friday, when Asani tried to lead prayers (it was Adeosun's week) on the basis of his election of the previous week, Adeosun and his sons stormed the central mosque and broke the microphone. The police marched in to dispel the riot and locked up the central mosque. Until 1977, Friday prayers were held in two different sectional mosques.

Asani went back to the courts in 1967 to ask that Adeosun be restrained from posturing as chief imam. The case went before Mr. Justice E. O. Fakayode in the High Court of Justice, Oshogbo Judicial Division. Here Adeosun counterattacked, claiming that in 1965 the balogun of the mosque had called a meeting of the leaders of the sectional mosques and twenty out of twenty-nine had voted for him to be chief imam. The balogun then turbaned him. He also claimed that Asani was not fit to be chief imam as he had a crooked finger (the imam, by Islamic tradition, should be physically normal) and had been arrested in 1949 (as a follower of R. A. Fani-Kayode—grandson of the catechist, who became a lawyer and a politician—in a demonstration against the government demanding social amenities for Ife). Asani, however, claimed that he fulfilled the requirements demanded by Judge Coker of Lagos and that a proper election had substantiated his claim.

Fakayode was unimpressed with both arguments, and attempted to settle the issue on his own. He therefore brought his court to Ife on 23 June 1967 to collect evidence. While Nigeria was bracing itself for a civil war, Muslim Ife was thoroughly mobilized for a crucial election; sound trucks blared as both sides rallied their forces. The judge ordered all Muslims to go to their sectional mosques on that day and stationed police to assure that there would be no movement among Muslims between mosques. He then polled all twenty-five mosques and found that sixteen supported Asani, eight supported Adeosun, and one was divided. With that evidence, he ruled, "I have no doubt in my mind at all that Asani Bello is a popular candidate . . . Therefore I hereby order that [he] be appointed Chief Imam."[33]

Adeosun's group immediately appealed the Fakayode decision to the Western State Court of Appeal in Ibadan. The three-justice appeal court overturned Fakayode on procedural grounds. First, the trial judge had not adequately described "how the views of the majority of the muslims in each sectional mosque were ascertained, whether the worshippers there were genuine and regular muslims or whether they were merely produced for the occasion." The electoral procedure was therefore considered of dubious value. Second, the trial judge had gone to Ife improperly. "[W]e find it extremely difficult to resist the conclusion," the Ibadan justices declared, "that the visits were more in the nature of an investigation by the trial judge than an extension of the *locus* of the trial."[34] Other procedural irregularities by Fakayode were mentioned, and the Ibadan court declared that the central mosque in Ife should remain closed "until the final determination of the case."[35] The issue was never settled in the courts.

With the central mosque at Enuwa locked, the two factions continued to pray at separate sectional mosques every Friday. Asani Bello died in 1971 and was succeeded by Y. A. Balogun. In 1977 a group of conciliators, seeing that Adeosun was soon to die, arranged a settlement. Adeosun would become chief imam and Balogun his naibi, with the promise that Balogun would succeed Adeosun. Adeosun's health allowed him to be undisputed chief imam for only a short time, and he was indeed succeeded by Balogun. The Islamic community, fearing another such battle, has eliminated the office of naibi. It has not developed a clear procedure for succession. Most elders say that the most qualified man will follow, hoping that history will not repeat itself. The substantive merits of any putative leader rather than the mode of his selection remain uppermost in their minds. In Islam, the legitimation of authority is less on procedures than on the merits of an officeholder or office seeker.[36]

The mode in which authority is legitimated has implications for the way it is exerted. The Anglican church as bureaucracy differs from the mosque as club. The imam at Enuwa Mosque was not an appointed civil servant to minister to the salvation of his congregation; rather, he was a member of a local community who had earned its respect. Members of the mosque visiting the imam called him Baba (father) out of intimacy and respect. In contrast, the vicar at the church was referred to as "Sir" or "Master." Moreover, the imam, and more obviously the tafsir, exerted authority more directly than did the vicar. In his collection of contributions, the tafsir not only exhorted but insulted, caressed, humiliated, and honored his fellow Muslims. His commanding presence, loud voice, large body, and intense eye contact with his audience all demonstrate a view that authority ought to be exerted.

The club atmosphere pervades the Muslim community in Ife. Compare the way collections are taken, for example. In the church, accountants record each collection with double-entry techniques. In the mosque, the imam, the tafsir, the treasurer, and a random set of other officers dump the day's collection on the floor just in front of the platform where prayers were led. They all sit in a circle, tell jokes, and push the money back and forth as if distributing stakes in a card game. The imam takes his share, and others who have provided special services (such as amplification equipment) are given their payment right from the "pot." Such techniques can of course lead to abuse. The local chapter of the Ansar Ud-Deen society was in total disarray—and lost great opportunities for the promotion of education among Muslim youth—when its chairman had absconded with the society's funds. Nonetheless, comraderie pervades collective action in the mosque.

In sum, the Christian society in Ile-Ife has developed a functionally specific institution in which roles are legitimated through the development of procedures. This authority structure parallels the practical religion of Christian corporatism. The Muslim community, on the other hand, has developed a functionally diffuse organization in which roles are legitimated through the substantive claims of an incumbent. Muslim authority structures in Ile-Ife are compatible with the practical religion of Muslim contractualism.

Sermons demonstrate the differences between Christian corporatism and Muslim contractualism as authority structures get legitimated in the two subcultures. I recorded three typical sermons at St. Paul's and three at Enuwa. In the church sermons I found six references to the church itself as an institution; in the mosque sermons there was no comparable reference. The vicar could speak of "confusion" in the church" and of "many churches where the work of God is not going well,"[37] because in Christianity the church itself is a commanding social reality. The institution is real. In the Muslim sermons, there were no such references; but contractualism was clearly evident. I coded the sermons for "If . . . then . . ." references, which demonstrated authority through contract. The vicar never used such rhetoric, but the chief imam used it eleven times in the three sermons I recorded. "All of you who are contributing money to this mosque, God will not let your pocket run dry," the Muslims were admonished. Or again: "If you have money and you are doing bad things, people will be regarding you as a good person but God will regard you as a bad fellow."[38] This is not to deny that there is a long tradition of similar sorts of admonitions in the Christian tradition—witness especially the parable of the talents (Matthew 25:14–30)—What I am suggesting is that the individual believer's relationship to Jesus is only in a limited way based on a bargain.[39] A more careful distinction needs to be made between "legitimacy" and "authority." Let us define "legitimacy" as the "legal right to rule." "Authority" can then be conceived of as the ability to command compliance without much resort to coercion. In the language of political exchange, an authority is a dominant figure with a high credit rating. That is to say, he will receive support from his followers without need to expend valuable resources in order to demonstrate his power. High credit ratings are a function of having cultivated a committed core of followers who see some moral worth in their leaders' incumbency.,[40] As legitimacy is opposed to illegitimacy, so authority may be contrasted with "pure domination."

The data presented in this section suggest that a leading point of concern within Christianity was to avoid "illegitimacy" by emphasizing correct procedure in choosing new leadership. A leading point of concern within Islam was to avoid pure domination by emphasizing the moral worth (or high credit rating) of the incumbent. Political authorities in the church can therefore be seen as acting to enhance their legitimacy while their Muslim counterparts are acting to protect their authority. Different conceptions of what authority is and how to protect it, nurture it, grasp it, and exert it are embedded in the subcultures of Christianity and Islam in Ife.

Equality

The corporate nature of Occidental Christianity made hierarchy a fact of life. Institutional hierarchy legitimates political inequality and makes it seem at best a necessary evil. The battle against inequality has usually been associated with rejection of the legitimacy of the church itself. Those Christians who have gone back to the founding doctrines and seen in them a call for the equality of all believers have been compelled to renounce their institutional membership. In the Nigerian context, the church hierarchy was associated with a foreign and politically dominant elite, which employed a social Darwinist ideology bordering on racism to legitimate its continued political control over the religious institution it created. In the practical religion of the converted, then, the tendency toward hierarchy was reinforced by colonialism and racism.

Islamic contractualism has a definite egalitarian thrust. To be sure, in many Islamic communities, including some emirates in northern Nigeria, the grossest inequalities have been common. But, because attention was rarely focused on institutional needs, the question of social equality remained a central point of concern among Muslims. Gross inequalities within the Islamic community appear to need justification; they can be challenged without requiring a new founding.

In Yoruba society before the advent of Christianity and Islam, inequality was accepted. The Yoruba polity was gerontocratic and recognized certain lineages as royal. The society was fraught with status differentiation; the economy permitted vast discrepencies of wealth. But in recent decades there have been moves toward equality. In Yorubaland during the Second Republic, the leading political party (the Unity Party of Nigeria) had a progressive social program consisting of universal free education and health care. Its leader, Obafemi Awolowo (who in the course of demonstrating his economic achievements displayed his personal wealth with outrageous insouciance), has long been an advocate of social programs that offer equal opportunity to the poor.

In the Muslim community of Ile-Ife, consistent with the practical religion of Islam, some of the more apparent manifestations of Yoruba inequality have been muted. All believers sit on prayer mats on the floor. Higher-status men and titled officers do, it is true, sit closer to the imam, and the more affluent believers bring, or have lower-status men carry for them, their own thick rugs rather than use the general prayer mats. Nonetheless, the seating boundaries are fluid, and nontitled adherents have little difficulty in penetrating the front rows. Furthermore, the floor is a great equalizer. In some Muslim societies, male status is exhibited through the use of expensive perfumes; but Ile-Ife Muslims were no more ostentatious about perfumes than were Christians. Perhaps because of the floor, or because of the call for simple white robes in the Islamic tradition, the sartorial splendor of expensive lace, so dominant among the rich in Yoruba society, is muted at the mosque. While occasionally I did observe Muslims dressed rather expensively for Friday prayers, more often I observed wealthy men wearing simple robes. Among the leading indicators of wealth and success is contemporary Yoruba society, dress is less differentiated among the Muslim believers.

Yoruba customs for greeting require younger men to prostrate to their elders. Today, men will bow to demonstrate respect for all those above them in the status hierarchy. In the mosque this norm is temporarily suspended. Greetings are in Arabic, and both greeters are required to bend their knees to an equal depth so that they are mutually deferent. Dress codes and greeting rituals are but two examples of how customs reinforcing inequalities in secular life are muted within the confines of the mosque.

In the Anglican church, in part because of its corporate tradition and in part because the missionaries were from a state far more powerful than that of the converts, the inegalitarian aspects of Yoruba society were reinforced. The minute social differentiations that characterize chiefly titles in Yoruba society are clearly evident in the church. There is a clear status hierarchy in the worth of jobs performed. Societies within the church are graded on the basis of their contributions and the status of their members. Seating within the church is differentiated for status groups. In many Anglican churches in Yorubaland (but not St. Paul's), the front pews can be purchased. Wealth is conspicuously displayed; Sunday is the day for expensive cars to be driven into the church compound and for the finest lace to be worn.[41]

Secular achievement is prized at St. Paul's. When members of the church attain high positions in civilian life, the church provides an ideal place to celebrate. Associated with the modern, the Anglican church makes a prestigious—and neutral—setting for fêting "strangers" to the town. A church member who received a major promotion at Radio Oyo wanted his fellow workers to celebrate with him at the church. The vicar turned the occasion into a religious celebration, lecturing to all worshipers that the member's promotion reflected glory on their church. The celebrants received special prayers. Richer members are undoubtedly encouraged to make large contributions for capital improvements because their worldly successes can so well be acknowledged on the church grounds. Once, when the Oyo State Head of Service appeared at St. Paul's, the vicar noticed her presence as he marched up to the altar. He prefaced his sermon by giving her special thanks for honoring the church by her attendance.

The church, always ready to celebrate worldly achievements, never became an arena where inequalities could be challenged. As we saw in chapter 2, challenges to racism and social Darwinism led to breakaway movements. The breakaway churches, however, while rejecting the idea of racial superiority, did not themselves reflect the equality of the early Christian communities. In the Aladura churches one finds "great attention given to these matters of rank, insignia, and privilege."[42] When one group feels relatively deprived in an Aladura church, it tends to break away and form a new church. In Yoruba Christianity, then, social inequality is not a major point of concern.

Two exceptions of the above generalizations glare out from my field notes. Both, I think, sustain my argument. In the mosque, a leading member once donated a considerable sum, far more than one of his elders. He publicly announced his apologies for embarrassing that elder by contributing more money. To demonstrate his respect for age, he said, he would prostrate himself before his elder—and proceeded to do so in the most obsequious of manners. The community laughed uproariously. A norm (that of all Muslims bowing to each other in equal measure) was clearly being broken for comic effect. The gesture was amusing only because prostration to a social superior appeared outlandish in a mosque.

My second example comes from my visit to the new burial ground. Transport to the new grounds was arranged on an ad hoc basis, and many people (including myself) arrived much earlier than the archbishop. This event attracted two sets of people: rich members with titles, who were at the ceremony ex officio; and underemployed urban members who had little else to do on a weekday morning. As we waited, it grew hotter and hotter. Rich and poor alike were exposed to the hot sun without shade. For the first time in a Christian environment in Ile-Ife, I observed the poorer people telling salacious stories, speaking onomatopoeically, and drawing social superiors into their ribaldry. Everyone was laughing together, and the hierachic Christian society was temporarily leveled. Social leveling can occur in a Christian setting, but it requires extraordinary circumstances. As would be expected, when the archbishop appeared, decorum and the status hierarchy were restored.

Status hierarchy bothersome in the Muslim context, is muted in the mosque but complemented in the church; Christians who wish to challenge the status hierarchy can do so only by leaving the church.[43]

Sexual Equality

Patterns of sexual inequality in the church and the mosque are harder to explain. Although I did not systematically investigate the female role in the two religious communities and did not interview Christian and Muslim women, I did observe sexual roles on the days of worship. Observing women in the Anglican church in Ile-Ife gave me a sense of irony; observing women at the central mosque gave me a sense of despair.

Women have played a remarkable role in Yoruba society. In traditional religion, women do not hold the highest positions. In marriage they have always been dependent on their polygynous husbands. Divorced women are social outcastes. Politically, however, women have done better, and in many cities they have cornered the market on certain titles. Economically, women have accumulated vast wealth as traders and have used their money with discretion. Wealth gives them an impressive social presence.

Missionary Christianity in Yorubaland was perhaps more Victorian than Christian. Believing that monogamy was a core value in a Christian life, they exerted great pressure on converts to renounce polygyny, but with little success. Motivation for an African (breakaway) church came largely from men who had become part of the religious hierarchy but could not advance in it because of their polygynous practices. Many of the men who remained in the CMS church had more than one wife; and in the outlying areas like Ile-Ife, as we have seen, at least one prominent Anglican was reputed to be a polygynist. It is, in fact, the size of a man's farm and the degree to which farm plots are dispersed that best explains the level of polygyny; religious affiliation has little to do with it. Although an Anglican pastor would not preside over a man's marriage to a second wife, Yoruba Christians have resorted to traditional ceremonies to marry their junior wives. It sometimes happens that a senior wife will attempt to stop her husband from taking a second wife by supplicating the pastor. But the aggregate effects of such actions are minimal. From my interviews in Ile-Ife, I found that the Christians on average had the same number of wives as the Muslims.[44]

Christianity has nonetheless won the allegiance of Yoruba women. Two-thirds of the regular worshipers are women, and their participation in mid-week church events far surpasses that of the men. The women dress magnificently for church. They have been given a significant set of chiefly titles and positions on the Parochial Church Council. Literate women were often invited to read psalms from the lectern. Their social preeminence, however, is belied by their lack of real power. Men control the religious hierarchy, and have the highest secular titles in the church. Even in the Aladura churches, where women have achieved considerable political power, taboos of ritual cleanliness prevent them from achieving their power until after menopause.[45] At St. Paul's, when the vicar was first introducing me to the church notables, he told me that women were of vital importance to his church. Yet each one of them was introduced to me as the wife of so-and-so. Women's power could only be legitimated through their husband's authority. Among the elders, virtually all of the men and few of the women were literate, which precluded their full participation in church services and other church-related matters. The Church invested primarily in the future authority of the men. In the past twenty years far more women have achieved literacy, but male power had already been institutionalized. Social preeminence but political dependence: this is the first irony of the Christian experience for women.

The second irony concerns the Victorian ideology of the family. Missionaries wanted families to attend church together. I was regularly encouraged by many of the men to bring *my* "madam" to the Sunday service. I think what they were asking me is what kind of *man* I was if I could not get my wife to accompany me. Yet I almost never observed a family going to church together or sitting together in the church. The women sat with their infants on their backs on one side, the men on the other side. Every once in a while a young married couple would sit together, but this was the exception. The virtues of families were extolled; the reality of a separate society for men was regularly displayed.

Christian ambiguity in this regard may be compared with Islamic domination. The position of women in the Ile-Ife mosque is one of complete exclusion. This of course could not have been predicted from the founding doctrines. Muhammad's views of women and family law were radical in his social milieu. Men were to be given full authority over the family and full rights to the children, to be sure. Yet, because all marriages were equal under the law and casual unions with free women were severely proscribed, all women were assured respectable social status. Furthermore, Muslim law gave a woman the right of inheritance, the (limited) right to divorce, and the right to retain her bridewealth if ever she were divorced. These were radical innovations for Bedouin society, with the purpose of protecting the "personal dignity of every individual, male or female."[46] But the monogamous tradition in Occidental Christianity and the evolving rights of women in its legal traditions made Islam seem retrograde in its treatment of women as far back as the eighteenth century. And in Yorubaland, Islam's concern for ritual cleanliness, while it may have brought a sense of dignity to the men, worked to isolate the women from the corridors of power.

Only about a quarter of the participants in the Friday prayers at the central mosque are women. This is in part due to the rather vigorous athletic demands of the Muslim *naflah* (genuflection), but the rules of ritual cleanliness have some import here. Menstruating women are forbidden in the mosque. Urine is considered unclean; hence, since most young women have babies on their backs, it is assumed that the baby will be unclean sometime during prayers. While Islamic law is not clear on this matter, most women pray at home while the men engage in public activity. In the Enuwa Mosque, the women are consigned to dark, dank rooms where they cannot be seen by the men. Even in contributing money, the Muslim women must sneak around to the platform area, curtsey to the imam, and quietly return to their section. Women who have made the pilgrimage to Mecca (*alhajas*) and who have thereby aided their trading empires, are never a part of the society of alhajis, who advise the Imam. I once observed a glorious ceremony to welcome back a woman from the pilgrimage, in which there were drum bands and the spraying of money. But in the mosque itself the woman received no public recognition.

Islam in Ile-Ife appears to be a man's religion; Christianity appears to be a woman's religion run by men.

Responsibility

As confessional religions, both Christianity and Islam attempt to instill in their believers a strong sense of personal responsibility. But what constitutes responsible action, and the standards by which it is judged, differ in these two world religions. In the mosque, all members have a moral responsibility to uphold community standards. In the church, all members have a moral responsibility to assure their own salvation, and only a few have the responsibility to assure community standards.

Personal responsibility for one's own salvation is a leitmotif in the Anglican church. In sermon after semon, that message is repeated. The vicar of St. Paul's lectured on Herod's imprisoning of John the Baptist because John told the truth about the questionable morality of Herod's second marriage. The purpose of this sermon was to teach the lesson that John was saved because of his fearless honesty. The vicar interpreted the story of Job to teach the lesson that ultimate salvation is possible for those whose belief is tenacious. In his sermons concerning illicit behavior in modern life, he emphasized that short-term gains through deceit will yield long-term costs at St. Peter's gate. Recounting the story of Adam and Eve, he kept repeating the question, "Where are you, and where are you going?" His message, I believe, was that his parishioners should take greater responsibility for their own salvation.

There are certain officials whose responsibility it is to see that their neighbors are acting correctly. In the church, decorum is enforced by "sidesmen" and "sidesladies" who, among other activities, collect screaming children off of the backs of mothers and carry them into the courtyard to cool off. They also make sure that latecomers do not disturb the service. Here responsibility is tied closely to institutional role.

In the Muslim community of Ile-Ife, a different conception of responsibility is evident. There, personal responsibility to uphold the reputation of the community is proclaimed. A recurrent theme in the sermons of the chief imam was that evil done by any Muslim affects all other Muslims. Once there was a bank robbery in the town in which a policeman was brutally murdered. The chief imam, hearing that the primary suspect was a Muslim, emphasized in his sermon the following Friday the threat to the entire Muslim community should any single Muslim be implicated in such a ghastly act. On another occasion, rumors had been spread—and had nearly created riots—that there were some strangers in Ile-Ife, proficient in *juju* (magic); if these strangers touched a man, he would lose his penis; if they touched a woman, she would lose her breasts. Many of the men in attendance were giggling like schoolchildren, in part because they themselves helped spread such rumors, some even claiming that they had seen a victim. The imam counseled that spreading false or unsubstantiated rumors runs counter to Islam, and for a Muslim to do so brings disgrace to his community. In his more regular denunciation of drinking, smoking, and theft, the imam's implicit message was that lawbreaking by Muslims gave a bad name to the community in general.

Decorum in the mosque, as would be expected from my discussion on authority, is not enforced by specific role incumbents but is a general responsibility. Once when I arrived late, and the privileged positions in the center front of the mosque were filled up, the tafsir suspended his money collection prayers, and began to redirect traffic, pointing to individuals to move so that a place would be opened for me. This was typical behavior: even unofficial members of the community would often stand up and take responsibility to help restore order in the mosque.

To understand the sources of this difference between the Muslim and Christian communities, it is useful to go back to the founding doctrines. The Muslim is seen by Muhammad as a vicegerent for God. The Muslim's personal responsibility for the maintenance of a moral order is a recurrent message in the Islamic experience. In Christianity, the focus is clearly on the individual's beliefs and actions, and whether they are consistent with Jesus' admonitions.

Complementing this difference, but on the level of the practical religion of the converted, Christians in Yorubaland have been imbued with a dualism between belief and action. It is their beliefs which are of ultimate concern to the church hierarchy. Christian concern for orthodoxy suggests that correct belief is more important than responsible action. Muslims have been exposed to a greater extent to the idea of orthopraxy. The doctrine of responsibility as heroic action to maintain the community standards is consistent with the practical religion of Islam.

Not consistent with the observed differences concerning responsibility is the differentiation on the level of practical religion between Christian corporatism and Muslim contractualism. Should we not expect Muslims to have a personal contract with God, that if fulfilled, will yield salvation? In the admonitions to donate to the Mosque, the tafsir regularly connects generosity with both worldly success (especially promising givers that their children will not be destined to deformity or early death) and salvation. Fulfilling a personal contract and reaping rewards suggests an individualistic notion of responsibility. Should we not expect Christians, with their characteristic corporatism, to worry about the reputation of the church? Indeed, members' contributions toward capital improvements for the church building precisely illustrates such behavior.

Cross-pressures of this kind, hardly surprising in a world religion, preclude a simple, one-to-one relationship between religious values and secular action. In the case of responsibility, within the Church and Mosque sub-cultures in Ile-Ife, the force of corporatism and contractualism played a less prominent role. Corporatism suggests an institution rather than a community; and the wider church institution appears impersonal to local Christians. Their actions seldom relate directly to the reputation of the church. By contrast, the clubby atmosphere of the mosque makes the community of believers more comprehensible to the individual Muslim. His personal contract with God could include the welfare of the community. The notion of responsibility, then, valued highly by both religions, provides the two subcultures with different points of concern.

SUMMARY

Christianity and Islam drew Yoruba converts for virtually the same reasons and generally from the same social strata. Yet the impact of these religions on Yoruba society was different. These differences manifested themselves in the two religious subcultures in Ile-Ife.

Christians in Ile-Ife are individuals associated with an impersonal and bureaucratic society; Muslims are members of a closely knit community. Christians have a role-legitimating view of authority in which roles are functionally specific. Muslims have an incumbent-legitimating view of authority in which roles are functionally diffuse. While Christians debate an incumbent's legitimacy (that is, whether he was chosen by proper procedures), Muslims debate his authority (that is, whether he has a moral right to rule). Christians do not worry over external manifestations of social inequality, while Muslims make conscious efforts to mute them. Christians give social prominence to women, while setting limits to their political equality with men; Muslims are consistent in their relegation of women to low social and political status. Christians see responsible behavior as those actions that enhance the opportunity for personal salvation; Muslims are acting responsibly when they take personal initiative to uphold the reputation of the community.

Christian and Muslim Yorubas, inside church and mosque settings, have commonsensical views of authority, of community, of equality, and of responsibility that are discernibly different. From the social systems perspective, we can postulate the two subcultures influencing the values in the wider social system in divergent ways.

4| Social Systems and Hegemony

Social systems theory posits that each subsystem within a social system is sensitive to changes in other subsystems. Regular adjustments by each subsystem to change permits societal equilibrium to be maintained. On the individual level, this means that when a person is, say, a member of a religious group and of an ethnic group that promote incompatible values, he or she will seek to find some point of compromise so that the two subsystems will be value-"congruent." Here social systems theory connects with the congruence hypothesis.

Most sophisticated proponents of the congruence hypothesis recognize that individuals may reject the values embedded in their cultures—perhaps for variety or perhaps out of rebellion. Yet all congruence theories hypothesize continued mutual adaptation of values among the cultural, political, and economic subsystems. The ever present relevance of one social subsystem for all others remains a central point in social systems theory.[1]

For the Yoruba case, this theory would predict that Christians and Muslims should feel at least some pressure to infuse their family or their government with the same pattern of relationships as they experienced in their churches and mosques. Alternatively, they should seek to infuse their religious communities with the values upheld in their families or their state. At minimum, Christian and Muslim Yorubas should feel uncomfortable living in two different worlds, and should exhibit crises of personal identity.[2] Among the prominent church and mosque elders I interviewed, one might reasonably predict that their religious points of concern would provide a framework for their political discourse and action.

In contrast to congruence theory, a hegemonic theory of culture would lead us to predict that mutual adjustment of values among subsystems is unlikely. Instead, a single subsystem—the one that is hegemonic—should provide a framework of values that any other subsystem either adapts itself to or loses its ability to guide action outside of its functional domain. The hegemonic subsystem provides the value basis for the "dominant symbolic framework that reigns as common sense," which is central to the definition of hegemony (see chapter 1). It will not be possible, given the research program involved here, to identify precisely the hegemonic subsystem in

Yoruba society. What will be shown is that the value framework embedded in the world religions does not affect the value framework in the political subsystem in Yorubaland. By demonstrating the irrelevance of the world religions in Yorubaland to political points of concern, I reveal the inadequacy of social systems theory.

EARLIER SURVEY RESEARCH

Two earlier studies, focusing on questions related to the ones asked here, demonstrated that differential attachment to one of the world religions in Yorubaland could not explain any variance in political values. Donald Morrison organized a massive survey of political attitudes throughout Nigeria, in which nearly 2,000 Yorubas were interviewed. His data do not allow us to reject the null hypothesis that would claim that religion has no impact on core political values. Christian and Muslim Yorubas, for example, were both very open to change and modernity. Both groups would take considerable advantage of free education and agreed that higher education was a prerequisite for the assumption of authority roles. Both groups reported willingness to try new foods and new farming techniques. Muslims were perhaps more fatalistic: they were more willing to "accept one's lot," and placed a lower value on "hard work" than on "government planning" or "God's help" as necessary conditions for a better future for Nigeria. The Muslim sample saw the world as more predictable than did the Christian sample. But these differences were small. The overwhelming evidence suggests a Yoruba outlook on change that overrides religious differences.[3]

Equally, Christian and Muslim Yorubas both favored democracy while recognizing the need for strong leaders and political guidance from the government. Both groups claimed to be open to a variety of political viewpoints, and both wished strongly for the end of military rule. Both rejected the idea of "union government"—which would have legitimated military oversight of civilian politics—as undemocratic, and both asserted that democracy required more equality and concern for the common man. Christians tended to see democracy as a conflict between government and opposition while Muslims tended to see it as the development of consensus; but these differences too appear to be small.[4]

P. C. Lloyd, in a survey of urban workers, also found that the differences among Yorubas based on their connection to a religious subsystem could not explain differences in outlook in the political subsystem. For some questions, such as the value put on monogamy, there were differences based on religion (obviously a higher percentage of Christians valued monogamy). But in matters not directly related to religious membership, Lloyd found no difference in response patterns between Christians and Muslims. When he asked whether "hard work" or "having a helper" brought success, for example, most respondents answered the latter, Christians to the same degree as Muslims.[5]

FINDINGS AND NONFINDINGS IN ILE-IFE

From the point of view of social systems theory, these findings are indeed anomalous. It was my initial belief that Morrison's data and Lloyd's findings were inadequate because the hypotheses did not tap in a sensitive way the potential differences in political orientation between Yoruba Christians and Muslims. Furthermore, neither study pressed the Yoruba respondents to provide a justification for their political values. The religious subsystem provides a commonsensical framework in which to think about political relationships. Since justifications for political beliefs are built on common sense, it is reasonable to infer that religious differences would be more easily detected in the realm of political discourse than in "yes, no" answers to political questions.

I geared my own questions, therefore, to the differences in political relationships that I had observed in church and mosque. Furthermore, I invited respondents to give reasons for their answers, so that I would get a better sense of the commonsensical framework that underlay their political values. In order to develop questions, I needed to paint in broad strokes— if the congruence hypothesis were to be sustained—a picture of how I thought religious points of concern would be transferred to the political subsystem. I therefore hypothesized that Yoruba Muslims would worry more than their Christian counterparts about the personal qualities of their political leaders. They would feel more comfortable responding to moralistic appeals from heroic men for direct action. Nonequivocation about moral action would be the rule, but egalitarian claims could arouse much worry and disputation. Yoruba Christians would want to hear about proper legal rights and duties from the leader of a well-organized, hierarchical organization. Careful equivocation about substantive issues—especially concerning the role of women—would be seen as natural. Yoruba Muslims would take full responsibility for the actions of members of their community; Yoruba Christians would be more attentive to their own political responsibilities.

To put the social systems perspective and the congruence hypothesis to test, I interviewed thirty-five elders from the church and thirty-five from the mosque where I conducted my field research, confronting them with questions concerning national politics. Although there were some subtle differences in approach between the Christian and Muslim samples, no major differences exemplifying their different religious points of concern could be detected. My results, consistent with Morrison's data and Lloyd's findings, gave virtually no support to the congruence hypothesis. To illustrate this point, I shall now summarize the responses I received in regard to authority, responsibility, and equality.

Authority

I asked two distinctly political questions, designed to pit the two different approaches toward authority—the (Muslim) substantive and the (Christian) procedural—against each other. Both of my questions built on the conflict in Nigeria's Second Republic concerning the fact that the president represented a political party that had virtually no support in Yorubaland and that the states within Yorubaland were controlled by a party deeply opposed to that of the president. In one question, I raised the issue of the Lagos state governor, Lateef Jakande, who was a strong supporter of the Yoruba party's plea for free education at all levels. Jakande feared that if free education were implemented on the state but not the federal level, youth from all over the federation would migrate to Lagos. He therefore announced that his free education plan would apply only to children born in the states that already had a free education program. This announcement was doubly troubling for the federal authorities. First, it was probably unconstitutional; second, since Lagos is the federal capital and Nigeria's commercial center, many children from all over the federation lived there. Implementation of this scheme would create chaos in Nigeria's largest city.

My observations in church and mosque led me to hypothesize that, if asked how Jakande might be defended, Yoruba Christians would emphasize procedural issues (the law does not prevent Jakande from making such a regulation) while Yoruba Muslims would emphasize substantive issues (the regulation is fair, because Jakande could not fulfill his campaign promises unless he preemptively warded off the deluge of potential migrants).

In my interviews, 13 Christians and 9 Muslims made procedural claims; 20 Christians and 21 Muslims made substantive claims. Interestingly, even though all respondents were encouraged to make a brief for their fellow Yoruba, Jakande, against their non-Yoruba president, very few did. In the presidential campaign which had just finished, the immensely popular leader, Awolowo, whose support was very strong within Ife among both Christian and Muslim respondents, had built his program on the premise of free education as the minimum essential public good. This stance was supported throughout Yorubaland, and worked against Jakande's gambit. Out of the 70 respondents, only 9 Muslims and 6 Christians made claims to support Jakande's position. In rejecting Jakande, 8 Christians but only 1 Muslim held that free education is an absolute good and all 9 argued that no one, especially a member of their own party, should set limits to it. One Christian respondent maintained: "Who said to do free education did right, because if somebody sent his children to school without paying money, he gets a great advantage" (C-20).[6] Another responded similarly: "He who brought free education did a good thing because he let the poor people have rest of mind on the payment of school fees" (C-30). The overwhelming response, however, was that everyone in Nigeria should be treated equally. Fifteen Muslims and 12 Christians emphasized this point. In the words of one respondent, "What I will say is that it is better to go round to everybody. Nigeria is only one and it is not good to differentiate the people if we want peace among ourselves. It is not good if some people enjoy it and other people do not" (M-22). Most of those who sought equality for Nigerians foresaw the potential for conflict among "tribes" if educational resources were distributed unequally. Here images of Nigeria's civil war (1967–70), in which Igbos, who thought they were not getting a fair share of government revenues and jobs, and other Nigerians who believed the Igbos wished for too many, were clearly in the back of the respondents' minds. The marginally greater support for Jakande among the Muslims may be attributable to the fact that the Lagos governor is a Muslim; indeed, their statements of support are stronger than those of the Christians. But the difference is not great.

The responses support the conclusion that two overriding values—free education is good; differential treatment among members from different tribes is bad—were shared by both Muslim and Christian Yorubas, and any differences between them on how to view authority became insignificant in light of their political agreements. More important for the congruence hypothesis is the fact that Christian Yorubas did not concern themselves with the procedural niceties of the issue, as might have been expected from their commonsensical view of authority within their church environment.

Respondents were also asked to advise their governor, Bola Ige of Oyo State, on how to handle a similar problem. The Nigerian president, Shehu Shagari, in an attempt to develop reliable lines of communication with the states, had appointed "liaison officers." Governors from states controlled by opposition parties saw these liaison officers as potential spies, and questioned the right of the president to appoint them. I asked the respondents what their governor should do if the president put pressure on him through his liaison officer to emphasize housing construction (the program of the president's party, the NPN) over medical care (a key program of the governor's party, the UPN). Here too we have a procedural question about authority (Does the constitution give the president the right to appoint these officers?) intersecting a substantive question (Will UPN governors be able to fulfill their oppositional programs in an NPN-dominated federation?). Again, the overwhelming percentage of respondents (69 percent of the Muslims and 82 percent of the Christians) spoke to the substantive issue that medical care is more important than housing.

Echoing themes from the campaign, most respondents quipped that ill or dead people cannot enjoy a house, and therefore medical care must take priority. (Nearly all of the respondents were living in their family-owned compounds and had no compelling need for new housing.) If anything, Christians took the "Muslim" view of authority more often than did the Muslims; but the point remains that the respondents' common adherence to the UPN led both groups to address the question not as Christians or Muslims, but rather as members of the Yoruba-dominated UPN.

The responses to two other questions gave limited support to the idea that authority is viewed differently by Muslims and Christians. Respondents were presented with the hypothetical situation of their being the party chairman when a group of women came to petition that they had not received a sufficient share of positions in the new state government. The respondents were asked how they would respond to the women. I coded answers according to whether the suggested remedy had a basis in the institutional structure of government (e.g. to contest elections) or did not have such a basis (e.g. work harder; do good work; join together for collective action). Of the 14 Christians who suggested a remedy, 64 percent suggested an institutional one; of the 18 Muslims who suggested a remedy, 94 percent suggested a noninstitutional one.

I asked each respondent what should be done if he, as an assistant minister of finance, saw that another assistant minister who was a member of his church or mosque was embezzling monies. Eleven of the Christians mentioned the role of a particular political institution (such as the police, the courts, prison, a judge) for resolving the problem. "Who did this type of thing," answered one Christian (C-4), "should be sued in the *courts*, and for him to pay the money back or for him to be put in *prison*." Another Christian responded, "He is a thief. I will tell him that what he did is not good. *Police* should arrest him and put him in *prison*" (C-27). Only one Muslim respondent mentioned a specific institution. The more typical response, "Who stole the government money, it is better to get it from him and do to him any punishment that he deserves (M-2), suggests an institutional occasionalism typical of Islam. I found some areas where the religious subsystem influenced reasoning about authority in the political realm. But in general, the procedural versus substantive approach to authority, so clear in the religious domain, did not divide Yoruba Christians and Muslims when they defended their political views.

Responsibility

The question concerning embezzlement was also designed to see if the Muslim respondents would take greater personal responsibility for bringing their fellow minister to justice. If so, it would be congruent with the Muslim concern for the upholding of community standards as opposed to the Christian concern for personal salvation. The data did not support this difference. Only 6 Muslims and 7 Christians suggested that they would intervene personally to bring the problem to some resolution. Furthermore, only 1 Christian but 2 Muslims denied responsibility for remedial action toward the guilty party. "Who stole the money," that Christian argued (C-11), "I don't know him. This one is not of concern to me." Among the Muslims, 1 respondent (M-4) pointed out that "government will do the right thing for him. I cannot do anything about it because I am not a government." Another (M-35) reasoned that "He is a thief. The Prophet doesn't like this. They must do the right judgment for him. There is no help that I can render him."

More consistent with the congruence hypothesis is the fact that 9 Muslims but only 5 Christians analyzed the theft in terms of some community being harmed. "It is everybody's money," commented one Muslim (M-9); it is our "neighbor" who is hurt, argued another (M-10), and, therefore, "I will fight with this person." Yet another Muslim (M-15) responded: "Who steals the government's money, he kills the people. It let the people become poor. He let the people go hungry. Everyone owns this money." But the five Christians who made similar points relied on the same moral framework: "I will tell him that he is a thief because it is all our money that he stole. We are all the government" (C-21); "Who stole the money deserves a rightful punishment because the money he stole belongs to everybody" (C-28). This pattern of responses hardly demonstrates that Muslims are more concerned than Christians about preserving their community's moral standing, while Christians are more concerned than Muslims about enhancing their chances for personal salvation. (Interestingly, although there were a number of religious references in the answers, no respondent defined the aggrieved community in terms of his religious affiliation; but an interpretation of that fact is the task of a theory of the second face of culture).

Equality

As with responsibility, I found no congruence between the views of equality in religious and political subsystems. The respondents were invited to react to a hypothetical proposal involving a substantial inheritance tax which would be transferred to the poor. My observations in mosque and church, as well as the fact that Muslim law demands greater spread of inherited money to a wider social network, led me to expect less outrage by Muslims toward coercive leveling. What I found was that a significant majority of both Christians (63 percent) and Muslims (88 percent) was opposed to the idea. Most of the respondents of both religious affiliations claimed that their kinsmen deserved the money and not the government or the poor. "I cannot agree with this type of program," answered one

Christian respondent (C-17), "because only his children have a right to his goods. Government has no right to give it to the poor, because they did not help him when he was working to get his possessions." A Muslim respondent (M-34) answered similarly: "I cannot agree to it. It is not the property of the dead to be given to the poor. If the government wants to help the poor, let the government help them." If anything, it was the Christians—who display their wealth more conspicuously in their place of worship—who were more receptive to the proposal (and this would be the reverse of what the congruence hypothesis would predict); but both groups shared the Yoruba sense of the family as a corporate unit, which surpasses in importance government's transfer policies.

The relationship between money and equality in church and mosque was very different. In the church, individual displays of wealth—driving expensive cars to church, wearing expensive clothes—were common. Yet the money itself was collected and counted discreetly. In the mosque, personal wealth was less conspicuous, but paper money was openly displayed and counted. Muslims, I assumed, were less squeamish about stating the clear relationship between money and power. Christians, on the other hand, by ritually severing that connection, would more easily be able to accept vast differences in private wealth. I therefore juxtaposed two well-known Yoruba proverbs and presented them to the interviewees for comparative evaluation: (1) "An elder who does not have money may as well not be wise. A rich man can go anywhere" (Agba ko l'owo a ni ko gbọn; olowo nṣe bi ọba l'oko); and (2) "Reputation is better than money; courage surpasses medicine" (Gbajumọn ju owo lọ; aya nini to oogun lọọ). I hypothesized that the Christians would find comfort in the equivocation of the second proverb, and the Muslims in the unambiguous recognition, in the first, of what money could buy. Again the data did not support my suppositions: 20 percent of the Muslims and 11 percent of the Christians supported the proverb extolling money. While in this case the distribution is in the predicted direction, the overwhelming majority of both groups emphasized the power of courage and fame. Among the Christians: "If someone is brave, he will not be afraid of anything" (C-1); "If someone is brave, he . . . can conquer his enemies with this" (C-13); "Only those who are brave can do many things" (C-27). Similarly with the Muslims: "If somebody is brave, he will be able to save himself in anything that happens" (M-5); "If someone is brave, he will not suffer" (M-6); "If somebody is brave, he will not run away if anything happens. If they want to cut off his head, he will not run away and those who want to harm him will be afraid of him" (M-23).

Discourse about money had similar emphases among the two groups. For the Christians: "If I rely on money, what other people will buy for 50 kobo [100 kobo = 1 Naira] they will sell to me for two Naira" (C-19); "If somebody has money and he is not popular, he just has the money for nothing" (C-24). And for the Muslims: "If a gentleman wants to make a celebration and has no money, many people will help him to do it. But he who is not popular and says that he has money, he just has money for nothing" (M-16); "Anybody who does not have good behavior he can have anything, but people will not like him. If he has money, they will tell him to eat his money" (M-22). The differential role of money in church and mosque rituals did not substantially affect views about money for Christians and Muslims when they discussed it outside of the religious environment.

The question about women and their petition for a greater role in government was also intended to tap views concerning sexual equality, where I had found differences in the church and mosque environments. Indeed, Muslim and Christian men demonstrated a different understanding of the basis of institutional authority in responding to this question. Their responses, however, demonstrated no fundamental difference concerning the role of women in society. Only 5 percent of the Muslims and 13 percent of the Christians argued that women should keep silent and accept their lot. The remainder felt that the situation should be (or at least might be) remedied. As in many of these questions, the differences, however small, go against the predicted direction. More Christians were bluntly opposed to an enhanced political role for women; while more Muslims than Christians (23 versus 14 percent) put themselves in the quasi-hypocritical position of supporting greater women's roles in government while advising them merely to be more patient. I had observed in the religious setting that Muslims were blunter about rejection of female equality and Christians were more hypocritical in establishing remedies.

The responses to my questions corroborate Morrison's data and Lloyd's findings: among the Yoruba, religious differentiation has not led to a concomitant adjustment of political discourse and action. Why should this be so? The most obvious answer is that these world religions are but a thin veneer on a strong society so that their values could scarcely have influenced Yoruba adherents. This answer is inadequate. The considerable percentage of their disposable income and spare time that Yorubas expend on the church and mosque demonstrate far more than a thin veneer. In chapter 7, I will rebut the claim that the world religions are "thin" in ideological penetration. For the remainder of this chapter, I shall discuss two approaches that might salvage the social systems perspective. I shall then demonstrate why they fail, and therefore why the theoretical postulation of a social system in which subsystems mutually adjust to each other will have to be dropped. Finally, I shall propose a model of "culture and hegemony" that better accounts for the apparently contradictory findings of this chapter and the previous one.

Evidence demonstrating religious syncretism could help save the social systems perspective. Suppose Yoruba traditional religion so heavily influenced Christianity and Islam that the two merged products looked more alike than different. In that case one would not expect to find different political views emanating from Christian and Muslim Yorubas. Or suppose that Christianity and Islam in Yorubaland were in such dynamic interaction that a religious synthesis developed? Again, social systems theory would be saved. For then the two religious subsystems would have created a syncretic world religion that would have had a single impact on the wider social system.

That there is abundant evidence demonstrating a syncretic effect between the Yoruba traditional religion and the world religions can be of no surprise. In *Islam Observed*, Geertz focused his entire attention on the way Atlas culture in Morocco and Javenese culture in Indonesia shaped Islam very differently.[7] In Yorubaland, Muslims were highly influenced by Yoruba divination, and Muslim teachers developed a parallel system and subsequently claimed that both the Muslim and the Yoruba systems originated in Arabia.[8] Other Muslims have woven into their rewritings of traditional history close contacts with Mecca. Muslim festivals have a distinctly Yoruba ring.[9] In mosques today, the hymns in praise of money can only be comprehended from a Yoruba cultural viewpoint.[10] Contemporary advertisements in the press for a "Mecca Pack" (food rations for the pilgrimage—see fig. 4.1) are comprehensible only from a viewpoint that understands the Yoruba love affair with commercial capitalism.

Christian syncretism shows similar patterns. Samuel Johnson and other Christian Yoruba historians are quick to point out how Yoruba cultural themes are consistent with Christianity.[11] In the churches, the proliferation of ẹgbẹ (societies) as the major activity centers suggests that the church has responded to traditional modes of urban organization among the Yoruba.[12] In the Anglican church that I attended (and all churches I visited were similar in this regard), the organist plays a Yamaha organ with a mambo beat, and he is surrounded by a coterie of "talking drums." As the ẹgbẹ members move to the altar to be blessed, they swing their hips and dance as they would in a traditional festival.

Social systems theorists could argue that Christianity and Islam in Yorubaland were so strongly imbued with Yoruba norms that they could not have had a different impact on the wider social system. They could also point to a more impressive example of syncretism—the mutual adjustment of Christianity and Islam in Yorubaland. Muslim adjustment to Christian value patterns is well recorded. As far back as 1895, on the celebration after the month of fasting, Lagos Muslims celebrated by throwing public

Figure 4.1 Advertisement for "Mecca Pack," *Daily Times* (Lagos), 15 May 1980

tea parties, modeled on the Victorian celebrations held by CMS missionaries.[13] More important, many of the Muslims who attended CMS schools became the leaders of the Muslim Reform Movements in Yorubaland.[14] In many Muslim schools, the curricula of the Christian missionary schools served as a model.[15] Chief Abiola, chairman of ITT (International Telephone and Telegraph), in Nigeria, is a leading Muslim in Yorubaland. He got his early education in a Baptist school, and in his public appearances one hears him quoting the New Testament with some authority.[16] At Enuwa Mosque, the Christian impact on the Muslim community was very much discernible. Its most obvious manifestation was in the innovations in money collection. The Muslim community saw that the oral urgings of the tafsir every Friday were inefficient. They began to print up envelopes for individuals to make pledges. The inspiration for this was the common practice in St. Paul's and many other churches. Perhaps more consequential is that Muslims in Yorubaland—largely because of their knowledge of the Christian experience—see Islam as a religion rather than as a civilization. In this regard, Yoruba Islam differs most greatly from the Islamic societies in North Africa and the Middle East.[17]

Christians have been heavily influenced by Muslims in Yorubaland as well. J. F. A. Ajayi, in his seminal history of Christian missions in Yorubaland, asserts that the Islamic expansion into southern Yorubaland legitimated for the urban kings the idea of a foreign church. The church was perceived in Yorubaland, then, as a different sort of Islam.[18] The model of Islam was most influential in motivating early twentieth-century Christians to experiment with an independent or African church.[19] An early Yoruba Christian leader, James Johnson, made quite explicit his respect for the Muslim model: "Every Mohamedan regards himself a missionary to his neighbours: he constantly manifests a strong desire for prosperity of the religion which he regards as his own. We want to see more of this in our Christian converts."[20] Johnson, who remained loyal to the CMS, was nonetheless an inspiration for what became the African church movement.

Islam had a strong impact not only on the African church but on the Aladura church as well. Many students of these Christian prayer-oriented churches have noticed the impact of the Muslim model. The very word distinguishing them—adura, meaning "prayer"—is of Arabic origin. Aladura prayers, their concern for cleanliness, their banning of tobacco, their fasting, and their restrictions on liquor and pork are all modeled on the Muslim religion.[21] Finally, the Muslim pilgrimage has influenced Yoruba Christianity. The Aladura churches have regular pilgrimages to holy sites. Even the Anglicans have made pilgrimage to Jerusalem an honored part of their religious experience.[22]

Not only have there been Christian influences on Islam and Muslim influences on Christianity, but there have been dynamic interchanges between the two subcultures. In the earliest years of Christian evangelization, Samuel Crowther took it upon himself to read the Qur'an so that he could debate with the Muslims.[23] Debates between Christian missionaries and Muslim teachers became a regular feature of market place discourse in the early twentieth century. In the University of Ibadan's journal *Orita* this discourse between the two religious communities has taken on a new (academic) form. But the principle is the same: ideological dialogue between competing groups forces each group to understand and even to adapt to the premises of the other. A dynamic synthesis of values can emerge from such a debate. It could be argued that because of the dialectic between Christianity and Islam in Yorubaland, and their mutual adaptation, both religions exerted a common influence on Yoruba society. By this argument, it could be maintained that the social systems paradigm has been confirmed.

However plausible, the syncretist argument cannot successfully account for the apparent anomaly in the social systems perspective. It has already been demonstrated that (Anglican) Christianity and Islam have developed their distinct cultures in Yorubaland. The descriptions in chapter 3 should make clear that the practical religions of the Christian and Muslim subcultures are indeed different, even if there have been mutual influences. To some extent, every social movement, every idea, every language, is a combination of a variety of influences and is therefore syncretic. But that cannot mean that different cultural or ideological forces cannot have their independent societal impact. Surely there have been mutual influences between Judaism and Islam in Palestine; of Hinduism and Islam in India; and of Protestantism and Catholicism in Northern Ireland. To infer from these examples of syncretism that members of these different communities should have no different points of concern in their political lives is to abandon completely the social systems approach to politics, an approach which takes seriously the substantive aspects of culture.

EVOLUTIONARY FORCES WITHIN THE WORLD RELIGIONS

Another approach toward explaining the apparent nonexistence of religious impact on the wider Yoruba social system is to argue that religions will not have that sort of impact until they reach higher levels of integrity. Relying on Nock's approach toward conversion, it could be maintained that the world religions have not been in Yorubaland long enough to have societal influence. While the religions are no longer quarantined, evolutionists would see both Islam and Christianity in today's Yorubaland in the late period of accommodation. What follows in both world religions is what some theorists call "scripturalism" and others "reform." In this culminating period of conversion, religious virtuosi go back to the founding doctrines of the religion and attempt to purge from their religious enterprises all manifestations of the traditional religion of the previous age.[24]

Like the syncretic approach, the evolutionary perspective is plausible. When St. Augustine went to proselytize in England, he was instructed by the pope to destroy idols but not temples. Thus in Anglo-Saxon Christian poetry, the cross of Jesus was metaphorically connected with the warrior's sword. In the early parts of *Beowulf*, Jesus also is placed within the warrior tradition; but by its end, the Christian author gives this description of the hero: "They said that he was of world-kings the mildest of men, and the gentlest and kindest to his people.[25] We see in the development of the *Beowulf* epic, then, the gradual infusion of the Christian message into the Anglo-Saxon tradition.

One can see in the work of present-day religious scholars in Yorubaland a certain contempt for accommodation, and an interest in reform.[26] Other data demonstrate that greater education correlates with greater religious chauvinism among the primarily Yoruba student body at the University of Ibadan.[27] Mosque and church officials have an even greater interest than scholars in scripturalism. Once I observed the tafsir of Enuwa Mosque, who was a charismatic figure inside the mosque, at a traditional ceremony. He sat glumly in a corner, not drinking the beer that was so plentiful. Mosque and church authorities, who command such respect in their own domains, are often odd men out in these ceremonies. They therefore have an interest in redefining culture so that religious adherence becomes a dominant social metaphor. That is the route to the expansion of their own authority.

Evolutionists accept with syncretists that different religious traditions interact with and mutually influence each other. But, unlike syncretists, they postulate that religions have a symbolic integrity that eventually will emerge. The force of Christianity and Islam on Yoruba society has not been dissipated through religious melding, which is merely a historical stage preceding the full development of the world religions. Social systems theory can therefore be saved: it could simply be held that I did my research in Ile-Ife one century too early.

Religious evolution theories, however, are subject to the same criticism faced by the syncretist theory. After all, we have seen that Christian and Muslim points of concern have already taken hold in church and mosque. Why should these changes not have broader effects now? Furthermore, to argue that scripturalists or reformers must follow accommodationists does not tell us how long that sequence takes. Like their counterpart theories of modernization that predict that religious societies will evolve into secular societies, evolutionary theories face too many anomalies.[28] If we don't get religious revolts at specified periods after conversion, it is because the religious vision must be embedded into a larger political program. This program requires an organization forged by an elite that sees some advantage in infusing the political system with religious symbols. Scripturalism does not evolve; it is forged.

With syncretism and evolution unable to save the congruence hypothesis, the law of parsimony should invite us to consider if there were any plausibility to the social systems perspective in the first place. Why should anyone have assumed that changes in the religious compartment in people's lives would have any independent ideological impact on the way they thought about political issues? In his polemic against the Weberian tradition, Maxime Rodinson examines carefully the Qur'anic ideology of equality and of wealth sharing. He then points out that, in actuality, "the traditional Muslim states offer throughout history the spectacle of a poignant contrast between the astonishing luxury that prevails at the courts and among the rich, and the most abject misery in which the mass of the people are sunk." Governments, representatives of the rich, made only token payments to the poor. Religious theorizing, he concludes, "did not challenge the fundamentals of economic activity."[29] To be sure, Rodinson did not examine what I have called the practical religion of Islam.[30] Nonetheless, his point that there seem to be no systemic constraints set by Islam, even in the most religious Muslim environments, is well taken. Why should we even postulate an interpenetrating social system?

With studies such as these available, it is hardly surprising that Geertz has recently begun to rethink what in fact "congruence" might explain.[31] However far Geertz himself might go, the law of parsimony solves the problem of no congruence by rejecting entirely the basic assumption of social systems theory.

HEGEMONY

The inadequacy of the syncretic and evolutionary approaches—in which the social systems perspective was merely amended—suggested the need for a new theoretical perspective. And to assume the nonconnectability of the social subsystems was as good a start as any. Without people or situations forging connections between subsystems, it is best to assume that there will be no adjustment. But this does not mean the irrelevance of one social subsystem for another. Contradictory symbol systems can easily exist side by side even within a single religion. But each of these symbol systems remains a resource to be exploited.[32] Once any symbol system becomes part of a political arsenal, the relevance of its message for other subsystems can be made clear.[33]

The crucial factor missed by social systems theory is that a cultural system will infuse other parts of the social system with its symbolic framework only under specific political conditions. Political leaders must demonstrate that the symbolic framework embedded in a cultural system is "obviously" a model for political life. Social science theory must learn the conditions under which this becomes possible.

The theory of hegemony that I am proposing as an alternative to social systems theory focuses its initial attention on the interests of a variety of social forces within a society. Rather than see marginal and evolutionary adjustment among competing subsystems, this approach postulates that social upheaval is necessary for there to be a major impact of a nonhegemonic subsystem on the society as a whole. An excellent model for this approach is provided by Karl Mannheim in his *Ideology and Utopia*. He looks at periods in which political change occurs, when new coalitions are forming and old alliances shattering. This is the period in which political entrepreneurs have an opportunity to create new visions and state new truths. But where do these visions come from? Mannheim portrays the Anabaptists as an ideal typical case in which a religious vision imploded onto the political stage when German society was already in a revolutionary situation. Not so much their ideas as the Anabaptist frame of mind was seen by Mannheim as influencing the direction followed by the oppressed strata of the population, who were predisposed by structural conditions to rebel.[34]

Aristide Zolberg suggests a similar pattern. In revolutionary situations—"moments of madness," as Zolberg calls them—when the population suspends normal routines and develops the belief that all reform is possible, utopian projects play an important social role. These utopian projects instill into the political system a "torrent of words" that creates new societal goals, new agendas, and new social networks.[35] Since politics in Yorubaland has followed a normal and incremental course ever since the world religions became established there, there have been no "moments of madness" in which Christianity or Islam could come onto the political stage as utopian projects. These institutions remain backstage, as it were, waiting for their cues.

One can only speculate about how this Mannheim-Zolberg approach might fit the Yoruba situation. One might consider the intense religious upheavals in northern Nigeria as a potentially strong destabilizing factor for the highly secular political arrangement since independence. Poor, lumpenproletariat Muslims had been organized by a self-proclaimed prophet who represented a challenge to the Hausa-Fulani aristocratic control of northern Nigerian society. Should this upheaval spill over into Yoruba towns, and should revolutionary religious prophets in the north begin to successfully claim authority in the Nigerian arena, a social cue could well be delivered to religious entrepreneurs in Yorubaland to expand their own realm of authority by articulating a full-fledged religiously oriented Utopian project.[36] From this perspective, social systems theory would be amended so that a utopian subsystem would be seen not to have a *persistent* effect on the wider social systems, but, rather, to have *major* effect if the conditions should be ripe.

This approach, focusing on social upheaval, is more adequate theoretically than the evolutionary model because it suggests a set of factors that retard or encourage the infusion of a symbol system into the wider social system. From this viewpoint, one can begin to see how a coalition of powerful social groups—a historical bloc, in Gramsci's terms—gains legitimacy through appeals to cultural values. But cultural values are multifaceted and contradictory. It is the task of the leadership of the hegemonic bloc to choose one major strand of the culture and to make it the privileged locus of symbolic infusion. If the bloc is then identified as a carrier of that aspect of culture, it will appear obvious and commonsensical that its leadership is the natural leadership of the society, and the values espoused by that leadership should be congruent with other social subsystems.

While it is possible for a historical bloc to forge a connection between one cultural subsystem and political life, it is beyond the ken of all but the most totalitarian of blocs to eliminate all the cultural strands that have politically irrelevant. This insight led Gramsci to contend that any revolutionary group, before it could adequately challenge a historical bloc, must develop a new framework—a "counter hegemony." In Gramsci's terms, revolutionary programs require leaders to counter the hegemonic conception of common sense with an alternate conception.

Alternative conceptions of common sense are not easily found. In chapter 3 I suggested that the practical religions of Islam and Christianity have indeed provided the basis for different commonsensical views of authority, responsibility, equality, and community. These alternative commonsensical perspectives cannot by themselves influence the Yoruba social system. The putative hegemonic elites of the Nigerian state are attempting to infuse in the population—by drawing on common cultural threads that surpass Yorubaland—their own common sense. And, as we shall see in the forthcoming chapters, the common sense of the British hegemonic bloc remains powerful, itself drawing on powerful indigenous conceptions of common sense—for example, that ancestral city attachments are "really real" in Yorubaland but that religious attachments are "thin veneers." Thus there is more than one cultural candidate for political relevance in Yorubaland.

The vision of the social system I am suggesting is one in which competing social forces with different interests vie to associate themselves with a cultural framework and to make their framework the relevant one to inform political discourse. What is commonsensical in politics is the core of the ideology of the dominant social groups. Ideological competitors appear to be utopian and irrelevant. Religious fundamentalists in a secular society, if they wish to be considered normal, will act as if religion is a hobby, of no particular political relevance. If they don't, they are liable to be considered abnormal or religious fanatics. But if the political system faces upheaval, religious entrepreneurs might seek to infuse the entire social system with a new common sense—a counter hegemony—that would make religious-political congruence appear to be normal.

The hegemonic theory of culture, unlike the social systems approach, does not expect all subsystems to interpenetrate. In the hegemony model, one expects to find a single source of symbolic production that infuses the entire social system. This source is the privileged subsystem and is backed by dominant elites interested in its ideological force.

Summary

In part 1 of this book I have demonstrated that Islam and Christianity make available to Yoruba society different points of concern, but I have also shown that these religious subcultures have little relevance outside of religious life. That religion can provide a basis for a particular vision of political life demonstrates its potential ideological force. That the very different frameworks in which church and mosque elders think about authority, community, responsibility, and equality did not infuse the secular political realm suggests that both the congruence hypothesis and social systems theory are inadequate to explain the relationship between culture and politics. A full view of the first face of culture requires more than a description of the symbolic framework embedded in any cultural system. To understand the conditions under which a cultural system such as religion will inform political discourse and action, one must examine the way a historical bloc forges a connection between one aspect of culture and the political system.

This introduction of the idea of hegemony into an analysis of the first face of culture provides a preliminary theoretical statement. In the following chapter, the model of hegemony will be elaborated. That done, we shall be able to address with some theoretical rigor the question of why Christianity and Islam in Yorubaland have not become mobilized by religious entrepreneurs. To explain the political irrelevance of religion in Yoruba politics—the central question raised by the second face of culture—is the task of part 2.

II | The Second Face of Culture

5 | The Benthamite Tradition

Part 2 focuses on the question of how cultural identities become markers for collective political action. In the context of Nigerian politics, Muslim and Christian Yorubas see themselves culturally as Yorubas rather than as Muslims or Christians. In the context of Yoruba politics, Yorubas organize collectively on the basis of their ancestral city, or subtribe (a category of membership that will be explained more fully in chapter 6), and not on the basis of their religious identification. A theory that merely predicts political organization based on cultural sharing, however, is inadequate for my purposes, since the question here is, *Which aspect of one's cultural identity becomes the basis for collective political action?* This is the central problem for students of the second face of culture. Whereas social systems theorists have little to say about why certain aspects of "primordial" identities become politically consequential and other aspects do not, rational choice theorists provide a compelling model to explain the conditions under which cultural identification relates to political organization. I aim to demonstrate the power of rational choice theory in making sense out of the second face of culture. It will then be possible to go beyond rational choice to explain the Yoruba case, and thereby to develop more fully the hegemonic model of culture. This model should incorporate the insights of both social systems and rational choice theory and thus provide a focal point from which culture's two faces can be resolved.

THE VIEW FROM CULTURE'S FIRST FACE: THE THEORY OF PRIMORDIAL LOYALTIES

Students in the Weberian tradition—Clifford Geertz among them—were examining the persistence of culturally based political movements at a time when many sociologists were expecting class ties to erode ties to culture and nation. Marxists belittled the importance of culture, and explained the weakness of class ties by suggesting that members of the local classes suffered from "false consciousness." Geertz, however, saw culture as providing the basis for "primordial" ties, argueing that these were sociological "givens" or unquestioned aspects of individual identity. Those who share primordial ties share a common culture; and cultures themselves are tenacious. Social system theorists—as we have seen in part 1—emphasize the interconnections between the economic, social, political, and cultural subsystems in order to demonstrate a homeostatic equilibrium within society. Cultural ties are therefore but one component of a complex system. Since systems need stability, each component supports the integrity of the other components; thus primordial ties are reinforced by the entire social system. Homeostasis (and not false consciousness) explains the persistence and strength of a culturally based politics.[1]

This social system perspective, therefore, provides an explanation not only of how culture molds political values (the first face of culture) but also why cultural diversity divides people politically (the second face). "In modernizing societies," Geertz suggests with some concern, "primordial attachments tend . . . to be repeatedly, in some cases almost continually, proposed and widely acclaimed as preferred bases for the demarcation of autonomous political units . . . It is this crystallization of a direct conflict between primordial and civil sentiments—this 'longing not to belong to any other group'—that gives to the problem variously called tribalism, parochialism, communalism, and so on, a more ominous and deeply threatening quality than most of the other, also very serious and intractable, problems the new states face."[2]

In some of his later writings, such as "Thick Description," Geertz eschewed disconfirmable statements such as the one quoted above. His greater attention to the hermeneutical method led him to seek interpretations of cultures rather than explanations for political outcomes. The interpretative method most certainly speaks to the first face of culture, where the central concern is one of *meaning*, and how meaning translates into political points of concern. But hermeneutics is less suitable to the concerns of the second face of culture. Here, we want to know which aspects of culture will become the symbolic basis for political organization. Not interpretation but explanation is required. It is therefore not surprising that, when writing about the political mobilization of culture (the second face), Geertz writes more in the social system and positivist mode than when he is writing about the political meanings embedded in culture (the first face).

Geertz's social systems theory, however, has been found, in a large number of studies, to be an inadequate explanation of communal politics. First of all, the dichotomy between tradition (in which case primordial politics prevails) and modernity (in which case civil politics reigns) began to collapse under the weight of disconfirming field data. In a study of the political mobilization of caste associations in India, in which these associations were seen to be useful tools for the attainment of certain political goals, the Rudolphs wrote of the "modernity of tradition." What they saw as "modern" (political parties) could easily be built on a foundation of what they saw as "tradition" (caste identification).[3] Furthermore, the "givenness" of primordial identities was put under question. Crawford Young, in his pioneering study of today's Zaire, found that at least one "primordial" group was of recent derivation and had developed its identity as the result of a conjunction between the colonialists' desire for control and the colonized's desire for greater resources.[4] In study after study, the politicization of communal identities was seen as a rational pursuit by actors seeking to maximize short-term goals. There was no need either for a theory of false consciousness or a theory of homeostasis.

THE VIEW FROM CULTURE'S SECOND FACE: THE RATIONAL CHOICE PERSPECTIVE

These findings—which were in search of a theory—fit in brilliantly with an emerging neo-Benthamite paradigm in other branches of the social sciences. The theory of communal action could easily be embedded in the more general theory of public choice, which itself has become a branch of microeconomics. Ethnic action from this perspective is seen as the rational pursuit of goals by value-maximizing individuals. Indeed, this was the perspective adopted by Abner Cohen, whose work was analyzed in chapter 1 in order to exemplify the second face of culture.

Because of the overwhelming evidence that tradition is less a constraint on action than a resource for political engineering, many other social scientists have become attracted to this neo-Benthamite paradigm. The sources of ethnicity from the perspective of the second face of culture differ substantially from the explanations of primordial conflicts by sociologists working within the social systems perspective. Ethnic (or tribal) conflict in the new states, from culture's second face, can be comprehended from the following rational choice paradigm (coded RC):

(RC1) Colonization created a new arena for political action. Imperial powers defined new boundaries, which brought together peoples from diverse cultures, and distributed resources from a new political center. Peoples who shared positive-sum trading relationships with other groups now found themselves in conflict with members of those groups for state resources.

(RC2) Exogenous social and economic change yielded a new pattern of rewards. Those groups who lived on mineral-rich land, or who could produce crops in high demand elsewhere, began to gain by comparison with their neighbors. Those groups who were on new trade routes, or whose urban areas became important new administrative centers, also gained. Sometimes gain came from a willingness to put up with missionaries, as European evangelists in Africa opened up job opportunities for their literate students. For a whole set of reasons, the broad social changes of the nineteenth century brought a new pattern of rewards in colonial societies.

(RC3) Rewards and resources were inevitably scarce, and competition for jobs, for status, and for other manifestations of "modernity" became intense. Individuals from areas which were not spatially favored migrated to other areas in order to gain the benefits of the changed environment. Migrants were discontent because of the uneven economic development of their country. "Sons of the soil" of those towns to which migrants came developed their own complaints as migrants successfully competed for local jobs. The stage was thereby set for ethnic conflict.[5]

(RC4) Political entrepreneurs found it cheaper to organize people on the basis of their ethnic identities than on the basis of their class identities. People who share ethnic identities often share a common language, and so translation costs are lower. They also share a myth of kinship, and so the symbolic basis of solidarity is already available.[6]

(RC5) The ambitious entrepreneur will at some time attempt to broaden the boundaries of the ethnic group he leads in order to enhance the geographic scope of his authority. Since "tribal" identities are fluid, and the myths of kinship are subject to manipulation, the boundaries of ethnic identification (and the symbolic core of the ethnic group) are subject to rearticulation by both entrepreneurs and members—in both cases to increase the opportunity for the successful pursuit of resources. Primordially based political action is thus a result not of "givens" but of strategic identity readjustments by self-interested individuals.

This instrumentalist perspective can be, and has been, formalized. For my purposes, however, its importance is that it has generated interesting, nontrivial hypotheses on the emergence of tribalism and the politicization of tribal identities. Thus hypotheses relating the number of communal groups formed within a single state structure to the continued coherence of the state have been proposed.[7] Also from this perspective (but adding the dubious assumption that communal pluralism necessitates a zero-sum view of virtually all collective goods), it has been hypothesized that democratic elections in a plural society tend to work towards societal disequilibrium.[8] Another approach suggests that the likelihood of communal action is related to the costs for any group of exit from the state in which it resides.[9] All these approaches hypothesize that under conditions of imperfect access to information, high risk, and uncertainty, individuals will adopt short-run political strategies to maximize their status, wealth, and power. Tribalism is the macrosociological outcome of rationally pursued strategies by individuals.

But just as the theory focusing on primordial identities faced the anomalies of identity readjustment and the apparent rationality of ethnically based political organization, the neo-Benthamite theory faces its own anomalies. These anomalies must be addressed if our theories are to be refined and advanced. The first problem that the rational action theories face is that of the *persistence* of communal identities. In another context, responding to arguments that political identities in Europe may, under certain conditions, transfer from the nation-state to the continent, Stanley Hoffmann pointed out that national identity is not like an onion, which can be peeled away into nothing, but more like an artichoke. People will transfer loyalty for purposes of political advantage only so far—i.e. until it reaches their heart.[10] Of course, the primordialists often assumed that the heart has an immutable reality. The data do not support this view. But, once the rational action perspective is adopted, what had been obvious to the primordialist, and therefore not requiring explanation, becomes problematical to the microeconomist.

Robert Bates, who is in the microeconomic or instrumentalist tradition, has argued that "ethnic groups persist largely because of their capacity to extract goods and services from the modern sector and thereby satisfy the demands of their members."[11] And Brian Barry, in a similar vein: "I would guess that ethnic groups will survive in the US just so long as it is a source of satisfaction."[12] Besides the fact that no data are presented to support these propositions, one easily sees how strained and unconvincing they are. People do not quit their ethnic groups as they do their jobs; nor do they change their ethnic identities in the same way they change their brand of beer. Because ethnic identity is believed to be a biological "given," most people at most times do not calculate how much satisfaction they derive from their ethnic identities. Without calculation and the weighing of satisfactions, economic paradigms lose their explanatory power. Persistence of ethnic identity without at least occasional calculation concerning its benefits is, then, a thorny problem for students of the second face of culture.

The second problem in the rational choice paradigm is in its inability to explain why some identity investments are made while others are abjured. In Abner Cohen's work, for example, we learn why it was rational (i.e. a route to power and wealth) for Hausas in Ibadan to become more religious than their counterparts in northern Nigeria.[13] In order to corner the markets in kola nuts and cattle, they adjusted their identities to become *Sufi Muslim* Hausas, instead of Muslim *Hausas*. Their culture not only differed from Hausa culture in the north, but these Ibadan Hausas had little desire to return to their homeland. They had become a "retribalized" and politically mobilized ethnic group.

The Yorubas, however, who constitute the majority in Ibadan, present a problem for someone working in Cohen's framework. Surely it would have been rational for (at least some of) them, to become Sufi Muslim Hausas in order to break the Hausa monopolies in trade. But, as we shall see, this did not happen. Furthermore, while many Yorubas (like Hausas) developed trading communities in "foreign" cities, few severed their ties with their ancestral cities. Why was it easy for Hausas to alter their ethnic identities and to break ties with their homeland, but difficult for Yorubas?

One way to pose the problem is to examine the tension between two neo-Benthamite points: (1) that tribal identities have lower organizational costs, and (2) that tribal identities are fluid. If they are fluid, then their organizational costs must be higher than assumed. If they are higher than assumed, why are they so easily mobilized in so many African contexts? Whether high or low, however, we still lack a theory to tell us which identities will become politicized.

Rational choice theorists can address this problem by arguing that success for a group in forming a viable political organization is contingent on political entrepreneurs who understand the "Olson" problem of organization. Since political entrepreneurs are offering their constituencies a "public good," why should any follower be willing to incur a specific cost? Shouldn't all prospective followers wish a "free ride" by watching others pay for what all will have to share? A good entrepreneur, from this point of view, is one who knows how to provide "selective incentives" to particular individuals to join in the group effort. Communal groups will politicize when there is an entrepreneur who (perhaps instinctively) understands the constraints placed by rational individual behavior on organization.[14] This is a powerful response, and it would be considerably enhanced as a theoretical contribution if it were possible to establish from independent data the quality of the strategic calculations of entrepreneurs before one assesses whether their organizations were successful.

Nonetheless, the response which emphasizes selective incentives tends to miss broad contemporaneous patterns over a number of similar countries. Why did Europeans in so many countries from 1580 to 1648 participate politically primarily in terms of their religious adherence? By the end of the nineteenth century, Europeans considered their national leaders to represent their primordial political group. Why were religious elites skillful political entrepreneurs in the sixteenth to seventeenth centuries but national elites more skillful in the nineteenth? Why did so many entrepreneurs attempting to organize peripheral nationalities in many places in Western Europe suddenly become moderately successful all in the same period in the 1970s. Why are religious entrepreneurs without large political constituencies in Europe today, though they cannot be contained in the Shi'ite world? Or, in the case under discussion, why in postindependence sub-Saharan Africa have tribal entrepreneurs been more successful then religious entrepreneurs in mobilizing political constituencies? Certain aspects of identity become crucial at certain times and politically irrelevant at others. These global patterns cannot be successfully addressed by the instrumentalists, who focus on the logic of individual cases.

BEYOND RATIONAL CHOICE

Communal identities are more fluid than the primordial theorists could acknowledge, but their source is more subject to a broader explanation than instrumental theorists have yet attempted. Indeed, a number of important studies have rejected the static view of identity inherent in the theory of primordial identities, yet have gone beyond rational choice.

These theorists have demonstrated that the politicization of communal identities cannot be fully understood by examining the logic of individual choices. The structure of opportunity faced by the wider group largely determines when it is worthwhile for members of that group to emphasize their primordial identities. Michael Hechter, for one, in a study of peripheral nationalism in the Celtic fringe, argued that communal identities would become salient when peripheral groups were locked into a low-status job category. He has hypothesized that where laborers work in geographical proximity (as in mines) and where there are few management-level jobs which would enable the better workers to break away from the lowest-paying jobs (and thereby be subject to cooptation), workers will rearticulate their cultural differences from the culture of the capitalist center. This Hechter called the "cultural division of labor." The theory leads us to predict that successful politicization of communal identities is at least in part a function of a community being isolated in the larger labor market.[15]

Peter Gourevitch, another student of peripheral nationalisms in Europe, also abjured the focus on individual choice that is embedded in the neo-Benthamite tradition. He coded regions within a country based on criteria of cultural differentiation. Within a peripheral region, the greater the differentiation, the greater their "ethnic potential." Next, Gourevitch determined for a number of European states whether "political leadership" and "economic dynamism" take place in the same region. He then argued that where there is ethnic potential, and where political leadership and economic dynamism occur in different regions, "the latter region is likely to develop strong, politically relevant, nationalism."[16] Like Hechter, Gourevitch found that separate regional identities were a function of their role in the division of labor. Both suggest a process of identity creation and reinforcement that is best explained by social forces that go beyond individual choice. The resurgence of Welsh and Basque nationalism, according to Hechter and Gourevitch, has been less a function of clever entrepreneurs solving free rider problems than a result of problems and opportunities that faced the group as a whole.

Other theories emphasize a related point: states have enormous power to restructure culture.[17] While states are not always successful in these sorts of endeavors, and while their strategies may backfire (for example, imperial divide-and-rule strategies in South Africa that led to a more congealed black African nationalism),[18] it would be imprudent to develop a theory of ethnicity that did not highlight the interest and the enormous relative power of the state to remold identities. Many of the apparently "natural" nation-states of today, in which a single national culture coincides with state boundaries, are the result of elite strategies to enhance cultural similarity and to eradicate differences.[19]

The work of Steven Lukes and John Gaventa can give some theoretical coherence to those studies that have gone beyond rational choice.[20] Lukes, in his study of power, divided it along three dimensions. The first dimension relies on theories of pluralism. These theories assume that all societal groups who want to articulate their interests will in fact be able to do so; and state action is seen as the vector sum of the pressure of societal interest groups. These theories are closely linked to rational choice theories of ethnicity.[21]

In most societies, of course, at least for some strata, the pluralist assumption does not hold. The second dimension of power is operating when the state "mobilizes bias" so that "some issues are organized into politics while others are organized out."[22] Furthermore, when power "influences, shapes or determines conceptions of the necessities, possibilities, and strategies of challenge in situations of latent conflict," then we are facing power's third dimension. "This may include," Gaventa suggests, "the study of social myths, language and symbols, and how they are shaped or manipulated in power processes."[23]

Gaventa's study—of the political quiescence in Appalachia in the face of enormous inequality and resentment—demonstrates that powerful economic and political forces structured for residents a clear sense of the spectrum of political possibility. He therefore maintains that an understanding of political action by aggrieved groups demands "consideration of the social forces and historical patterns involved in Gramsci's concept of hegemony."[24]

To be sure, an examination of the behavior of powerful actors could easily demonstrate that they are acting "rationally." They have an interest in political quiescence among coalminers. In what sense, then, has Gaventa gone beyond rational choice? He has in two ways. First, he provides an historical analysis to demonstrate how the political marketplace was created, and how the rules stacked the deck against certain sorts of action. Microeconomics takes market rules as givens—as constraints to rational action—and does not know how to theorize about their origins and biases. Second, Gaventa permits a focus on the creation of rules of thumb—ideologies and myths that are the source of common sense. While a microeconomic perspective can see ideologies as devices to reduce information costs, it cannot comprehend the mechanisms by which ideologies structure goals and perceived opportunities. Because of its power to go beyond rational choice, it is to the concept of hegemony that we now turn.

A MODEL OF HEGEMONIC CONTROL

The model of "hegemony," although too often invoked and used as a sobriquet, can, like the rational choice model, be stated in a paradigmatic set of related propositions. Relieved of some claims that cannot be sustained, Gramscian analysis retains much that can help make sense of the nature and form of political conflict among cultural groups within a society. Furthermore, conjoined with the notion of hegemony used here to address culture's first face (see chapter 4), it will allow us to reconcile (in chapter 8) the Janus-faced image of culture and politics. Let us begin with the Gramscian paradigm of hegemony and political action (coded H):

(H1) Hegemony creates a unified moral order or, in the words of Gwyn Williams, "an order in which a certain way of life and thought is dominant, in which one concept of reality is diffused throughout society."[25] This concept of reality infuses all aspects of civil society—for example, the schools, the churches, and trade unions.

(H2) Hegemony, residing in civil society, provides a bulwark in support of political society. Political domination requires a mixture of coercion and consent, and hegemony provides an ideology that encourages consent by the lower strata to rule by the political authorities. Thus, where hegemony in civil society is strong, there is little need for coercion in political society.

(H3) The moral order, which serves the interests of the ruling strata, is accepted by the lower strata out of "false consciousness," which allows the ruling strata to rule through consent rather than relying too heavily on coercion. The masses, according to Gramsci, will give "spontaneous consent" to the higher strata because of their prestige and position. Consent comes from the lower strata not because it is in their interest to give it but because they have "adopted a conception . . . of the world . . . which is not [their] own but is borrowed from another group."[26]

(H4) Political action by the masses can never be understood in terms of rational calculation of costs and benefits because, as Joseph Femia puts it, summarizing Gramsci's ideas, "the very definition of what constitutes costs and benefits necessarily presupposes some framework of value and categories which does not itself merely reflect 'external reality'. That is to say, political and social preferences . . . reflect a man's assumptions about how society is and should be run, and in capitalist societies these assumptions are largely set by the ruling class through its highly developed agencies of political socialization."[27]

(H5) Latent in the lower strata, however, is a critical consciousness, "one which unites . . . the active man-in-the-mass . . . with all his fellow-workers."[28] Gramsci recognized the fragility of the so-called liberal consensus, and saw in the masses a "contradictory consciousness" with the critical element being latent.

(H6) The latent critical consciousness can become manifest if it is elaborated and fully articulated. This elaborated doctrine is called a "counter hegemony," and it is the social role of the intellectuals to develop and propagate it, in an activity that Gramsci felicitously refers to as the "war of position" on the cultural front. When civil society is strong, the development of a counter hegemony is a necessary precondition for revolutionary action.

This model of hegemony has been attacked on virtually every front. Perry Anderson, for example, has demonstrated that the dichotomy Gramsci proposes between the hegemony that resides in civil society and the coercion that resides in political society cannot be consistently maintained. Among other telling problems with this dichotomy is the fact that it is the state that has the greatest resources to sustain and/or reestablish culture and common sense.[29] Hegemony resides at least as much within political society as it does within civil society.

Another major argument made against the hegemonic paradigm concerns its claim about the false consciousness of the working classes. Who is to say that the workers have an interest in revolution over trade unionism? Many observers, not themselves caught in an ideological net, who calculate the fate of the workers after a revolution is made in their name, could well conclude that it is the radicals who suffer from false consciousness.

Furthermore, any empirical examination of the culture of the poor will demonstrate that the lower strata consistently ignore or mock the ideological bulwarks of the ruling strata. They mimic with bitter irony the hypocritical justifications for authority that come from the ruling classes. They articulate their own visions of a just society (especially through millennial movements). Folk religions, as James Scott points out, "contain, almost inevitably, the seeds of an alternative symbolic universe, one that makes the social world in which peasants actually live less than completely inevitable."[30] There is no compelling evidence that the calculations or consciousness of the lower strata are "false."

With these criticisms in mind, it becomes necessary to shear the hegemonic model of its excesses. First, the rigid distinction between the locus of ideology and that of coercion is unnecessary.[31] It seems clear that blends of coercion, cooptation (with bargaining between classes) and ideological production go into the making of a stable social system, one in which the lower strata give some degree of consent to the social order.[32] Hegemony requires a dominant symbolic framework that provides a cultural context within which cost/benefit calculation can take place. Hegemony does *not* require ideological production to reside only in civil society.

Second, the notion that there is "one concept of reality" under hegemony cannot be sustained. Instead, consistent with the Gramscian point about "contradictory consciousness," hegemony must be understood in terms of a "dominant" ideology about the nature of the social system. From this point of view, the lower strata should be seen not as merely sharing a dominant ideology with the ruling strata but, instead, as being in simultaneous possession of ideas that support *and* challenge political authority in their society.[33]

Third, the notion that there is a single "order" that results from hegem- ↙ ony is misleading. The notion of "order" suggests that under hegemony there is a normal state of harmony and political consensus. Relying on the insights of Thomas Metzger (see chapter 3), however, we see that all political cultures reveal internal struggles among conflicting elite groups. What makes societies, or cultures, differ, is the issues people think are worth struggling over. A successful hegemony, then, doesn't yield "order"; rather, it yields a set of conflicts that automatically and common-sensically stand at the top of the political agenda.

Fourth, the concept of "false consciousness" is a red herring. Lower strata will operate within a dominant ideological framework because they can, within it, achieve short-term gains and avoid risk. Why should this be considered "false"? Risk aversion by the poor appears to me to be ra-tional. It is best to claim that the lower strata accept a dominant ideological framework if within it they have some room for bargaining and can make some claims successfully for the resources controlled by the upper strata.

Even with these concessions, the model of hegemony still has explana-tory power. Let us apply a revised hegemony paradigm to the problem of the politicization or nonpoliticization of cultural identities:

(H*1) In all societies, cultural subsystems are diverse and divide up the ↙ population along different dimensions. Language, religion, kinship, and occupation are categories that combine and divide different subsets of a single society.[34]

(H*2) As any elite group (or historical bloc) attempts to achieve domination over society, it will seek to lower the costs of compliance by developing an ideology of its own legitimacy. One method of lowering the costs of control is to view the society from the lens of a single sociocultural divide. All political conflict can then be interpreted in terms of that divide. Cultural hegemony has been established when members of all social strata interpret politics and choose strategies of participation in terms of the divide favored by the elite group. (This does not preclude the existence of a latent set of membership categories that cross-cut the chosen dimensions of conflict: all citizens have "contradictory consciousnesses.")

(H*3) The elite-preferred dimension of conflict is sustained by the state. It becomes commonsensical to both upper and lower strata that the chosen cultural divide is real, while other cultural markers are thought of as superficial or shallow. Political conflict can be intense; it will, however, be fought along a single dimension, one that had originally been favored by the hegemonic bloc.

(H*4) Culturally based political action on a nonpreferred dimension is not easy to mobilize. Simple cost/benefit calculations are insufficient to activate people on a different dimension of conflict. Putative elites at-tempting to mobilize a constituency based on membership in a nonpreferred dimension must successfully establish a "counter hegemony" and fight a "war of position" before their messages can yield a political following. (We can assume that cultural elites interested in establishing an alternative framework are not lacking. Many virtuosos in a nonpreferred cultural domain will see great opportunity if their cultural domain becomes the leitmotif for political action).

This paradigm, by focusing on elite forging of a single cultural framework from a number of possible frameworks within their society, enables us to study cultural conflict historically. We can thus observe how political resources are employed to alter the pattern of symbolic interpenetration within a social system. We can also understand why certain cultural calculations are not made, even if they could yield added utility.

It will be the task of chapters 6 and 7 to show how hegemony was established in the Yoruba case and to show its implications for the political mobilization of ancestral city and religious groups. The promise of this book is that the model of hegemony elaborated here will enable me not only to explain why religious adherence to Christianity and Islam has had so little impact on Yoruba political life, but also to show the potential of these world religions to provide a framework for an alternative political ideology, or counter hegemony. If successful, the model of hegemony will enable us to reconcile the Janus-faced image of culture and politics.

6| Competing Cleavages:
Ancestral City and Religion

A ki i gba akaka lọwọ akiki, a ki i gba ile baba ẹni lọwọ ẹni (You cannot cure a monkey of squatting, so you cannot take a man's ancestral home away from him).
Yoruba proverb, cited in J. O. Ajibola, *Owe Yoruba*

In Yorubaland there is a social basis for political conflict both between religious groups and between members of different ancestral cities. Ancestral city has remained an important category for collective political action in Yorubaland; yet membership in a world religion has never become such a category. What is this ancestral city, and what is its meaning in Yoruba society? The first section of this chapter attempts to answer these questions.

The second section poses the sociological puzzle that forms the problematic of part 2 of this book. It will be demonstrated that the rational choice perspective, exemplified by Abner Cohen's framework, would have led us to expect the politicization of the religious cleavage in Yorubaland. Yet this has not occurred. The study of religion and political organization in Yorubaland is therefore a "critical case," allowing us to develop our theories of culture's second face.[1] It will then be possible to demonstrate the power of the model of hegemony to make sense of the politicization of ancestral city but the nonpoliticization of religion in Yorubaland (see chapter 7).

ANCESTRAL CITY AS A CULTURAL SUBSYSTEM

By "ancestral city" (see map 1-2), I mean the city in which a Yoruba traces his family origins after the conquests of today's Yorubaland by the descendants of Oduduwa, the mythical founder of the Yoruba people. The Yoruba word for city, *ilu*, like *polis* in Greek, connotes "community" and is the root of the Yoruba word for politics, *iṣelu*. A Yoruba's "ancestral city" is referred to in the phrase *ọmọ ilu* (son of a city). If a Yoruba's city of residence (*ara Ife* means a resident of the city of Ife) is different from his ancestral city, he is considered to be a stranger (*alejo*).

An *ilu* is an aggregate of corporate descent groups or lineages (*idile*) that has an organized government of king (*ọba*) and chiefs. Under certain conditions, a Yoruba will claim the capital city of his kingdom as his ancestral city (e.g. Oyo, Ijebu-Ode, Ile-Ife). Under other conditions, he will claim ancestral city membership in a subordinate town. Most Yoruba farmers who have city compounds also have huts in small hamlets (*aba*) near their farms. When these hamlets grow in population and commerce, corporate development may take place, with new chieftaincy titles and thus a new ancestral city.[2] A variety of symbols, rituals, and institutions distinguish each ancestral city. Each city-kingdom has its own myth of origin (heralding a different son of Oduduwa), and a particular design of facial markings incised on the young. Each city is also associated with a distinct dialect of what is today called the Yoruba language. The priests (*babalawo*, "father of the secrets") in each city kingdom, though all practitioners of the same divination system (*ifa*), pay obeisance to their own subset of the Yoruba pantheon. Some divinities (*orişa*) are worshiped throughout Yorubaland, but each city also has divinities of its own. Burials take place in family compounds, so the land in each city has sacred appeal to those whose ancestors were buried there. Festivals, too, have special local forms. Finally, each city kingdom has somewhat different political structures and titles. Because members of an *ilu* share these myths, rituals, and institutions, and differentiate themselves from other *ilu* by virtue of them, it is consistent with the criteria set in chapter 1 to call ancestral city a Yoruba cultural subsystem.

It ought to be emphasized, however, that a Yoruba's *ilu* is subject to redefinition, for a number of reasons. The myths of the migrations of Oduduwa's descendants have many versions, each yielding a different picture of the development of subsequent "city-kingdoms." As is well known to anthropologists, political entities are regularly subject to fissions and fusions. Leaders of a rival satellite city to a major capital of a city kingdom will often reformulate the "tradition" to make their city historically more important. Individuals will then begin to consider themselves sons of the satellite city rather than identifying with the capital. In the case of fusion, the reverse will happen. For political or economic reasons a man may be considered a native son (*ọmọ ilu*) in a town different from that of either of his parents. Intermarriage among people from different ancestral cities provides opportunities for identity adjustment by the next generation. Among the southern Yoruba, individuals can emphasize their identification with either of their parent's lineages (this is called "cognatic descent"). Other Yoruba children of such mixed marriages will normally see themselves as descendants of their father's ancestral city, but it is not uncommon even for a northern Yoruba to consider himself a son of his mother's *ilu*.[3] Despite the biological ambiguities, I shall refer to a Yoruba's *ọmọ ilu* as his "ancestral city." Let us now put this concept into historical perspective.

Ancestral Cities in Yorubaland: Historical Background

The first indigenously written account of the history of the Yorubas claims that Ile-Ife is the cradle of civilization. Oduduwa is said to have crossed the African savannah from the Middle East some time in the twelfth century and arrived in what is today Ile-Ife.[4] Oduduwa's descendants eventually spread out across the savannah and into the forest, founding imperial outposts for Ile-Ife. Oranmiyan, Oduduwa's youngest son, is said to have remained in Ile-Ife, become its king—the Ọọni of Ife—and ruled over the religious and political center of the satellite kingdoms.

By the fifteenth century, the city of Oyo was founded. Oyo eventually established political control over both the complex pattern of cities which traced their ancestry to Oduduwa and a number of other cities that had no particular relation to Oduduwa. Oyo was to become a centralized empire of great territorial expanse; Ile-Ife long remained the religious center of those cities whose elite lineages traced their ancestry back to Oduduwa.

In each of the cities founded by the descendants of Oduduwa, Yoruba traditions suggest that the conquering band incorporated many indigenous peoples into their social and political system. Yoruba, the language of Ile-Ife, became the language of the conquered cities; as did reverence for the tradition of Oduduwa, which formed the basis of a complex and theologically rich religion. A family's identification with a particular city became, over the centuries, the determining characteristic of any individual's political identity.[5]

These myths (which of course have considerable meaning among Yorubas today) have been contested by much scholarly research. The connection between Oduduwa and the Middle East has no historiographical support. More probably Oduduwa (if he was an outsider) migrated from the less distant Nupe or Borgu areas.[6] Also, it is doubtful that the indigenous peoples in Yoruba cities adopted the language of their conquerors. The Yoruba language is closely related to its next-door neighbors Edo (Benin), Nupe, Igala, Idoma and Igbo, and there is evidence that before the fifteenth century there was already a large, settled population in today's Yorubaland. One can therefore infer that Oduduwa's band of conquerors learned the local language rather than the other way around.[7] Another anomaly for the Yoruba foundation myth is that central aspects of the religious rituals and chieftaincy titles associated with Oduduwa have been recorded in the eastern kingdoms around Akure before the founding of Ife.[8] Also, the political structures in Sabe (a city in western Yorubaland) have been found to have had little connection with Ile-Ife. Twentieth-century attempts to demonstrate a direct line of descent between Sabe and Ife are now believed to be "late fabrications to plug the loopholes in the Ife traditions."[9]

The very use of the term "Yoruba" to describe the common culture zone is itself an anachronism. Those peoples who claimed descent from Oduduwa had no name for their collective identity, and no ideology that their common cultural characteristics had any relevance for political organization. It wasn't until the anticolonial movement of the nineteenth and early twentieth centuries—after the collapse of the Oyo Empire—that the activities of the descendants of Oduduwa were compiled into a unified history.

Anomalies weighed too heavily on the Ile-Ife tradition; Robin Horton's inventive reassessment was long overdue.[10] Horton argues that early Ife was an important commercial center from about A.D. 1000. Since it was the closest forest point due south of the eastward bend of the Niger River, it played a key role in the riverine trading system. Ife, and its market at Apomu, became a center for trade in cotton, *akori* beads, and copper (and thus the famous Ife bronze statues). Its key location led the people of Ife to establish political dominance over a wide area. Ile-Ife became a magnet for artists, craftsmen, and iron workers. Meanwhile, Ife kings sent out royal relatives to govern conquered towns.

But these princes ruling the satellite cities eventually sought to challenge Ife's supremacy. By 1500, Oyo and Ijebu-Ode were well-placed to make a successful challenge. The old city of Oyo was north of Ife, on the border between forest and savannah, and could therefore maintain a cavalry to conquer and control cities at great distances from it. (Because the forest-dwelling tsetse is a menace to horses, cities in the forest like Ile-Ife could not maintain cavalries.) Also because of its location, Oyo became an entrepôt between the Saharan trade and the forest, and its trade far surpassed Ife's. Ijebu-Ode, south of Ife and closer to the coast, was better able to procure guns from the European traders on the coast, and it, too, began to surpass Ife as a trading center.

Oyo, Ijebu-Ode (and nearby Benin) all developed trading specialties and spheres of influence among the cities that traced their origins to Oduduwa and Ile-Ife. Because of a desire for trade stability, these cities accepted Ife's role as a "buffer" or "mediating center." They embroidered a myth of Ile-Ife's greatness to enhance Ife's legitimacy as a neutral party among the new great powers. Ife had not the military power to defend Apomu, but the new commercial centers did not challenge Ife, according to Horton, because the stability of Ife symbolized a peaceful balance of power among the nouveaux riches city-kingdoms. Ife, with its declining economy, accepted the role of buffer and refocused itself into a city which could specialize in oracular services. Ile-Ife thus became the religious center of Yorubaland, and it is probably in this period when the religious significance of Oduduwa's role in Ile-Ife became a central part of the "tradition."

Oyo overcame the balance of power and became a new imperial center because of its excellent commercial and military position.[11] Its merchants sold slaves on the Atlantic coast (bypassing Ijebu-Ode), and bought horses from the Saharan trade. The Oyo empire, especially under *Alaafin* (King) Abiodun, who ruled from 1774 to 1789, was most successful, and his reign was remembered for peace and prosperity.

Oyo's rulers relied somewhat on the Oduduwa myth—and therefore on identification with ancestral city—to establish their legitimacy. But Yorubaland as a common culture zone was not a dominant theme within the Oyo Empire. Although the *Alaafin* (Oyo's king) claimed descent from Oduduwa, there was no cultural criterion for membership in the Oyo Empire. Some Yoruba areas, especially on the coast (such as Lagos and Badagry) were never under Oyo's rule, and this was not seen as a problem of unredeemed territory. Many Yoruba city-kingdoms, such as Ilesha and Ijebu, although they acknowledged the Alaafin's seniority and high status, were autonomous from Oyo. Still other Yoruba cities, such as Owu, Ketu, and Sabe, were allies rather than subjects of Oyo. Furthermore, a number of non-Yoruba speaking areas, in Dahomey to the west and some Fulani areas to the north, were subject to the Alaafin's authority. With a multinational subject population, and no ideology of common "Yoruba-ness" as a basis for membership, ancestral city identification—and Oyo's key role in the Oduduwa foundation myth—was only a minor theme in the legitimation of Oyo's domination.

The basis of the Alaafin's domination lay at least as much in the development of a cavalry and an open trade zone than in the legitimacy and magical powers afforded by his claimed descent in the line of Oduduwa. Oyo sent tax farmers to provincial cities, but this taxation in agricultural produce had more symbolic than economic value. More important, subject cities on main trade routes supplied slaves and tolls to the Alaafin. The primary source of revenue from cities off of the main trade routes came from fees paid to the Alaafin from men and women who achieved new titles, whether of religious or of political significance.

Within Oyo city, the Alaafin shared power with a governing council known as the *Qyọ Misi*. The Qyọ Misi were made up of the autocthonous priests of the cities incorporated into the empire. There was thus a natural basis for conflict between an Alaafin and his Qyọ Misi, especially since the head of the council, the *Baṣọrun*, was the ex officio commander of the metropolitan army. The Baṣọrun tended to support ever expanding circles of military conquest and plunder, which would enrich the army; the Alaafin tended to support increased control over the long distance trade, which would enhance his revenue. In the eighteenth century, Oyo's Alaafins and Baṣọruns were continually attempting to depose each other.

Complicating matters, Alaafin Abiodun sought to weaken the Baṣọrun by creating a new political office, the Provincial Military Commander (*Arẹ Ọna Kakamfo*). This commander was forbidden to enter Oyo proper. Abiodun thereby sought to institutionalize a tension between the Baṣọrun and Arẹ Ọna Kakamfo. Abiodun's successors were, however, less skillful at this political game, and many cities began to defy Oyo's leadership. In 1793, in an attempt to reassert Oyo's supremacy, Alaafin Awole ordered the attack on Ife's Apomu's market. Ife's control over Apomu, as was noted, was symbolic of the balance of power within the Oyo Empire and associated city-kingdoms.

For the next century, virtually all the ancestral cities connected with the Oduduwa migrations were involved in a series of civil wars. Although alliances were fluid and changing, and although old cities were abandoned and new ones created, the key units for political and military action in these wars were ancestral cities. A city may have been created by a congeries of refugee lineages from a variety of razed towns, but that city would be described in contemporary accounts of the wars as having an acknowledged social reality. These wars were devastating to Ile-Ife. On two occasions Oyo refugees overran Ile-Ife, whose citizens were compelled to live as exiles in shacks on their farms.

It was not until the late nineteenth and early twentieth centuries, when it became of interest to many Yorubas to demonstrate to the British that there was a united "Yoruba" state in ancient times, that the Yorubas began to pay attention to the myth of Ife's past. Within Yoruba society, the Ife people have a distinct identity and a clear sense of their central role in Yoruba history. Their myth of Ile-Ife as the cradle of Yoruba civilization and the home of their deified founder is a part of their cultural identity. The Yoruba foundation myth therefore provides for any Yoruba a historical connection with an ancestral city. Any Yoruba's connection with Oduduwa is immediately understood once he is placed as an Ife, an Oyo, an Ekiti, an Ijebu, or a member of any satellite city-kingdom.

The Fall of Oyo and the Rise of Ibadan as a Quasi Empire

The fall of Oyo and the rise of Ibadan represented a new founding for the Oyos and other Yoruba peoples.[12] The social significance of ancestral city began to dissipate under Ibadan's rule. Military skill rather than proper descent became the criterion for domination in the Ibadan quasi-empire. The sociological "fall" of ancestral city is a key link in the argument of this chapter: its story requires some detail.

In the early nineteenth century, turmoil in Oyo city and the Alaafin's attempt to depose Afonja, his Arẹ Ọna Kakamfo stationed in Ilorin, were the precipitating factors in the fall of Oyo. Afonja, his life in jeopardy, and recognizing the Alaafin's weakness, decided to challenge him with a newly constructed coalition. He first recruited Alimi, a Fulani who had been active in the jihad of Uthman Dan Fodio in which orthodox Fulani Muslims defeated and unified the peoples in the desert to the north of Yorubaland. Afonja then mobilized Hausa slaves working in Ilorin and the small community of Yoruba-speaking Muslims in Oyo. Afonja, Alimi, the Hausa slaves, and the Yoruba Muslims together formed the nucleus of a force which ransacked (but did not then conquer) Oyo. But Afonja lost control of the movement when he attempted to name himself Alaafin, and eventually Alimi's son, 'Abd al-Salam, captured control of Ilorin and became recognized by the Fulani authorities of the jihad (who were in Sokoto) as the first "emir of Yoruba." Afonja was not himself a Muslim, which may be the reason he was deposed; but Solagberu, the military leader of the Oyo muslims, who was a Muslim as well, was also liquidated by the Fulanis. While the original Afonja coalition was a provincial assault on an imperial center, the fall of Afonja was a result of a coup organized to establish Fulani control over Ilorin and perhaps even further to the south.

By 1830, Fulani-controlled Ilorin made another attempt to conquer Oyo. This time it succeeded, and the Alaafin escaped and established his court in a barely cleared settlement halfway to the coast, now called "new Oyo." For several decades it was known as *Agǫ d'Qyǫ*, "the camp that became Oyo.") Ilorin, under Fulani leadership, could not extend its authority beyond its own city limits, and had little success in replacing Oyo as the imperial center for much of Yorubaland. Its forces were defeated in a famous battle of Oshogbo in 1843.

Ibadan, a city that rose in the wake of the destruction of Oyo, inherited a large part of old Oyo's authority. Before Afonja's attack, with the status of Oyo already in considerable question, the Alaafin encouraged an allied city, Owu, to help in the capture of the Apomu market. Attempting to defend itself, Ife allied with the Ijebu Kingdom, which was trying to assert itself more forcefully in the Atlantic trade. The combined Ijebu and Ife armies, which then surrounded Owu, began to offer rewards to the Oyo refugees to join their forces. The recruitment effort was so successful that eventually the army had a predominance of Oyo refugees. Once victorious over Owu, the newly constructed army, homeless, moved southward toward the Egba ancestral towns to increase its size and power. After destroying the Egba heartland, the army met resistance near Ibadan, then a small village abandoned by the Egbas, and settled there. Many Ijebus returned home; many Egbas escaped southward and settled in Abeokuta. But the victorious army incorporated refugees from virtually all the ancestral cities. It became a congeries of ambitious warrior groups with no systematic connections to any descent group. Ibadan was the melting pot of the civil war refugees.

By the mid-1870s, Ibadan had established some control over an area of its own which may have covered more of Yorubaland than the former Oyo empire. It controlled Ibadan city, its countryside, and other Yoruba-speaking areas such as Ibarapa, Ife, Ilesha, Ikiti, Igbomina and Akoko; it also had influence in the upper Ogun area. This made up a considerable geographic unit. But Ibadan, largely because its war chiefs were often at war with each other, did not control this area sufficiently to be called an imperial center (and thus I call it a "quasi empire"). As we shall see, Ibadan took on some characteristics of an ancestral city on the Oyo model. But its very existence—a population with a mixed heritage and without royal ancestry—challenged whatever legitimacy the ancestral city framework had.

Ile-Ife as an Ancestral City

Because the research for this study was carried out in Ile-Ife, the discussion about ancestral cities in Yorubaland should be put into local context.[13] As we saw, Ile-Ife was the founding city-kingdom in Yoruba tradition, and identification as ọmọ Ife, a son of the city of Ile-Ife, carried rich cultural weight. With the breakup of the Oyo Empire, Ile-Ife suffered greatly from the civil wars, in large part because Afonja's rebellion against Oyo created a major refugee problem in Yorubaland. Very few Oyos joined the Alaafin in his exile. Many more sought protection in neighboring cities such as Ile-Ife and were initially welcomed by the Ọọni. In 1839, Oyo refugees sided with the Ọọni in a revolt by his chiefs, and the refugees were rewarded with official titles and a separate settlement, called Modakeke. This was the seed of a long and tense conflict within Ile-Ife between "natives" (ọmọ Ife) and the Oyo "strangers" (alejo).

In 1850, when Oyo and Ife became enemies, the Oyo strangers supported their ancestral city and turned on their hosts, forcing the Ifes to evacuate their own city. Ibadan intervened, however, and helped the Ifes to return to their own homes. A peace between Ife and Modakeke lasted for a quarter-century.

In 1881, however, the Ifes refused to help Ibadan extend its empire over a coalition of ancestral city-kingdoms to the east, known as the Ekitiparapọ. In the following year, an Ibadan contingent set to pressure the Ifes into compliance overzealously killed an Ife chief. The Ifes responded by breaking off ties with Ibadan and declaring for the Ekitiparapọ.[14]

The Modakekes sided with Ibadan, and were now encouraged by Ibadan to challenge Ife. They burned the sacred city, drove out the inhabitants, and sold many Ifes into slavery. It was not until 1894 under the Pax Britannica that the Ifes were able to return to their homes. So twice in a half-century Ile-Ife was defeated in war, and both times the town was occupied by the Oyo refugees of Modakeke.

Corporate interests as members of a set of interrelated lineages, combined with a common devotion to a king, formed the historical basis for ancestral city attachment. In this sense, ancestral city—symbolically rich and essential to personal identity—is a Yoruba cultural subsystem, even though built on a foundation of myths, political strategies, and instrumental identity readjustments. The subsequent section of this chapter demonstrates that while the social basis for ancestral city identification has, since the rise of Ibadan, declined, the political relevance of ancestral city for Yoruba collective political action has remained strong—a puzzle that rational choice models are unable adequately to solve.

THE SOCIOLOGICAL PUZZLE

In order to illustrate the significance of the puzzle, four separate arguments must be presented: (1) that although ancestral city once had great social and political significance, there has been significant decline in its sociological relevance; (2) that despite the decline in the *sociological* relevance of ancestral city, there has been no decline in its *political* relevance in Yorubaland; (3) that over the past few generations, religious differentiation among the Yoruba has created a socioeconomic divide; and (4) that despite this *sociological* divide based on religion, there has been no concomitant *political* divide between Christians and Muslims in Yorubaland.

One important caveat must preface the analysis. "Sociological decline" means that the material base for a certain cleavage has begun to erode. It does not imply that the meaning of that cleavage to the Yorubas has declined. We are here concerned with another line of cleavage (based on membership in a world religion), orthogonal to the major line of cleavage in past time (ancestral city), which has both a material and a cultural aspect. Both lines of cleavage are "real." The sociological question concerns which line of cleavage will form the basis for collective political action.

The Decline of the Sociological Significance of Ancestral City

The rise of the Ibadan quasi Empire challenged the elites most interested in preserving the integrity of ancestral city politics. In the numerous wars of the rapacious Ibadan armies, many old cities were destroyed; new cities attracted mixed populations. The city-kingdom of Owu was utterly destroyed. Its people were dispersed among Ijebus, Egbas, and Oyos. To legitimate their presence in the Ijebu and Egba kingdoms, a fiction was created so that they soon were considered "an 'original' land-owning group."[15] Few Yoruba migrants ever returned to their ancestral cities; most of them intermarried with the local population and members of other refugee groups. One important people, the Egbas, moved southward en masse and established a new urban center at Abeokuta. Other migrants assimilated into the "cultures" of different ancestral cities. As one Yoruba historian concludes from his study of this period: "It is surprising how little it is usually realized that each of the Oyo, Ekiti, Ijebu or any other Yoruba sub-group today is really a synthesis of fragments from almost all parts of Yorubaland."[16] This reshuffling of identities, especially because so many refugees saw strategic advantage in downplaying their former connections, should have reduced the relevance of ancestral city as a mode of political characterization. Indeed, the evidence of this reshuffling demonstrates the inadequacy of the primordial theory of identity. Identities are not always "given"; often they are "taken."

The consolidation of Ibadan's domination in Yorubaland was also a threat to the ancestral city framework. By tradition, Ibadan, when still a small Egba village, should have been subservient to Ife and Oyo; but the Ibadan army challenged that system. Ibadan introduced a new structure of authority, in which achievement rather than social position within the ancestral city framework was rewarded with political advancement. Since the social background of the Ibadan elites was substantially irrelevant for mobility, Ibadan was built and sustained on the merit principle, which meant that the most efficient warriors advanced quickly up the ladder of chiefly titles. Although historians can identify the leaders in Ibadan's imperial period on the basis of their ancestral cities, the political practice within the empire made that identification unimportant for career advancement. Furthermore, royal lineages did not hold the same status in the eyes of Ibadan authorities as they had under Oyo's rule. Under Ibadan, then, the ancestral city framework was challenged.

The mechanisms Ibadan used to control subject areas, while relying on some Oyo patterns, became a further threat to the ancestral city authorities. Local histories in the eastern provinces are replete with stories of local chiefs being treated with contempt by the Ibadan ajẹlẹs (high-powered representatives). These ajẹlẹs were assigned to areas with no regard to traditional city boundaries. "Towns within the same kingdom were allotted to different guardians and had different Ajẹlẹs appointed to them. The size of the town alone seems to have been the deciding factor in considering whether it should have an Ajẹlẹ or not." And, of course, ajẹlẹs were often "strangers" coming from other Yoruba areas; this exacerbated the mixing of peoples that already occurred at the height of the civil wars.[17]

The Ibadan system, involving the consolidation of new refugee cities, and the attachment of captured slaves from one city to war chief compounds in other cities changed fundamentally the nature of the family. The new trading household had up to several hundred slaves coming from different ancestral cities. Many of these slaves were incorporated into the family. The more slaves were incorporated, the more the blood basis of ancestral city identification became fiction. Newly constructed cities, newly constructed families, and incorporation of slaves into both further challenged the primordial reality of ancestral city identification.[18]

British political and economic influence in nineteenth-century Yoruba-land also threatened the material base for ancestral city politics. After the Napoleonic wars, Britain attempted to curtail the slave trade internationally, and her navy blockaded the West African coast. This new trade policy may have made Ibadan less able to establish itself as the exemplary center of the Yoruba peoples. The slave trade required large convoys and could only operate economically with state protection of roads. Traders were more willing to put up with Oyo's suzerainty during the slave trade than during the palm oil trade, in which smaller convoys could work their way to the coast more surreptitiously. A larger number of trading families, each able to provide protection itself, meant less need to obey the king from an imperial center.[19] In the 1890s, the British were able to broker a peace to the civil wars that had ravaged Yorubaland for more than a half-century.[20] The Pax Britannica supplanted an important role that ancestral cities had played during the nineteenth-century wars. Refugees on the coast acted as middlemen supplying modern weapons to their ancestral city brethren; in return, refugees received the right of sanctuary if hostilities erupted in their cities of residence. Yorubas of all ancestral cities by the early twentieth century could live in any city under British protection.[21] Perhaps more important, British imperialism opened the gates for larger British firms to invest inland. These firms were not interested in royal prerogatives but in profits. If Oyo could not produce cocoa or groundnuts as well as cities to its east, its claim to authority in Yorubaland had little meaning to investors. Also, since neither new Oyo nor Ife fell on the direct route to trade with the north, these cities could be ignored by traders and railroad investors. Therefore it was in Ibadan, near the cocoa-growing center, easily accessible from Lagos and with a large internal market, that a major railroad station was constructed and the international banks and trading companies settled.[22]

The ties that bound Yorubas to their ancestral cities—ties so important during the civil wars—began to develop strains. As early as the 1880s, when the civil wars were still raging, Egba traders in Lagos heard rumors that their "brothers" in Abeokuta (the Egba center) were negotiating with the French about exporting goods through the French-controlled port of Whydah. Such an arrangement would have threatened the middleman role of the Egba Lagosians. Consequently, they sent a delegation to Abeokuta to urge reconsideration. They received this response:

> We thank you for the solicitations you have manifested for your fatherland. You have done well in that, though living out of home, you have not forgotten the homeland and its interests. You call yourselves our children, but what have we, your parents, ever received from you? But immediately you heard that others have made us a few presents, you hastened to show us the danger of lurking in

their gifts . . . Have you not observed the short weights and the short lengths in the folded cloths? Have you not noticed that the English cloths contain increasingly more chalk . . . the price of our produce always falling and never rising? What have you done to help in these things to make our labour more remunerative? Nothing. It strikes us that you only concerned yourselves in competing with the white men to make your own profits out of us . . . No sooner we attempt to try for a profitable trade with another people than you hasten to warn us of the danger that lies herein. We thank you for your anxious care, but neither to the French nor the English are we giving our country.[23]

Ambitious men in the late nineteenth and early twentieth century saw clear advantages in divorcing themselves from the constraints of their ancestral city ties.

By the late nineteenth century, at least within the Ibadan quasi empire, attachment to a particular ancestral city was based less on lineage than on social and political fiction. This of course is not entirely new. The construction of one's descent was never based purely on blood. Yoruba cities from their earliest times had incorporated people into their communities for political purposes.[24] But by the early twentieth century, when kings of the ancestral cities no longer controlled many resources and were no longer necessary for providing sanctuary, identity readjustment was less costly and more often made.[25]

The Continued Political Significance of Ancestral City

Continued identification with an ancestral city, however, still has its uses. In each ancestral city, the myth of common descent is sustained by regularly scheduled rituals honoring the gods of special importance to that city. The festivals associated with those rituals bring back many emigrants and their families.[26] In these festivals, successful members of the city's diaspora get showered with status rewards, especially if they have performed services in support of their "home" cities. Yorubas who live in anomic cosmopolitan centers such as Ibadan or Lagos derive great pleasure on return to their ancestral city to see the people bowing to them, and to have praise singers follow them through town extolling their origins and worldly successes. These émigrés believe the king of the town will grant a prime plot to them for their retirement home if they should make such a request. Despite the Pax Britannica, which virtually ended the Yoruba civil wars by 1892, Yorubas remain security-conscious and see their ancestral cities as their only true safe haven.[27]

To say that ancestral city is an important category for politics because it is "traditional" is inadequate; the tradition itself has been in flux. Yet ancestral city remains the primary focus for political identification within Yoruba politics: nearly all political actions and positions are examined in Yorubaland through the lens of an ancestral city's colors. Since identities are always multistranded, it is significant that a Yoruba's ascribed tie to his ancestral city has remained the primary clue to interpret his political actions.

In 1947, Obafemi Awolowo returned to Yorubaland from England with a law degree. In London, he had organized a cultural society. Ẹgbẹ Ọmọ Oduduwa (Society of the Descendants of Oduduwa), which aimed to unite all Yoruba-speaking peoples. Although an Ijebu, Awolowo inaugurated his practice in Ibadan. In an early political stand against the British, he advocated that all Yorubas should be considered natives (i.e. have full property rights) whether they were sons (ọmọ ilu) or merely residents (ara) of whatever town in Yorubaland they lived in. This action could well have been interpreted as the practical outcome of Awolowo's belief that all Yorubas were equally sons of Oduduwa. This was a mighty concession for an Ijebu man, as the Ijebus distanced themselves from Oyo authority even during the height of the Oyo Empire. Nonetheless, some Ibadans interpreted Awolowo's position as a particularistic Ijebu demand to secure for his people a better opportunity to speculate on Ibadan land.[28]

This was but the start of political conflict among Yoruba ancestral cities transferred to the modern Nigerian state. Despite Ibadan's mixed heritage, it became the center of "Oyo" interests. The Oyos found themselves in political battle not only with the Ijebus but with the Ekitis as well. This became the stuff of modern Yoruba politics.

In this period, Ibadan sought to limit the power of Ijebu dominance in Awolowo's political party, the Action Group (AG), which became the political expression of the Ẹgbẹ Ọmọ Oduduwa. Under the populist leadership of G. A. O. Adelabu, the National Council of Nigeria and the Cameroons (NCNC) established itself as a force in Ibadan politics. The NCNC was one of the parties that had pan-Nigerian aspirations even though it recruited most heavily in the Igbo areas of the Eastern region. Its founder, Nnamdi Azikiwe, was himself an Igbo. Ibadan was a natural point of penetration to fracture Yoruba unity for a leader as knowledgeable about Yoruba politics as Azikiwe. Although originally a melting pot for all Yoruba refugees, it eventually became the place where Oyo discontent with Ijebu domination in the Action Group was strongest. In the 1954 elections, Adelabu's Grand Alliance defeated the Action Group in Ibadan. In 1958 Adelabu died in an automobile accident, and the Action Group was able to reestablish itself as the dominant party in Ibadan. Much of the bitterness between Ibadan and the AG remained.[29]

The second threat to Action Group dominance in Yorubaland came from the United People's Party and the Nigerian National Democratic Party, both led by Chief S. A. Akintola, who was from the Oyo-related city of Ogbomosho. This conflict had its roots in the period just after independence, when Awolowo and Akintola were allies in the Action Group. Awolowo, the leader of the party, chose to become leader of the opposition in the federal parliament. Akintola would become premier of the Western Region. But soon the two were quarreling and Awolowo sought to depose Akintola as premier-elect of the Western Region. The debate in the Western House of Assembly on the no-confidence vote got so heated that a riot broke out. This battle was in part responsible for the state of emergency called by the federal government in 1962, and planted the seed for the constitutional crisis that culminated in a coup d'état, toppling Nigeria's civilian government in January 1966. Endless intrigues and a few real issues caused this split within the Action Group. Awolowo believed that the AG should use its resources to challenge the north and thereby create a progressive Nigeria. Akintola did not wish to challenge the north, and was content with the idea of a progressive Western Region. Thus Awolowo chose to operate politically at the federal level, consigning Akintola to the regional level. Whatever the substance of the debate, the implications of the conflict were very deep for ancestral-city politics. Ogbomosho became a bastion of anti-AG sentiment, and the crisis hardened the already bad feelings between the Ijebus and Oyos.[30]

In 1964, Akintola helped organize a new party, the Nigerian National Democratic Party (NNDP). He allied with the Northern Peoples' Congress (NPC), the major party of the Northern Region, to oppose the AG in the federal elections scheduled for December of that year. That election campaign was marked by great violence and thuggery. Leaders from virtually every Yoruba town had to declare for one party or the other and then protect themselves from violent assaults by mercenaries of the opposition party.[31] (Interestingly, a major reason for the AG success in this election was that Akintola's alliance with the NPC was considered un-Yoruba, even among most Yoruba Muslims). This was the last election before the coup d'état that led to thirteen years of military rule.

Under military rule, Awolowo (who had been convicted and incarcerated for a "treasonable felony" based on charges put forward by the leaders of the First Republic) fared better. The federal military government convened a conference of Yoruba elders in which Awolowo was elected to the title of "Leader of the Yorubas." He became federal minister of finance, and he helped to build unity among the Yorubas. Nonetheless, the Ijebu-Oyo conflict festered. Awolowo's successes under military rule were ominous signs to the Oyos. An "Oyo Central State" movement began to grow, with a secret charter decreeing that if a new state were created, all the Ijebus would be banished from Ibadan.[32] Their demand for statehood was eventually met. The Western Region was carved up into three states in 1976 (Lagos was made a separate state in 1967): Oyo (Ibadan, Ijesha, and Ife); Ogun (Egba, Egbado, and Ijebu) and Ondo (Ekiti, Owo, and Ondo).

In 1979, when the military government gave way to electoral politics, the Yorubas were unified in the first election of the Second Republic. Awolowo carried the flag for the Unity Party of Nigeria (UPN), the successor to the AG. As a presidential candidate, he won an overwhelming victory throughout Yorubaland, collecting 85.8 percent of the vote even in Oyo State.[33] The only cracks in the unity of the Yorubas are to be found on the divide of ancestral cities. In Ogbomosho, the ancestral city of Chief Akintola, the UPN candidate for governor received only 16.6 percent of the vote, and Awolowo received only 15.9 percent for the presidency. Underneath the impressive display of Yoruba unity in the first elections of the Second Republic, there remained the political divide of ancestral city.

The persistent ancestral city conflict between Ife and its sister village Modakeke serves to demonstrate the political explosiveness of ancestral city identification in Yorubaland. This conflict, as we saw, goes back to Oyo migrants settling in Modakeke in the nineteenth century, and these migrants, with the support of Ibadan, occupying and controlling the city of Ile-Ife.

The Ifes faced better times under British colonialism. They used their new legitimacy under indirect rule to evict the Modakekes from Ife town in 1909 and to send them back, after three generations away, to their "homeland" on the outskirts of Ibadan. The Modakekes, who had established homes and a community in Ife, were outraged. In 1910, the Qoni (king of Ife) was about to reconsider his eviction order. But one of his military officers, who was opposed to the return of the Modakekes, was found murdered. The Ife people suspected a Modakeke plot, and this delayed the return for a decade. By 1923, however, the Modakekes were back, and two Modakeke chiefs were given special titles and salaries within Ile-Ife.

The Modakeke-Ife conflict has ramified in all important areas of Ife politics. From the moment of their return in the 1920s, Modakeke Muslims were pressuring for their own Friday mosque. Since each town, under Muslim tradition, has a single Friday mosque, the Ife people saw the Modakeke Muslims as making a symbolic attempt to define themselves as living in a separate town. It was also a material threat, for Modakeke—and Oyo in general—had a higher proportion of Muslims than did Ife. Should the Modakekes have their own Friday mosque, the Ifes reckoned, Modakeke's alms would no longer be available to Ife Muslims to appropriate as they wished. By 1934, a compromise was worked out, which essentially permitted the Modakekes to have their own mosque, but not without a lingering hostility between Ife and Modakeke Muslims.

In land politics especially, Ife-Modakeke conflict has been manifest. When, in the late 1940s, the cocoa trees harvested by Modakeke tenants on Ife land began yielding greater profits, the Ifes attempted to raise rents. The Modakekes then claimed that the rent they were paying was itself unwarranted, since they were virtually the owners of the land on which they were working.[34] The Ifes responded by importing Urhobos from the Niger Delta area to work their land in Modakeke, which led to riots.[35] This issue was brought to the courts, and the Ọọni retained the services of Obafemi Awolowo, then a brilliant young lawyer just back from England, where he had been studying, to argue the Ife case. Awolowo helped win the case for the Ife landlords and, in so doing, cemented a tie with Aderemi, the Ọọni of Ife. This rent issue remains a very tense one in Ife, and many Modakeke people stopped paying it in the wake of a Land Decree written by the military government in 1978. Court cases are pending. Whatever the substance of the issue, it will be fought out as one dividing the area between "Ife" and "Oyo" (and other stranger) interests.

In electoral politics of the 1950s and 1960s, the Ife-Modakeke conflict, exemplifying the ancestral city divide, determined political alignments. The powerful alliance between the Ọọni and Awolowo meant that in the 1950s, when a young Ife lawyer, R. A. Fani-Kayode, began to challenge the "traditional" and authoritarian power of the Ọọni, he received little support from Awolowo and other Action Groupers, who were supposedly "modern." Kayode led a movement, Ẹgbẹ ọmọ Ibilẹ Ifẹ, (modeled on Awolowo's old London society), seeking more popular participation in Ife affairs.[36] Although an Ife native, Kayode found that as he stood for candidacy for a number of political positions, his support came from Modakeke and not from Ife proper. Modakeke had already become an NCNC stronghold, in alliance with Adelabu, the populist leader of Ibadan. Kayode followed his supporters after a gentleman's agreement with the Ọọni broke down in 1959. He had been promised by the Ọọni that there would be no opposition if he contested the election for a seat in the federal House of Representatives. But the Ọọni crossed him, and Kayode lost the seat, winning only in the Modakeke ward. Kayode then allied with the Akintola and NCNC forces.[37] Meanwhile, as governor of the Western Region, the Ọọni collaborated with Awolowo to seek the vote of no-confidence in premier-elect Akintola. It would be hard to find a wide ideological divide between Awolowo and Kayode, both progressive lawyers who had received degrees in London. It would be equally hard to dispute the popular political analysis of the Kayode-Awolowo split, which was ultimately framed as one that pitted the Ijebus (Awolowo) and Ifes (the Ọọni) against the Oyos (represented by Kayode). Although an Ife himself, Kayode's only basis for a real challenge to the Ọọni was by portraying himself as a champion of Oyo interests.

A similar sequence of events occurred in the 1960s, when Oladipo Akeredolu-Ale was attempting to organize a radical farmers' organization, the Nigerian Farmers Union. He faced trouble in Ife, because E. T. Latunde had already organized a more moderate cooperative movement. Rather than convert Latunde, Akeredolu-Ale moved cross town to Modakeke and had considerable success there.[38] The political cleavage of the town compelled Aderedolu-Ale, as it had Kayode, to organize not according to political principles, but according to identification with ancestral cities. The Modakekes did not live in Oyo; but political circumstance continued to reinforce the "Oyo" aspect of their complex social identity.

The battle between Ife and Modakeke still rages. In the early period of the Second Republic, Modakeke attempted to establish itself as a separate city with its own local government. The Ọọni was against the idea and influenced Awolowo's UPN, which controlled the Yoruba-populated states, to oppose Modakeke's application. The Modakekes, not surprisingly, were rebuffed, and when Awolowo visited Ife some time later, he was heckled by the Modakekes. He returned only to be blockaded at the gates of Modakeke. This incident precipitated a bloody conflict between the two communities in early 1981 in which hundreds of people were killed. In the 1983 elections the NPN dominated in Modakeke, and in one of the electoral contests, Modakeke produced more NPN votes than the estimated population of the entire city of Ile-Ife.[39]

Meanwhile, Modakeke remains the pariah section of Ile-Ife. Although paved streets and other public services have come to Ife, Modakeke still lacks piped water. The differences are stark, and the conflict is deep. Virtually all the political issues which concern Ife people—chieftaincy titles, public services, land tenancy, and alliances within regional and Nigeria-wide politics—are guided by the terms of this ancestral city conflict.

Throughout Yorubaland, there continues to be conflict among ancestral cities in the race for civil service jobs. At the University of Ibadan, the most prestigious university in Nigeria, Yorubas are predominant. Students there have organized themselves according to their ancestral cities and prepare themselves to compete against rival ancestral cities in the race for good grades and important jobs after graduation.[40]

Survey researchers have confirmed that Yorubas evaluate equity in terms of ancestral city distributions. When asked to divide the population according to the greatest differences among the people, Yorubas answer largely in terms of ancestral cities. In one study, although most respondents admitted that there were hardly any real differences among members of the various ancestral cities, they were nonetheless able to name the ancestral city of virtually all of their co-workers. "Ethnic differences are cited," the author concludes, "not only because they undoubtedly exist, but also because they are felt to be important."[41]

The Growing Social Relevance of Religious Differentiation

That there has developed in Yorubaland over the past century distinct religious subcultures was the principal finding of chapter 3. The differences adduced there, however, do not capture the concomitant and growing differences in social, economic, and political power that divide Yoruba Christians from Muslims. In the race for jobs in the civil service sector, the key to social mobility in the colonial world, Christian Yorubas soon outran the Muslims. Largely because the education provided by the Christian missionaries was tied to the job requirements in the colonial civil service, Christian converts had an immediate advantage. Students at Christian schools found themselves with a monopoly of access to the English language, which assured young Yorubas good jobs in the modern sector, and provided to them the crucial skill in combating colonialism. The anticolonial battle against liberal Europe in most of middle Africa was fought by lawyers and not guerillas. Thus Christian Yorubas captured leadership positions in the nationalist movement.

In 1870, according to Gbadamosi's data, only 9 percent of the students in the Lagos missionary schools (virtually the only places to acquire English literacy) were Muslims; by 1893, the figure was only 13 percent. The Muslims tried to counteract this inequality by building their own schools, but their efforts brought only marginal improvements. Data collected by Van den Driesen in rural Ile-Ife show that even in the present era of government schools and free education, Christians maintain their advantages in school enrollments. Among the farmers interviewed, 58.7 percent were Christians, but their children accounted for 63.7 percent of those attending school.[42] In my survey of church and mosque elders, 75 percent of the Christians but only 23 percent of the Muslims claimed competence in English.

I visited the local Ansar Ud-Deen primary school in Ile-Ife, a school organized to provide better education to Muslims. Only three of the thirty-seven teachers were Muslims. The headmaster's car sported a "Jesus Loves Us" bumper sticker. In a small school, originally built by the CMS, that I visited in a local farm community, the entire teaching staff was Christian and lived in the mission compound. Even though formal ties between education and religious organization had been severed years earlier, education remained in the hands of the Christians.

Even those Muslims who have gone through school have nowhere near the proficiency, in English as the Christians whose parents have experienced mission education. Attempting to counteract the tide of Christian publications with one of their own, the Ibadan branch of the Islamic Youth League of Nigeria created a journal, *Darul-Salam*. The malapropisms were often amusing and reflected a poor foundation in the language of economic power. The journal's first editorial gave "praise [for the] scheming ability of the members who for responsible . . ." (*sic*), and the lead writer congratulated "the Editorial Board on its success in publishing the maiden issue of our quarterly magazine . . . It reflects the twilight of Islamic renaissance in this part of the globe."[43] I remarked regularly in my notebooks on the deficiencies of the Muslim Yoruba schoolchildren in the English language in comparison with the Christian Yoruba schoolchildren.

In a comprehensive study of education in Yorubaland, Fafunwa speculated that "it is perhaps safe to say that at least one out of three Christians has been to school while the Muslim ratio is likely to be one out of five or six." And at the University of Ibadan, where Yoruba students predominate, some 92 percent of the students questioned in Fafunwa's survey claimed to be Christians, while only 6 percent claimed to be Muslims.[44] Many Yorubas have used their salaries or their retirement benefits from their modern-sector jobs as investment capital. It was access to the skills provided in missionary education which provided the opportunity for capitalizing on new trade opportunities.[45]

Available data on farm wealth are sparse. In land ownership, however, Christians appear not to have achieved supremacy. This is largely because the distribution of land has not become a key issue for Yorubas seeking to establish themselves economically or politically. Van den Driesen's survey of 267 farmers in the periphery of Ile-Ife shows comparable percentages of Christians and Muslims for each size farm. For example, 84.2 percent of the Christians and 82.3 percent of the Muslims had less than ten acres of land. Yet in studies of elite farmers, a different picture emerges. In the politically important Cooperative Committees, Beer has shown, Christian Yorubas accounted for 63.4 percent of all members and 100 percent of members who were literate. Berry's data demonstrate that it was the Christian Yorubas who were the first to take advantage of, and continue to profit by, the investment potential in cocoa. The Christian-Muslim cleavage, then, is manifest not in the ownership of land per se but in the pattern of wealth and political influence among farmers.[46]

The cleavage dividing Christian from Muslim Yorubas is far more manifest in commercial life. The Ijebus, who have taken the greatest advantage of the commercial opportunities in Yorubaland since the advent of the colonial state, have a large Muslim population. Yet one study of the Ijebu traders in Ibadan, one of the more prosperous centers of the Ijebu diaspora, found that nearly 80 percent of them were Christians, a near reversal of the percentage within Ijebu-Ode proper. These are the rich traders who have triggered such antipathy from the Oyos in Ibadan.[47]

The socioeconomic preeminence of Christians in Yorubaland is clearly demonstrated in Donald Morrison's massive survey conducted under the auspices of the University of Ibadan, with a subsample of nearly 2000 Yorubas living in Yorubaland. Of the Muslim respondents, 48% were illiterate and 2% had a university degree; of the Christians, only 36% were illiterate, and 10% had a university degree. Only five of the respondents' parents had completed university, but all of them were Christians. A higher percentage of the parents of the Christian respondents were literate than the parents of the Muslims. Thus, 60% of the Christians but only 35% of the Muslims claim to read a newspaper every day. A higher percentage of Christians claim to have a radio, a wrist watch, a gas cooker, a refrigerator, a sewing machine, an electric iron, a car, a house or land, an electric fan, and a clock. On no consumer items did the Muslims have an advantage.[48]

Not only economic benefits but political benefits as well have gone to Yoruba Christians. Of the 61 inaugural and executive members of the Action Group, only 2 were Muslims. Only 3 Muslims were identified among Sklar's tabulation of 33 Western Regional personalities in the Federal Executive Council of the Action Group in 1958, and only 1 Muslim was among the 12 regional ministers. Finally, there were only 5 Muslims among the 75 constituency and divisional leaders of the Action Group.[49] Among the members of the delegations from the Yoruba states in the Nigerian Constitutional Drafting Committee in 1977, 74 percent of those delegates whose religion I could identify were Christian.[50]

In Ile-Ife, where Christianity and Islam have developed at comparable rates, the pattern of Christian dominance in the elite holds. In a dissertation on political power in Ile-Ife, using Robert Dahl's techniques to identify the political elite, Oyediran enumerated eight leaders, all of whom were Christian. The only prominent Muslim who appeared to play a role in the political conflicts within the town was illiterate, and could not sustain himself on the political stage.[51]

In my own observations in Ile-Ife, where I regularly attended both central mosque and a centrally located Anglican church, I found the weekly voluntary contributions at the church to be commensurate with the quarterly sum of the mosque's capital improvement fund. Within six months, the Anglican church was able to raise 26,000 nairas for a new marble floor while the mosque was well behind in its goal for 10,000 nairas to build a second story. The differences were quite conspicuous: the Anglican churches on Sundays had many cars parked around them, while most Muslims had to walk or take public transport to the mosque.

To be sure, Nigeria has provided substantial mobility opportunities for citizens. A civil service which has been growing since the completion of the railroad in 1911, the expanding educational opportunities in the wake of independence, the presence of multinational firms seeking alliance with "bridgehead elites," and of course the new oil economy have all provided outlets for many Nigerians with ambition. Nonetheless, the relative advantage of Christians in capturing those opportunities among the Yoruba is clear.

These differences have coincided with some minimal social tensions. In a study of the growth of Islam in Oyo Province, Adelowo demonstrates that from the last quarter of the nineteenth century there was friction between Christians and Muslims. He records Muslims portraying the CMS as "enemies of the truth," and the CMS counterattacking, calling Islam the "greatest obstacle to progress of civilization." Over the years, Muslims have complained that their children have been under unfair pressure to convert as they sought to improve themselves through exposure to mission education.[52] More recently Christians have chafed at the government expenditures for the Muslim pilgrimage, and the unfair trading opportunities that the foreign exchange available to Muslim pilgrims provided.[53]

There has been as well an undercurrent of suspicion. Public figures often admonish citizens to abjure incidents that might incite religious tensions.[54] In my research and in Van den Berghe's as well, our informants gratuitously confessed to their own fears of members of the other religious group.[55] When a prankster posted a sign at the University of Ife welcoming visitors to "Jesus University," the registrar took immediate action, fearing an outbreak of religious violence.[56] Stereotypes have already developed. For example, some Ife Christians told me that the Muslims were inferior because they can never agree among themselves. The Modakeke mosque will celebrate a Muslim holiday one day, the Hausa people the next, and the Ife people yet a third day, "while we Christians all celebrate Christmas on December 24th."[57]

Each religious group has generated a healthy supply of leaders whose ambitions for expanded social and political authority can be fulfilled by the redefinition of political consciousness among their constituents, making religious affiliation a core component of individual identity. These religious leaders have a career interest in organizing followers politically as Christians or Muslims. The supply of religious entrepreneurship constitutes a social fact—a necessary outgrowth of mass conversions into institutionalized religions. Their interests provide social pressure for expanding the relevance of religion into other social subsystems.[58]

The Nonpoliticization of the Religious Cleavage

Despite the socioeconomic cleavage separating the two religious subcultures in Yorubaland, the differences have had little political or ideological resonance. Although political entrepreneurs have tried to mobilize Yorubas on the basis of religious identification, Yorubas themselves have not used that identification for purposes of political alignment.

The most common interpretation of Ilorin's challenge to Oyo supremacy in the nineteenth-century civil wars concerns the Islamicization of Ilorin and the concomitant continuation of the Fulani jihad into Yorubaland with Ilorin as the base camp.[59] This interpretation ignores the social realities in Ilorin and Oyo. First, Afonja, who allied with Muslim forces to challenge Oyo, was not himself a Muslim and refused to destroy the sacred groves and other symbols of the Yoruba traditional religion. Second, after Ilorin's victory, Muslims in Oyo suffered no discrimination, nor were they seen as potential fifth columnists. Many Oyo Muslims eventually supported the Ilorin forces, but their actions were perceived as anti-Alaafin rather than pro-Muslim. Third, Solagberu, the military commander of Ilorin, a Yoruba Muslim, was liquidated by the Fulani advisers. The war was perceived as one of Fulani control over Ilorin rather than Muslim control over Oyo. Robin Law concludes that Islam was central to this rebellion only insofar as "it provided a basis upon which disparate elements—Fulani, Hausa, and Yoruba—could be united in a common loyalty for an assault upon the established order." But even this is too strong, because it does not acknowledge how ephemeral that alliance was, nor does it point out that the Muslim Yorubas in Ilorin refused to integrate socially with the Fulanis. And Babayemi, whose work shows an even greater influence of Muslims in the outbreak of the civil wars than does Law's, emphasizes that both Oyo and Ilorin received Muslim military aid. For Babayemi, the wars never involved a Muslim side versus a non-Muslim side.[60]

In the course of the twentieth century, the Fulani overlords in Ilorin adopted the Yoruba language and have been assimilated to some degree into Yoruba society. Muslim-Fulani leadership continues, and there are no churches in the center of the town. Meanwhile, Yoruba strangers live on the town's periphery, and there church life abounds. Despite some Christian-Muslim tensions, however, the major political upheavals within Ilorin have united Christian and Muslim Yorubas in an attempt to wrest control of Ilorin from the old Northern Region. The creation of Kwara State (which includes a significant majority of non-Yorubas in Ilorin's hinterland) during the period of military rule was the reward for many years of united (Yoruba) Christian-Muslim political action in Ilorin.[61]

Another place in Yorubaland where Muslims might have become mobilized qua Muslims was Ibadan. In 1954, Awolowo's Action Group attempted to win an electoral victory in Ibadan over the favored NCNC. The AG, hoping to divert support from the NCNC, surreptitiously supported a prominent Muslim from Ibadan running under the banner of the

United Muslim Party. Adegoke Adelabu, however, the Yoruba leader of Ibadan's NCNC, and a Muslim, decried the strategy, and roundly defeated the AG at the polls. In 1956, Adelabu, by now in a weakened position, attempted to revive his own political fortunes by making the pilgrimage to Mecca and then mobilizing Yoruba Muslims as Muslims. This time Awolowo copied Adelabu's rhetoric of 1954, and the Adelabu-supported National Muslim League felt compelled to change its name to the National Emancipation League in the 1958 election. But it still polled less than 1 percent of the total vote in the local government elections that year, and failed to win a seat in the 1959 federal election. It was the Oyo-Ijebu cleavage, not the Muslim-Christian one, that affected Ibadan voters.

The nonpoliticization of religious differentiation in Yorubaland is also discernible in the politics of distribution. In the 1950s, when Yoruba Muslims complained that they were relatively disadvantaged in the race for jobs, and pointed to the mission schools as the culprits, the Western Region government enacted an Education Law which contained a formula for special funding for Muslim educational agencies.[62] In that same period, Chief Awolowo, who is a Christian, worked out an inventive program to subsidize Yoruba Muslims on the pilgrimage to Mecca, without a complementary program to mollify the Christians. Administrative formulas easily satisfied the religious organizations before their complaints became grist for the political mill.

Yet there were opportunities for religious politicization. In 1950, Aminu Kano, a Muslim from the north, attempted to break from the Sokoto elite that controlled the Northern Peoples' Congress (NPC). He helped organize the Northern Elements Progressive Union (NEPU), and tried to expand his support by recruiting into his movement Adelabu from Ibadan and the Ilorin Muslims. The Yorubas were not enticed. Nonetheless, in the wake of the Nigerian civil war of 1967–70, Kano tried again. This time he approached the Yoruba Ahmadiyyas in an attempt to expand his constituency. Again he failed.[63]

In 1965, the last election before military rule, and in 1979, the first election after military rule, no parties attempted to bifurcate the Yorubas on the religious dimension. In 1979, the National Party of Nigeria, built on the old NPC base, had a great interest in penetrating the Yoruba states. The new electoral laws of the Second Republic required the winning party to win 25 percent of the vote in two-thirds of the states. NPN strategists might have sought that 25 percent by seeking support in the Yoruba states among fellow Muslims. Instead, they worked through the ancestral city divide, hoping to recruit Oyos and Egbas in a common stand against the Ijebu, Awolowo. Indeed, NPN strategists had learned in the course of the Sharia debate (see chapter 1) that Yoruba Muslims would not respond to political pleas based on their Muslim identity.

In the 1983 elections, the second and last of the Second Republic, the NPN did in fact make significant inroads in Yorubaland. Yet its successes were entirely based on the exploitation of ancestral city fissures. Yorubas who identify with Oyo were mobilized again to counter alleged Ijebu domination of the UPN. In Ibadan, violence between Oyos and Ijebus broke out in the wake of the voting. In Modakeke, the "Oyo" ward in Ile-Ife, as has already been noted, there were more NPN votes than the estimated population of the entire city.[64]

An important dissertation written at the University of Ibadan had as its opening chapter a full discussion of "patterns of communal conflicts in Western Nigeria." In that chapter, five important cleavages were addressed: city of origin; sides in the nineteenth-century civil war; settlement patterns; strangers and natives; and class. This Yoruba political scientist did not even mention the potential of religion as a source of electoral division.[65] Other studies that have examined political rhetoric in Yorubaland are equally silent about religion.[66] And research that has sought to explain the sources of conflict in Yoruba towns also ignores religion, and does so without losing any explanatory power.[67]

Even Morrison's data, though demonstrating a clear socioeconomic cleavage among Yorubas of different religious affiliation, shows that the Muslims do not feel aggrieved politically. While Christians and Muslims are equally satisfied with their lot, the Muslims are less critical of the Nigerian state. Muslims see themselves as benefiting from government services and trust government more than do Christians. Muslims are less critical than Christians about the distribution of wealth in Nigeria, and are quicker to point to improvements over the past decade.[68]

Religion, then, has little strategic import in Yorubaland. More than 80 percent of Morrison's Yoruba respondents said they saw virtually no effect of religion on politics. My research in Ile-Ife substantiates this. Interviewing a prominent local notable, I asked him for the religious affiliation of two leading Yoruba politicians. He had to recollect their first names—one Richard, the other Mashood—before he could answer. It is not that he did not know their religion: it just wasn't part of his normal coding of their identity. And of the seventy church and mosque elders I interviewed, not one made a reference to his religious organization as a source for political mediation.

I also questioned my respondents in an informal way about electoral strategies in the Second Republic. The Yoruba-dominated party, the UPN, had been unable to build an electoral alliance with any region, and lost the presidency and control over both the Senate and the House of Representatives to the National Party of Nigeria (NPN). The NPN originated in the populous Northern states, and although it managed to win in two non-Muslim southeastern states, it was perceived to be the party of the northern Muslims. The NPN tried a variety of strategies to incorporate Yoruba groups into its electoral coalition, but outside of a few prominent figures with virtually no electoral base, it failed completely to develop a foothold in Yorubaland. When I pointed out to my Muslim interviewees that joining with the NPN might entail a variety of payoffs to Yoruba Muslims which would not be available to them if they remained loyal to the UPN, they implied that organizing politically as Muslims was not in their realm of calculation at all.

I have thus far produced a plethora of examples to demonstrate that religion has not provided a basis for political organization in Yorubaland, and this in the face of differential economic performance between Muslims and Christians and, as van den Berghe's data show, some religious chauvinism at the elite level. My discussion (in chapter 1) of the Sharia debate showed that it was Yorubas of both religions that snuffed out the religious fire that brought such heated exchanges in the Constituent Assembly debates of 1979. One other occasion on which latent religious conflict in Yorubaland might have become manifest was amid the Nigerian civil war of 1967–70, a period I shall now turn to.

YORUBALAND AND THE NIGERIAN CIVIL WAR

In 1967, the Eastern Region of Nigeria declared itself the Republic of Biafra and attempted to secede from the Nigerian state. The causes of the secession are many and complex.[69] The Igbos, the largest national group in the Eastern Region, had taken the fullest advantage of Mission education, and they advanced brilliantly through the Federal Civil Service. However, in the 1950s, when the Western Region profited greatly from a surge in world cocoa prices and Yoruba politicians used that money to enhance educational opportunities for their people, the Igbos saw this as a challenge in a race for educational excellence and jobs. Although relatively poorer, the Igbos nonetheless did very well in educating their people and in procuring high positions on the civil service ladder.

Igbo stranger communities were therefore visible in virtually all administrative centers. With Igbo civil servants everywhere, Igbo traders rounded out the communities. These people were economically successful and socially arrogant. In 1953 and again, much more fiercely, in 1966, northerners took to violence to rid their cities of Igbos.[70] The massacres of 1966 led to a mass return migration from the north back to the Eastern Region. Since educated Igbos were unwelcome in the north, their economic incentive to be loyal to the Federation was seriously undermined.

In the mid-1960s, the discovery of oil in the Eastern Region further reduced Igbo interest in the Federation. The revenue allocation formulas provided for regional control of the major part of agricultural earnings but for federal control of the major part of mineral earnings. The Igbos thought this unfair: they could not do with oil in the 1960s what the Yorubas had done with cocoa in the 1950s. Oil gave them the resources to make a go of it as a separate country; the revenue allocation formula gave many of them the motivation to try.

To garner international support for their effort, Igbos portrayed themselves as victims of genocide in the Muslim north. They argued before the court of world opinion that Muslim hordes would complete the genocide of Igbos in the name of Nigerian unity. It must be pointed out that the Igbos did not have much of a claim on this score, even if they were able to convince the pope, the *New York Times*, and Kurt Vonnegut that they were fighting a rear guard action against a northern jihad.[71] In fact, the federal army was under the command of a Christian, Yakubu Gowon, from the Middle Belt—an area in Nigeria that had successfully resisted complete Islamic penetration in the nineteenth century. The greatest interest in the integrity of the Nigerian state came from the "minorities" in each of the regions. These peoples often felt oppressed by the dominant nationalities in the regions but free to compete on the federal level. Unlike the minorities, many of the Muslim Hausas of the north were quite willing to let the Eastern Region secede.[72]

Nonetheless, the Igbos presented a view of Nigeria that pointed to the united Muslim north oppressing the Christian south. To make this claim credible to other Nigerians, the Biafran leaders needed Yoruba support, and Awolowo had hinted to them that should the Igbos secede, the Yorubas might follow suit.[73] The political rhetoric of the early period of the civil war concerned the unity of the "south" (the Eastern and Western regions) against the "north." The only characteristic shared by the "south" was that none of the people were under emirate control. Here was the opening for a "Christian" south, rich in oil, to separate itself from the "Muslim" north. No longer would southerners be subject to the political majority of the north or the indignity of having to accept the authority of people who were educationally and, from the southern point of view, culturally backward.

Yoruba politicians would not accept that gambit offered by the Igbos. Although Awolowo equivocated, the Yorubas stayed loyal to the Federal Republic. Whatever Awolowo's motives, neither Muslim nor Christian Yorubas ever saw the conflict in religious terms. After Awolowo, a Christian, had made peace with the military leaders of the Federation, the Yorubas as a whole gained considerably from the alliance. Substantial infrastructural investment in Yorubaland over the next few years gave the Yorubas a commercial edge over the East in the post–civil war years. Awolowo was able to deal so effectively with the federal leaders in part because the Yorubas themselves were not divided by the rhetoric of religious difference.

The fact that the Yoruba Christians and Muslims are geographically intermixed does not fully explain why the Biafran gambit was rejected. In India, the population divided itself geographically once it became impossible for Hindus and Muslims to live together politically. The Yorubas are no strangers to resettlement, and it is not impossible to imagine massive migrations within Yorubaland to resort the population. Yet it is unimaginable that *religion* would be the source of the divide.[74]

CONCLUSION

The socioeconomic divide among the Yoruba based on religion has not manifested itself politically. The socioeconomic divide based on ancestral city declined markedly in the nineteenth century; yet its political centrality persists well into the twentieth century. The dominant metaphor for political interpretation within Yorubaland, then, is ancestral city. How can this be explained?

7| Rational Choice and Hegemony

The theoretical anomaly of the nonpoliticization of the religious cleavage in Yoruba society has now been posed. There are two theoretical explanations for this outcome.[1] Social systems theorists who have concentrated their attention on the first face of culture will claim that certain ties are naturally strong: blood is thicker than water. Certain social cleavages result from deeply embedded personal identities. These "primodial" identities are thought to be the most difficult to shed. The more primordial the tie, the social systems theory predicts, the better candidate it is for political mobilization. Rational choice theorists, who focus their attention on the second face of culture, will claim that personal identification with ancestral city is rational; it is a strategic response to limited availabilities. The costs of politically reorganizing Yorubas according to religion, the theory predicts, are too high. In the following two sections, I shall discuss how each of these schools would attempt to make sense of the problem presented in the previous chapter, and I shall show why neither provides a fully plausible account. I shall then posit the hegemonic model and attempt to demonstrate its explanatory power for understanding the conditions under which cultural identities become politicized.

PRIMORDIAL TIES ARE REAL

Yorubas themselves usually explain the nonpoliticization of religion—and here they are consistent with social systems theory—by pointing out that ancestral city identification is real, while religious identification is artificial. Most Yorubas vigorously deny the idea that there is a real religious cleavage. They uphold a premise that in religious matters "we are all one family." Yorubas in all walks of life, stress the cultural importance of the family, which is divided by religion but tied together by blood. This premise of religious harmony has two components that can be separated analytically, but are rarely separated in Yoruba discourse about their religious life. First, it is argued that the world religions constitute a thin veneer pasted onto a thick social framework. Second, it is deeply believed that religion cross-cuts descent group, so that real family ties constrain the politicization of religion, which would inevitably tear families apart. Each of these components deserves elaboration and systematic rebuttal.

136

World Religions as Thin Veneers

J. S. Mbiti insists that the world religions have made very little ideological penetration into the African mind. They are the religions for only one day of the week, Mbiti asserts; for the other six days and for all times of crisis, the traditional religions predominate. Mbiti, a devout Christian, confesses that "a careful scrutiny of the religious situation [in Africa] shows clearly that in their encounter with traditional religions, Christianity and Islam have made only an astonishingly shallow penetration in converting the whole man of Africa, with all his historical-cultural roots, social dimensions, self-consciousness and expectations."[2]

Numerous examples support his thesis. Yoruba names retain their traditional significance: Muslim and Christian first names are socially irrelevant paste-ons.[3] Many Christians and Muslims still rely on "Ifa" divination; and most belong to traditional ẹgbẹ along with their affiliations to church and mosque societies.[4] Recent research has also pointed out that apparently devout members of the world religions continue to participate in traditional forms of sacrifice.[5] There appears to be considerable syncretism in Yoruba religious life, with the traditional religion paramount.[6]

The thinness of the veneer of world religions cannot, however, fully explain religious toleration, since there is no clear link in social theory between the degree of religiosity and the degree to which religion is politicized. One could hardly explain the degree of ferociousness in the Christian-Muslim conflict in Lebanon on the basis of the purity of the combatants' religious beliefs. Nor could the degree of Islamic orthopraxy among the Iranian masses have predicted the enormous popular support for Khomeini's movement for theocratic control over politics in Iran. The degree to which Yorubas are *really* Christians and Muslims should have no direct bearing on the nature of religious politics.

Even if it were possible to link religious commitment to religious politics, the "thin veneer" argument would not be persuasive. Any perusal of Yoruba life suggests that the world religions have penetrated Yorubaland with considerable force.[7] Mosques and churches abound, and on Fridays and Sundays many of them are filled to capacity. In every town, small shops, buses, and taxis sport signs expressing religious themes, many of them invoking the deities of the world religions—"Blessed Olu [God] Battery Charger," "Ola-Olu [Wealth of God] Pools Agency," "Owu Tutu [Raw Cash] Anchor in Christ," "Loruko [In the name of] Jesus," and "Alhaji Bismillah [Blessed Muslim Pilgrim]," and so forth.

The world religions have contributed to scholarship in Yorubaland from the time of their establishment there. In the early nineteenth century a man called Harun, a son of an Oshogbo chief, had accomplished so much in the development of Islamic education that "scholars came from as far afield, as the Sudan and Sokoto" to study with him.[8] The independent development of Islamic learning in Yorubaland was matched by the independent development of African Christian churches with their own theological traditions.[9] In the serials collection in the University of Ibadan, indigenous periodicals abound, such as *Nigerian Islamic Review; Nigerian Journal of Islam; Al Ansar, Lagos; Nigeria Ahmadiyya Bulletin, Lagos; Christian Student, Ibadan: The Nigerian Catholic Herald, Lagos;* and *Orita, the University of Ibadan Journal of Religious Studies.* There is some evidence of a vast readership for these journals.[10]

University life too demonstrates a "thick" affiliation with the world religions. At the University of Ibadan, one study found that in a request for religious affiliation of the students, only 2.3 percent of a random sample of over 3,000 students failed to give a religious preference, with no confessions of atheism or agnosticism, even though the form permitted such response. Van den Berghe, who led this study, interprets his finding in this way: "The expression of a religious affiliation [was not] the perfunctory kind of act of, say, a British student checking 'Church of England' on a questionnaire. There are five active student religious organizations out of a total of some 25 student clubs and voluntary organizations. These associations are affiliated with national organizations; one of them is Muslim, one is Catholic and three are Protestant. Informal prayer and hymn-singing groups of students form in the halls. The few expatriate students living in the halls express surprise that even in shower rooms much of the singing is religious."[11] And even though this university was created by expatriates, one of the important indigenous marks on the curriculum has been the development of two religiously inspired academic departments—one of them catering to Islamic, the other Christian, scholars.

Church and mosque membership is another measure of the penetration of the world religions in Yoruba society. A study of Yoruba peasants found that whereas 20 percent of the respondents belonged to farm cooperatives, 14 percent to other farmers' unions, and 13 percent to thrift groups, as many as 70 percent reported membership in churches or mosques.[12] In my survey of church and mosque elders in Ile-Ife, I asked respondents to name all the ẹgbẹ they belonged to and to state whether membership in these societies was limited by religious affiliation. Ẹgbẹ constitute a basic form of social interaction in Yoruba life, and membership is taken very seriously. At the very least it involves purchase of expensive uniforms. Among Christians, more than half of the societies were restricted to Christians; among Muslims, nearly 90 percent were similarly restricted.

Not only do the world religions attract high attendance in ritual activities and impressive membership in societies, but they seem to have made a deeper ideological impact on Yoruba society than anyone—including the believers—has acknowledged. Although I have hardly emphasized this point in the course of this study, some converts have reported that religious visions motivated them to forsake traditional religious authorities. These converts adopted and took seriously a new vocabulary of religious discourse, which affected other converts whose motivations were somewhat more instrumental.[13]

In a series of interviews with Yoruba healers (*oniṣẹgun*) in eastern Yorubaland, Barry Hallen has demonstrated considerable ideological adjustment in Yoruba society based on the missionary message. Hallen attempted to elicit from these men the essence of an indigenous Yoruba epistemology. Although he urged his respondents to purge what he, like Mbiti, considered to be the thin veneer of Christian ideology from their philosophic analyses, the theologians did not do so. One theologian, in responding to questions concerning *emi* ("breath"; missionaries used it to connote "soul"), suggested that one's *emi* could be resurrected (*jinde*). Hallen asked if the concept *jinde* were obtained from the Bible. The respondent answered that it was. Hallen urged that they should keep their discussion restricted to "traditional ways of thought." The respondent countered that "there is little difference . . . It is those who are wise before the Bible came, they are also the same set of people who believe in the Bible." The respondent then peppered his answers with references to "judgment day," "the Bible," and "Adam." And when asked the source for the many changes in Yoruba modes of thought and action, he was quick to attribute those changes to Christianity.

To be sure, many of the Hallen's respondents believed that Christianity was complementary to traditional beliefs, and therefore minimized the ideological influence of Christian theology. When Hallen urged one traditional theologian, after he used the missionary concept for God as creator, to restrict his responses to ideas before the missionaries came, the *oniṣẹgun* resisted Hallen's analysis: "No, I'm *not* talking about the Bible. You see, before we knew anything about Christianity . . . we knew that God existed . . . We knew that there is something which travels out after death." Another traditional priest confessed that he went to Church regularly. "To go to church is a modern thing here . . . In the church now people are even doing the traditional things which they previously preached against. Usually when you went to church before, all was silence; but now they dance and sing traditional songs. This leads us to think that time is 'flowing backwards.'"

Nonetheless, these *oniṣẹgun* were exposed to a new set of connotations for Yoruba words; connotations that led to assimiliation of Christian concepts. The very word for Christian, *Onigbagbọ*, involved a use of the word "belief" very different from its traditional usage. *Gbagbọ*, in traditional Yoruba discourse, means "knowledge that," as in "I know that the earth is round." It does not refer to experiential knowledge, for which the concept *mọ* is used, and almost always in the first person singular. Yorubas were therefore being asked to use *gbagbọ* to refer to a kind of belief that comes somewhere between *gbagbọ* and *mọ*. The very fact that Yorubas who have experienced Christianity must contend with the tension between the missionary meaning and the traditional meaning of Yoruba words—and Hallen's field data show that Yoruba theologians have indeed used old words with new connotations—suggests that the world religions have had a significant ideological impact on traditional thought.

One *onişẹgun* responded to Hallen's inquiry concerning the influence of Christianity in this way: "The fact is that what we had been serving did not bring progress. Our chairs and doors were made of rough unfinished wood, but later on they were made of planks. The wisdom which the Bible gave to us is more than we got from our own traditions." This materialist metaphor demonstrates a rather subtle understanding of ideological change. While some may argue that Yorubas always made chairs and doors and therefore there has been no change in Yoruba material culture, this respondent understood that the criteria for what constitutes an acceptable chair has indeed changed. Yoruba religious discourse and, consequently, religious belief have been modified by exposure to the world religions.[14] The presumption that the world religions are not taken very seriously among Yoruba adherents cannot therefore be sustained, and it cannot be used to explain the nonpoliticization of religion in Yoruba society.

Softening of Religious Conflict by Cross-Cutting Family Ties

Since religious affiliation involves choice, one's adherence to a world religion is considered to be contingent on circumstances. Therefore "real" social units, such as the family, can be divided by religion. That members of different religions can belong to the same families means to my Yoruba respondents and to a wide body of social science theory[15] that religious conflict will be somewhat softened.

When M. O. A. Abdul was engaged in his research on the development of Islam in Ijebu, he noted that the Anglican bishop of Ibadan had been born of Muslim parents in Ijebu-Ode but had become a Christian in the course of his (mission) education. In 1970, when the Catholic cathedral in Ijebu Ode was consecrated, the Catholic bishop there, the Right Reverend Anthony Salisu Sanusi, was the son of a prominent Muslim in nearby Iperu. His brother was then the Balogun of the Iperu Muslim community. He, along with an entourage of Muslim dignitaries, were honored guests at the consecration.[16] Yoruba political leaders, too, have had family members who were adherents of the other world religion. Adegoke Adelabu, the Muslim who had such influence in Ibadan politics, was brought up and went to school with his Christian cousin, Joseph Adelabu.[17] Chief Awolowo, the most prominent Yoruba politician of this century, has written about his father's devotion to Christianity dating back to the late nineteenth century. Awolowo's father attempted to convert all his family to Christianity, and Awolowo wrote that he "was made to realize quite early in life that Christianity was, of a surety, superior in many respects to paganism." Nonetheless, Awolowo's sister married a Yoruba Muslim, and she not only converted to Islam but has made the pilgrimage to Mecca.[18] In Abeokuta, a tense religious situation was brought under control after the bishop and the chief imam, both whom were from the same family, negotiated a settlement. I heard of many other instances of such cross-cutting family ties.

The evidence is insufficient, however, to sustain the theory that cross-cutting cleavages account for the nonpoliticization of religion. Since "descent" is a socially constructed rather than a biologically constructed reality, why is it that Yorubas have not "reconstructed" their families to make them religiously homogeneous? The fact that Yorubas consider members of different religions as bona fide members of their inner families is itself a reflection of the nonpoliticization of religion. At the birth of Christianity and Islam, converts were asked to redefine their families in order to make kinship commensurate with religious affiliation.[19] Rather than being an independent variable to explain religious toleration, the Yoruba emphasis on cross-cutting cleavages is part of the dependent variable. The Yorubas' continued emphasis on the cross-cutting religious affiliations itself demands explanation.

But this theoretical issue is only part of the problem. In fact, there is far less cross cutting than any Yoruba would admit. In fact, it would not take a great deal of "reconstruction" for Yoruba families to make themselves into religiously homogeneous units. To demonstrate this point I must return to my survey of the seventy church and mosque elders.[20] The data demonstrate that social solidarity based on religious similarity is strong, perhaps at least as strong as solidarity based on ancestral city. If cross-cutting cleavages have made the politicization of religion difficult, they should have made the continued politicization of ancestral city equally difficult.

The Social Reality of Religious Adherence

For both Christian and Muslim respondents in my survey, the degree to which immediate family members share religious affiliation is extremely high. Table 7.1 demonstrates that Yoruba families in the aggregate are religiously homogeneous. Nearly 90% of the Christians report that all their wives are Christians and over 90% of the Muslims report that all their wives are Muslim. About 70% of both subsamples report that their sisters' husbands (they could choose any sister)[21] were of the same religion as they. As I inquired about more distant relatives, the social fact of religious solidarity was confirmed. One hundred percent of the senior wives of the

TABLE 7.1. Religious Homogeneity in Respondents' Families

	Religion of Respondent	
Relationship:	Christian (%)	Muslim (%)
Wives of the same religion	88.6	94.3
Sister of the same religion	89.0	76.1
Sister's husband's present religion	70.4	68.4
Brother's present religion	89.7	93.5
Parents with same religion as each other	77.1	91.4

respondents' brothers who were Christian were themselves Christian; 95.7% of the brothers who were Muslim had senior wives who were Muslim (the other 4.3% adhered to the traditional religion). When I inquired about these brothers' junior wives, the respondents rarely knew the wives' religious affiliation. In 89% of the cases in which the respondents did know, the spouses shared the same religious affiliation. The likelihood of religious endogamy, as can be seen from table 7.2, is also high. About 70% of the respondents' sisters who were born into a world religion married a man of that same religion.

Social Regrouping Based on Religion

There is, as we have seen, some religious exogamy. However, my data show strong pressure in Yoruba society to homogenize the family religiously. First, most of the elders I interviewed were original converts to the world religions. Therefore their own fathers still adhered to the traditional religion when they converted. But, as table 7.3 shows, a considerable percentage of the respondents' fathers converted to the religion of their sons. Nearly all women who marry men of a different world religion

TABLE 7.2. Religious Endogamy: An Example

Respondent's Sister's Religion at Birth	Sister's Husband's Religion at Birth		
	Traditional (%)	Christian (%)	Muslim (%)
Traditional	*61.5*	23.1	15.4
Christian	17.6	*70.6*	11.8
Muslim	12.5	18.8	*68.8*

TABLE 7.3: Social Pressure toward Religious Solidarity

	Same as Father's Religion	
Respondent's Religion	At Birth (%)	Now (%)
Christian	11	69
Muslim	11	77

convert to the religion of their husbands, thereby making the nuclear family religiously homogeneous (see table 7.4). Outside of the pressures of the mission schools, the only source of conversion from one world religion to the other that I found was based on the need to create a fiction of religious endogamy.

Social regrouping based on religious affiliation extended beyond the family. I asked the respondents to list up to three friends. The Christian respondents listed eighty-two friends, 87.8 per cent of whom were Christian. The Muslim elders listed ninety-nine friends, 89.9 per cent of whom were Muslim. Religiously homogeneous family networks as well as wider social networks have indeed been created in Ile-Ife.

Religious and Ancestral City Solidarity Compared

Social solidarity based on ancestral city identification, which continues to have political meaning in Yorubaland, is barely greater than social solidarity based on religion. As is evident from table 7.5, the degree of difference between religious and ancestral city exogamy for each subsample is negligible. Christians are slightly more endogamous in regard to their religion; Muslims are slightly more endogamous in regard to their ancestral city. But there was no significant difference between religious and ancestral city endogamy among my respondents.[22]

TABLE 7.4. Endogamy and Conversion—Respondents and Their Wives

| | Religious Subsamples | |
Respondent's Wives	Christian	Muslim
Total number in sample	76	89
Religious endogamy	69.7%	65.4%
Converted to husband's religion	25.0%	32.3%
Remained of a different religion from their husbands	5.3%	2.3%
Converted to a religion different from husband's	0	1.1%

TABLE 7.5 Ancestral City and Religious Endogamy Compared

| | | Wives of a Different |
Religion of Respondent	Ancestral City (%)	World Religion (at birth) (%)
Christian	14	9
Muslim	37	40

A similar pattern appeared in the respondents' wider families. Among the Christian respondents, 85.7% of their sisters married a man of the same religion; 84.2% married a man of the same ancestral city. Among the Muslims, 78.6% of their sisters were religiously endogamous; 88.9% married a man of the same ancestral city. If we factor in conversion by wives, religious solidarity becomes of course far greater than ancestral city solidarity. For example, consider the respondents' brothers: in the Christian sample, 13% married women of a different ancestral city, while only 4.3% married women of a different religion who did not convert. In the Muslim sample, 8% of the respondents' brothers married women from a different ancestral city; none married women who now claim to belong to a different religion.

That a large percentage of the respondents did not know the religion of their brothers' junior wives reflected not the social irrelevance of religion but the social irrelevance of that particular relationship. Whereas 88.9% of the Christian respondents did not know the religion of their brother's junior wife, 100% did not know her ancestral city. Of the Muslim sample, 80.6% did not know the religion of their brother's junior wife; 82.8% did not know her ancestral city. The ability to code distant relatives according to religion is at least as good as the ability to code their ancestral cities.

Although my respondents lived in neighborhoods that were religiously heterogeneous but homogeneous in regard to ancestral city, their friendships were largely based on religious similarity. While 6.1% of the friends of both samples were of different ancestral cities, only 12.2% of the friends of the Christians and 13.1% of the friends of the Muslims were of a different religion. Only three of the seventy respondents mentioned more than one friend of a different world religion. Here, where proximity would suggest overwhelming predominance of ancestral city, we see that religious solidarity is not too far behind.

The data presented in tables 7.1–7.5 must be read with some care. One expert in Yoruba society, in reading these tables, argued that "there is a need to distinguish between what is statistically factual and what is unquantifiably truthful." Many of the conversions, he pointed out, especially of parents to the adopted religion of their children, were merely cosmetic (A. I. Asiwaju, professor of history, University of Lagos, personal correspondence). Careful readers of chapter 2 will understand that conversions were often "trivial" in the sense of not confronting the belief system of the convert. The point being made nonetheless stands: there has been pressure within Yoruba families to construct a reality of religious homogeneity that works the same way as the pressure within Yoruba compounds to construct a reality of ancestral city homogeneity.

To sum up: although most commentators on Yoruba society contend that there is religious heterogeneity within the Yoruba family, religious homogeneity is the normal pattern, with at least as much religious endogamy as ancestral city endogamy. Furthermore, Yorubas convert in order to create religious solidarity. Finally, Yorubas join societies (*ẹgbẹ*) and develop friendship networks that are religiously homogeneous. To be sure, there are cross-cutting ties within Yoruba society. But there is sufficient religious solidarity within family and wider social networks to support, if it existed, the politicization of religious identification.

Instrumental Management of Yoruba Identity

Theories that rely on the concept of "primordialism" must identify "real" social ties and distinguish them from the more instrumental ones. "Real" social ties are presumably those most subject to political organization. So far, I have demonstrated that religious ties in Yorubaland are a least as "real" as those to ancestral city. Now, I will return to a theme presented in chapter 6 in order to point out that Yoruba identification with ancestral city is far more subject to instrumental management than has previously been held. In fact, a careful study of Yoruba history demonstrates not the "givenness" of primordial ties but, rather, their changeability.

Consistent with data collected in other environments,[23] the Yoruba case provides abundant evidence of the fluidity of the social definition of identity. The development of Ibadan, discussed earlier, is an excellent example. Ibadan, originally a military camp with refugees from a variety of ancestral cities, soon began to develop its own "tradition," and its leaders fostered an Ibadan consciousness. Soon these leaders were making claims for higher-status titles in the "traditional" hierarchy. Abeokuta, another refugee city, also experienced instrumental identity management. Although numerous oral traditions suggest three different waves of migration into Abeokuta, each wave bringing a different set of lineages with virtually no familial connections between waves, by the time the missionaries came to Abeokuta in the mid-nineteenth century virtually all the town residents identified themselves as pure Egbas.[24] Even the "ancient" hierarchy of Yoruba cities was subject to instrumental manipulation. Recent historiographical evidence demonstrates that Yoruba kings from small towns were in regular negotiations with the king of Ile-Ife in order to rearrange their status in the "ancient" hierarchy of kings. The British colonizers paid kings salaries according to their positions on the hierarchy, and Yoruba kings had little problem in recreating their tradition to garner economic payoffs.[25] Deep cultural beliefs as well were subject to instrumental reformulation. In the early eighteenth century, twins were regarded in Yoruba tradition as a challenge to the established distinction between men and animals, and they were tabooed and systematically killed. But this "tradition" was subject to change. In the mid-eighteenth century, Yorubas became aware of a cult of twins, practiced in Dahomey, that held them to be sacred and not taboo. Christian missionaries in the early nineteenth century tried more directly to challenge the Yoruba taboo. By the mid-nineteenth century, amid the great population losses of the civil wars, the new cult of twins became widely accepted in Yorubaland. The tradition was not rejected but reinterpreted, perhaps to help shore up the declining population. Twins were seen as the product of the trickster god and as a sign to the parents that they would be served well by that god. The reformulation was a success, and the taboo reaction ultimately disappeared.[26]

Any theory that accords an eternal social reality to supposed ties of blood or to the bedrock of traditional culture is sure to be inadequate. This does not mean that myths of solidarity are not politically meaningful. Rather it means that the myths of solidarity are based on blood ties *combined with* a social idea about which blood ties are real. In the Yoruba context, the idea of ancestral city conjoins with lineage and compound relations to constitute a dominant ideology about identity. The social basis for religious identification could objectively (i.e., in blood) play the same role. It doesn't. To explain "why not" in terms of primordial identities is to be caught in an explanatory circle. An explanation is needed to understand why ancestral city identity is subjectively felt to be primordial while religious identity is not. Only an explanation able to do that will get us out of the circle.

CLEAVAGE PATTERNS ARE RATIONAL

These examples of the instrumental management of identity in Yoruba social relations appear to confirm the rational choice theory of the politicization of culture that was presented in chapter 5. Indeed, Yorubas appear to have assessed costs and benefits in their individual creation of their social identities.

As I indicated in that chapter and elaborated more fully in chapter 6, however, the rational choice paradigm faces a number of anomalies. Especially problematic for the instrumentalists in my case study is the political quiescence of the Muslim Yorubas. A microeconomic paradigm would lead us to suspect that there would be a sufficient number of Muslim entrepreneurs who would be willing to supply leadership to a coalition of disaffected people who saw themselves collectively as "Yoruba *Muslims*." Furthermore, since Yoruba Muslims have been relatively disadvantaged in the race for jobs and capital in comparison to Yoruba Christians, a rational choice paradigm would lead us to predict that individual Yorubas could be politically mobilized by the promise of special rewards to those who join a movement to foster equality for Yoruba Muslims. Given the data on the socioeconomic cleavage in Yoruba society presented in chapter 6, a rational choice theorist should predict a movement toward the politicization of religious consciousness among the Yoruba.

Not only has this politicization not occurred, but, even more anomalous for the rational choice perspective, the Yorubas interviewed for this study simply did not calculate the potential benefits of refocusing their political identities as Muslims. A neo-Benthamite approach would lead us to predict that, in the free market of identities, ambitious, investment-oriented Muslim *Yorubas* would consider presenting themselves as *Muslim* Yorubas. If the market presents opportunities but these opportunities are left unexplored, microeconomic theory cannot hope to explain the reason.

To these attacks, rational choice theorists have two lines of defense. The first involves an empirical reinterpretation of the Yoruba data already presented, to make sense of the anomalies within the rational choice perspective. The second line involves the implicit delimitation of the explanatory power of the rational choice perspective without abandoning it entirely. The following elucidation of the lines of defense will permit me to evaluate better the overall contribution of rational choice theory.

Empirical Reformulation within the Rational Choice Perspective

Rational choice theorists, armed with the data presented in chapters 2 and 6, can emphasize different aspects of Yoruba social and political history. First, it could be argued that all evidence points to high mobility prospects for Yorubas, from the enormous budget surpluses in the heady years of the cocoa boom in the 1950s, through the career opportunities available in the civil service and multinational corporations once the Igbos attempted secession from the Nigerian Federation, to the period of oil wealth subsidizing vast expenditures on infrastructure. Any Yoruba man with some wit, ambition, and luck—whether Muslim or Christian—has had a chance to become wealthy.[27] Because the social structure has not become ossified, it is perhaps irrational for any Yoruba man with ambition to seek changes in the nature of the ruling coalition. With so many aggregate rewards, the microeconomist can point out, it is rational to seek wealth and power within the present framework.

Second, rational choice theorists can emphasize the advantages to any Yoruba of continued identification with his ancestral city. I have emphasized the promise of physical security in the colonial state and within independent Nigeria. One can also highlight the security dilemma that many Yorubas face. Violence in the 1960s amid the fight between Awolowo's AG and Akintola's NNDP sent many Yoruba strangers back to their ancestral cities for a short period. In 1969, Yoruba traders were evicted from Ghana, and again found sanctuary in their ancestral homes. And in the early period of the Nigerian civil war, the uncertainty of the Western Region's role led many men to take their families back to their ancestral cities to wait the situation out.[28] A rational choice perspective would be saved if it could be demonstrated that Yorubas place a high value on a form of security that can be provided only by the perpetuation of one's ties to an ancestral city.

The third empirical line of defense for rational choice theory would be to ask why Yoruba political leaders reacted so strongly against mobilization strategies that involved religious identification. In fact, the early nationalists very carefully observed Indian nationalism.[29] Awolowo wrote that he was shocked by the massive killings associated with the partition, and believed that religious warfare should be avoided in Nigeria at all costs. One of the reasons he helped subsidize the pilgrimage to Mecca (and made sure that Yoruba Muslims got excellent accommodations and tour services in the Middle East) is that he wanted to preempt a Muslim political awakening. Awolowo thought Nigeria could avoid a replay of the Indian partition if Muslim needs were met before they organized to articulate demands. This was indeed a risky strategy, as thousands of Yoruba Muslims from a host of ancestral cities live together in hostels as they travel throughout the Arabian peninsula. In such situations, political programs and alliances are easily formed.

Finally, rational choice theorists could point out that the division of Yorubaland into two religious groups is less than a century old. The social cleavage that I have reported is probably even more recent. And the creation of religiously homogeneous family and social networks is more recent still. Strategic manipulation requires time. It took the American consumer over a decade to learn that Japanese cars were both cheaper and were of higher quality than Detroit-made vehicles. This fact does not mean that consumers did not want value for their money; it merely means that the information about value is costly itself. While consumers may be quick to see the relative advantage of a Buick over a Chevrolet, the costs of acquainting themselves with a different seller altogether are high. After a number of years when the information was fully disseminated, consumers indeed acted in a more rational manner. Rational choice theorists could make the same point in regard to the case at hand: the information required for rational action for Muslim Yorubas is costly. Large changes involve high "transition costs," that many political actors, like automobile consumers, may wish to avoid. Therefore there will be a lag before Yorubas strategically react to new opportunities in the political marketplace.[30]

Theoretical Delimitation of Rational Choice Theory

Rational choice theorists explaining the anomalies in chapter 6 could also refine the claims of their theory. They could point out that microeconomics is a theory of marginal decisions. It cannot tell us if ultimately butter is better than guns; it can tell us that at a certain point the production of a small number of guns will cost us a whole lot of butter, and at that point it is probably irrational to produce more guns. Within a political structure, individuals constantly make marginal decisions. Neo-Benthamite theories can give us a grasp on how individual political actors are likely to make choices within that structure.

Microeconomic theory cannot, however, handle long-term and non-marginal decisions. When market structures are themselves threatened, and people must decide whether to work within the new structure or hold on to the old—without any opportunity for a marginal decision—microeconomic theory is not applicable. In the case at hand, rational choice theorists could argue that their theory would enable one to predict whether a man born of a father from Ibadan and a mother from Abeokuta would see himself as an Egba or an Oyo, but not whether a Muslim *Oyo* would begin to see himself as a *Muslin* Oyo. Structural transformations—changing the basic cleavage structure in a society—are not amenable to the tools of microeconomic theory.[31]

The Explanatory Power of Rational Choice Theory

The empirical reformulation engendered by the rational choice perspective is plausible. There are very good reasons why Yorubas should eschew religious mobilization and equally good reasons to continue their associations with their ancestral cities. My purpose in setting up the problematic in chapter 6 was not to make the claim that religious mobilization would be more rational for individual Yorubas than ancestral city mobilization. Rather, it was to demonstrate that a structural transformation has been occurring within Yoruba society over the past century and to show that this social transformation has not translated itself into a political realignment.

The *level* of costs and benefits of different forms of political identification among the Yoruba is not at issue. For a Yoruba to reformulate his political identity on the basis of his religion would involve great uncertainty. To do so, then, any Yoruba would have to expect enormous potential gains, which are probably not on the horizon. It is therefore not irrational for a Yoruba to eschew such a reformulation of his political identity.

Acknowledging this point, however, does not mean that rational choice theory is particularly useful in understanding the pattern of political cleavages in Yorubaland. Why were there virtually no Yorubas testing the waters for a new form of political recruitment amid the civil war and the Sharia debate? Why were the informants in this study so unwilling to calculate increased emphasis on what is already a central component of their identity? Under what conditions do changing social structures lead people to refocus their identities entirely? While the neo-Benthamite paradigm can explain the anomalous findings presented in chapter 6, it does not push us to ask ever more penetrating questions about the potential politicization of new social cleavages.

Not Bentham but Gramsci provides the solution to the problematic of the second face of culture: under what conditions do what aspects of cultural identity become politically salient? The model of hegemonic control can help explain the reification of the "tribe" in African politics—why that cleavage became the dominant metaphor for political action and why it persisted.

To make the case for hegemony, I focus my attention on the transition from the Ibadan quasi empire to the British empire. As was discussed in chapter 6, for many parts of Yorubaland, political identification with one's ancestral city became less significant when Ibadan ruled Yorubaland. Warlords led armies of mixed ancestral city identification. Many traditional leaders of ancestral cities lost the resources necessary for maintaining authority, and Ibadan administrators refused to grant legitimacy to traditional boundaries or authorities. The king of kings, the Alaafin of Oyo, lived in a refugee encampment in near poverty. In spite of this great change, under British domination traditional kings were restored and ancestral cities were thereby given a new lease.

British action provides us with a clear example of what Lukes and Gaventa have called the third dimension of power, or what Gramsci meant by hegemony. In order to exert political control at low cost, the colonial administration needed to shape and manipulate social myths so that the social order they created would seem legitimate. Given the obvious illegitimacy of foreign rule, this task required some imagination. The near defunct kings provided for the colonial administration an unusual opportunity. The exploitation of that opportunity—the reestablishment of ancestral city kings by a hegemon—had vast implications for political organization in the Yoruba areas of Nigeria which have lasted to this day. The mechanisms by which the British did this deserve scrutiny.

In the late nineteenth century, Lord Lugard, who helped define and articulate the strategy of British administrative control over Nigeria and elsewhere in Africa, developed a strategy of "indirect rule." The core idea was to preserve local authority structures while the colonial authorities could "overrule"—that is, guide and manipulate local authority. Lugard, heavily influenced by Darwin, had an evolutionary view of society. Primitive societies were governed by tribal leaders, more developed societies by religious authorities, and fully developed societies by secular leadership. From this standpoint, British rule in northern Nigeria should be filtered through Muslim authorities, in southern Nigeria through tribal chiefs.[32] Indirect rule in Yorubaland meant that the kings of the ancestral cities were the "real" rulers of Yorubaland, who must be the intermediaries between the British administration and the people. In fact, what the

British did in Yorubaland was to create what historian J. A. Atanda has called "the New Oyo Empire."[33]

The alliance between the British and the ancestral city kings was politically interesting. The kings maintained some legitimacy in Yorubaland but lacked authority; the British had the coercive power for domination but lacked legitimacy. In combination, the British and the kings could exert legitimate domination. Both parties quickly learned the mutual advantage of this alliance. In 1888, Alfred Moloney, the governor of Lagos, attempted to enlist the support of the Alaafin in keeping French traders out of Yorubaland. The seeds of indirect rule were planted in his message, which was addressed to "Adeyemi, Alaafin of Oyo, and Head of Yorubaland, the four corners of which are and have been from time immemorial known as Egba, Ketu, [I]Jebu, and Oyo, embracing within its area that inhabited by all Yoruba-speaking peoples."[34] The provisions called for a nice "dash" (payoff) for the Alaafin if he used his influence to keep trade open for the British. At the end of the Kiriji war, the last of the great fronts amid the Yoruba civil wars, a treaty secured by British influence and power gave the Alaafin the responsibility of managing the final settlement between Ibadan and Ilorin. (He failed.)[35] That there was a mutually productive relationship between the Alaafin and the British became clear to both.

In 1895 the British nonetheless had to prove their superiority, but one short bombardment of new Oyo forced the Alaafin to flee temporarily and the town to submit. Despite this inauspicious event, the Oyos, destitute in their refuge, were quick to see the advantages to them of submission. To the eyes of the colonialists, Ibadan's power was thin, while Oyo's legitimacy was deep. Ibadan was noisy and rough; Oyo stable and orderly. When in 1898 the Resident at Ibadan, F. C. Fuller, visited Oyo, he described the Alaafin as "the most 'royal' native" he had "seen in Yorubaland." Atanda notes, "It was thought that great administrative advantages would be derived if the Alaafin's 'empty' appellation of 'Head of Yorubaland' was given some reality. The first step was to increase the territorial responsibility of Oyo at the expense of Ibadan."[36] For the Oyos, submission to the British meant overcoming the indignities of Ibadan's threat to ancestral city kingship.

When W. A. Ross became district commissioner for Oyo in 1906, the consequences of indirect rule for the relative status of Oyo and Ibadan were quickly revealed. Ross was an ardent advocate of indirect rule, and a Yorubaphile who deeply wished to enhance and protect the Yoruba tradition. An age-mate and friend of Oyo's crown prince, he was instrumental in getting the crown prince appointed as Alaafin when the latter died, though it took some creative reinterpretation of the Oyo tradition.

In Ross's grand scheme, he first had to overcome a treaty of 1893 in which the British conceded to Ibadan that it would be autonomous from

Oyo. He had to wait until he became Acting Resident over the whole region in 1912, and then he rearranged authority relations so completely that even the white missionaries found themselves subordinate to the Alaafin. When Lugard became governor of Nigeria that same year, and his doctrine of indirect rule became enshrined, Ross preempted Lugard's thrust by intervening in a succession battle for the leadership of Ibadan by making "loyalty to the Alaafin a *sine qua non* for election."[37] Lugard demonstrated his approval of Ross by transferring S. M. Grier to Oyo in 1913. Grier was one of the architects of the Indirect Rule system in Northern Nigeria, which served as a model for other colonial administrations. Lugard continued to infuse the south with the principles of administration from the north by promoting northern junior officers to senior positions in the south.[38]

Ross, now backed by a sympathetic governor, moved next to make Oyo the seat and headquarters of the entire province, with the Alaafin considered the "paramount chief." When the leader of Ibadan protested, Ross had him deposed. This became the key strategy in the application of indirect rule in Yorubaland. The "real" authorities were the ancient chiefs (who had virtually no power); the military junta that ruled Ibadan (that had considerable power) was not, from the standpoint of Africa's evolutionary progress, "real." Despite the fact that the British treaty with Ibadan authorities promised the Ibadan people autonomy, Lugard's administration sought to eliminate Ibadan entirely from the ruling paradigm. Where town authorities elsewhere were permitted to supervise day-to-day administration, a British officer in Ibadan took virtually all responsibilities directly into his own hands.[39] Indirect rule did not mean that colonial administration would rule not through the most powerful forces in the society but through forces it considered legitimate.

If Ibadan was destroyed as a power, Oyo was uplifted. The Alaafin's annual salary of £4,800 dwarfed the salaries of lesser kings. The king of Lagos, for example, then received a mere £300 per year.[40] Furthermore, Lugard gave Ross permission to grant the Alaafin the authority to impose the death sentence on rebels, and to exert judicial control over a wide range of issues. He could send his own residents (*Baba ni niki ọ*, literally "Father asked me to greet you") throughout the province, and many became high-handed marauders. Ross overlooked concomitant complaints, arguing that it was the Alaafin's duty to discipline his men.[41]

Ross's version of indirect rule significantly influenced the structure of cleavages in modern Yorubaland. First, Ross's policies enhanced the position of those elites who considered themselves "traditional authorities" in new Oyo, which helped to sustain an Oyo identity even though the people were living far from their ancestral home. If the notion of an "Oyo" identity was becoming more ambiguous in the wake of the civil war, that identity was reified and restored by British authority.

Second, other groups found that the only "legitimate" claims they could make within the colonial political system were based on the rights of their ancestral city. The king of Ife received considerable benefits from the British because Ile-Ife was the foundational ancestral city in the Yoruba tradition and specialized in religious services. Soon even Ibadan played the game, and its leaders petitioned the British to grant ever higher titles in the ancestral city framework for the leader of their city. The British, then, not only gave new power and meaning to the Oyo identity but also provided benefits to other groups that made claims in terms of their ancestral city identities.[42]

Third, the system of indirect rule induced groups which had no special claims by virtue of their authority in the old Oyo Empire to challenge the advances of Oyo and Ile-Ife. The only way they could succeed, however, was by making alliances with other cities or with outsiders (in the case of Ekiti and Ijebu, it was with missionaries) to capture greater resources. Catching up with Oyo became a dominant theme; but that theme itself acted further to reify identity based on ancestral city. Interestingly, the Ijebu and Ekiti alliance with missionaries paid off in the long term, as their sons procured civil service jobs more effectively than any other Yoruba groups, and the sons of Oyo found themselves playing catch up. Not Oyo's preeminence, but the very game of intercity competition is what became reestablished.

The reification of ancestral cities, even when many Yorubas had lost their geographic connection with them, was successful in part because the British strategy served a number of local interests. Yoruba kings never had autocratic power. By the late eighteenth century, their power relative to their military commanders was further reduced. After the complete breakdown of the Oyo Empire, kingly authority, as we have seen, was virtually crushed. Although it sometimes took a while for the kings to recognize the advantages of collaboration with the British,[43] they soon understood that the British were not only restoring their power but were promising them a degree of autocratic control over their cities that local kings had never previously enjoyed. When the Egba peoples fled south and settled in Abeokuta, they were ruled by coalitions of war leaders, *Ogboni* [a religious cult] officials, and traders. "It was only during the colonial period that the authority of the *Alake* (an office which became king of the Egbas, on the Oyo model, but had been a senior chief in the early Abeokuta years) was consolidated."[44] By the early twentieth century, the British and the chiefs had a shared interest in neotraditionalism. Chiefs in small towns sought British resources by fabricating myths of the ancient glory of their towns. The British responded favorably and subsidized these kings, thereby creating a whole class of "nouveaux rois."[45]

Meanwhile, claims based on religious identity were expunged from the political arena by British administrators. Even before the ideology of indirect rule had been articulated, British administrators shied away from the promotion of Christianity. Instead, they became arbitrators among the interests of Muslims and Christians. In 1875, for example, the governor attempted to settle an internal Islamic dispute in a sense of "fairness and freedom of worship." Again in 1902–3, a factional dispute among Muslims in Epe prompted the governor to bring in a group of Lagos Muslims to arbitrate.[46] Religious conflict required arbitration; but no resources were given to contending religious authorities in order to enhance their prestige and power in their own constituencies.

One British governor, C. A. Moloney, sought to preempt religious conflict through education. He subsidized Christian schools if they would accommodate their curricula to meet the needs of Muslim students. This failed, and subsequent British governors began to subsidize Muslim schools. In return for these funds, Muslims helped the governors bring peace to the country. Governor G. T. Carter recruited the chief imam of Lagos to appeal directly to the emir of Ilorin to make peace with the British; and Carter found himself being requested as an intermediary among Muslims in their internal disputes. Despite the protestations of the Christian missionaries that the government was giving "excessive deference" to the Muslims, it is clear that the preemption of political claims based on religion was the British goal.[47]

The British strategy was to defuse religious antagonism rather than to divide Yoruba country by religion. A major reason for their gingerly treatment of potential religious conflict was that British administrators, due to their recent experience with the Sudanese Mahdi, feared the revolutionary implications of religious fanaticism.[48] Lugard did not even permit the recruitment of Yoruba Muslims into the colonial army for fear that an alliance between northern and southern Muslims would have revolutionary potential.[49] But it never occurred to Lugard to use his indirect rule system to rule through the local religious elites: in Yorubaland's stage of development, tribal chiefs were the "natural" authorities. British colonial rule, then, politicized one cleavage (between ancestral cities) and depoliticized another (between religious groups).

Lugard's successors were not as ideologically committed to indirect rule as was Lugard; but his system remained the leitmotif of British administration in Nigeria. In each town, Native Authorities were created; and the towns were governed by their "natives." Some "strangers"—i.e., those from different ancestral cities or other regions—were housed in ghettos and had virtually no political influence in the towns in which they lived.[50] British Residents were solicitous of complaints by the native town dwellers concerning disruptions by strangers. Many of the political battles within Yorubaland in the post-Lugardian years concerned the rights of natives vis-à-vis strangers.[51]

Land law, which prevented the alienation of land from ancestral city ownership, consolidated the authority of ancestral city kings. Before British colonialism, "the status of stranger was a temporary one; either the stranger was absorbed into the community or he went home." Under the Native Authority system, introduced in 1917, severe constraints were put in the way of land alienation to strangers. British suzerainty, then, defined more sharply the boundary between native and stranger.[52]

After the Second World War, British administration created elected bodies in the towns. Electoral politics planted the seeds for the ultimate destruction of kingly authority. But other political forces within Nigeria sustained the political relevance of ancestral city. In the 1950s Awolowo's Ẹgbẹ Ọmọ Oduduwa became a political force in Yorubaland. What had been a cultural society in London became a political party in Nigeria—the Action Group. Party politics and elections threatened the authority of the "New Oyo Empire." Awolowo forged an alliance with the Ọọni of Ife (see chapter 6) early on his return to Nigeria, and decided to build on that alliance for his wider political ambitions. This strategy angered the Alaafin of Oyo, who tried to organize his local forces against Awolowo. The ensuing political battle was tense; but ultimately Awolowo's forces were able first to banish the Alaafin's son from Oyo, then to suspend the Alaafin's salary, and finally to depose him from office.[53] The British authorities were nonplussed. Politics in Yorubaland was getting out of hand. Awolowo's alliance with the Ọọni of Ife created its own counterforce. Groups in Ife, ideologically supporting Awolowo's reformism, attempted to do unto the Ọọni what had been done to the Alaafin. The British administration did all it could to save the Ọọni's skin.[54] It seemed to some observers that ancestral city kings had been surpassed completely and that the Lugardian system was about to collapse.

What saved it up through Nigerian independence was the fact that Yorubaland was part of a wider Nigeria. The Lugardian system in Nigeria had meant that three different administrations were created, with three different authority structures. So many resources were controlled by the regions that ultimate power in Nigeria required a politician to build from a regional base. The more unified a region, the more opportunities it had in claiming resources at the center. Awolowo had to build up a "Yoruba" constituency, Azikiwe an "Igbo" constituency, and Balewa a "Hausa-Fulani" constituency. These regional identifications were as artificial as the reestablished ancestral cities.

Lugardianism's apotheosis was the emergence of a "tribal" politics in Nigeria.[55] If the Yoruba "tribe" remained a political reality in Nigeria's First Republic, it had to rest on a foundation of ancestral cities. Nigerian politics itself became a blown-up version of colonial politics in Yorubaland. The pattern of tribal politics continued through the independence years and provided the ideological rhetoric of the 1967 civil war. Biafra claimed the Eastern Region had a right to secede due to the national distinctiveness of the Igbo people. The idea of a distinct "Igbo" identity reflected strategies of colonial control rather than any ancient political reality.

In the wake of the Biafran civil war, when the military government sought to create more states, it drew its maps commensurate with Lugardian boundaries and criteria. Oyo became a separate state. The group of cities that formed a united opposition to Ibadan (the Ekiti alliance) became the heart of the state of Ondo. The kingdoms of Ijebu and Egba were put together in Ogun State, and this has created some tension already. Breaking up Yorubaland on ancestral city criteria did not require military coercion: as we have seen, the Oyo people had long clamored to be separated from the Ijebus and the Ekitis. To all concerned, these boundaries were commonsensically legitimate.

Not only do representatives of ancestral cities continue to assert themselves politically, but potential representatives of aggrieved religious groups in Yorubaland remain politically quiescent. In 1980 and 1982, Nigerian state authorities ruthlessly repressed a religious sect in the northern states.[56] President Shagari, who was roundly criticized in Yoruba circles for almost everything else in his term of office, met virtually no criticism in Yorubaland for his police action. Intra-Muslim battles in the north fell on deaf ears in the west.

In this chapter I have highlighted the role of the British state as a hegemonic bloc in reifying a cultural framework for political action. It might therefore be useful to engage in a thought experiment: What if the British had not colonized Yorubaland? Would collective political action in Yorubaland then have had a different basis from common ancestral city ties? Three scenarios appear to be possible. First, because ancestral cities *did* have high legitimacy among many Yorubas, if Ibadan had been able to consolidate its rule its leaders might have modified the tradition by remaking Ibadan into a town with an ancient and glorious past. (As we saw, reworking the tradition is a central component of the tradition.) The leaders of Ibadan would then have created new chiefly titles, commensurate with old Oyo's, and held that their king was the supreme king of all cities. His lineage would be connected to one of Oduduwa's sons and he would have become sacred. If this had succeeded, it would have meant the continued importance of the ancestral city framework, as Ibadan would have been acting in a way similar to the way British authorities did in fact act.

Second, Ibadan authorities might have continued to abjure methods of indirect rule, and thereby ignore and/or degrade traditional authorities. This would have led to a Yorubaland of competing war chiefs carving out fiefdoms and attempting to consolidate their rule through alliances with multiancestral-city trading households. A new set of cleavages would thereby have begun to form, but the traditional criteria of ancestral city membership would have been antithetical to the interests of the new leaders and incommensurate with the new social realities.

Third, if the war chiefs of the Ibadan quasi empire had continued to fight each other and rapaciously to exploit their provinces, subject areas would likely have sought to consolidate a formal opposition. In the northeastern part of the quasi empire, ancestral cities formerly distinct had already joined together into a supra-ancestral city (the Ekitiparapọ, combining Ekiti, Ijesha and Igbomina). Each of these cities had already adopted many of the Ibadan military titles, which suggests the declining relevance of sacred kingship—the backbone of ancestral city legitimate domination. When British military authority intevened, Ibadan and the Ekitiparapọ were at a standoff. Had the British not intervened, it is likely that other ancestral-city coalitions would have formed; yet the Ibadan model of war chiefs maintaining political control would have fundamentally altered their basis of authority. There would have remained, then, an ancestral city cleavage, but of a new kind.

It is also possible that opposition to Ibadan could have been formulated on religious terms. The Ekitiparapọ, after all, started out as a Christian group in Lagos and held weekly prayer meetings.[57] It is not difficult to conceive of newly installed religious leaders organizing opposition to what they could have called Ibadan's "anti-Christian" assault on Yoruba life. They could clearly have gotten foreign military aid from European and North American church groups if they had made such claims. Meanwhile, Ilorin had not lost interest in challenging Ibadan, and its leaders were still able to call upon Fulanis for military support. It is therefore possible to conceive of a religious partition of Yorubaland, going northeast from Lagos, splitting Remo and Ijebu-Ode continuing up the Ọṣun river, and finally splitting the Yoruba zones in what is today Kwara State (see map 1.2). South and east of this line would be "Christian" Yorubaland; north and west would be "Mulsim" Yorubaland. Yorubas would have been compelled to convert or migrate. If this partition had occurred, world religion could have replaced ancestral city as the dominant framework for collective political action.

These hypothetical outcomes cannot be formally assessed, though I would suppose the first scenario to be the most plausible. The point being made is that the political situation in Yorubaland ws fluid at the point of British conquest, and that the British resuscitated a declining set of author-

no very persuasion — *but*
why did indirect rule lead
to political
n
other contexts?

*totally
circular
so*

e

*later
persist development*

ities in order to rule through them. In so doing, they created a cultural
hegemony of ancestral city membership. And this is why it seems obvious
to nearly all Yorubas that religious conflict is bloody and led by fanatics,
whereas regional (i.e. tribal) conflict is natural and led by responsible
authorities. This commonsense perception did not come from the free
marketplace of ideas; it was forged by British colonial strategy.

The Problem of Persistence

The colonial structure made indirect rule an efficient strategy of control.
Indirect rule involved the infusion of resources to politically defunct but
socially legitimate leaders. In Yorubaland, this strategy led to the reestablishment of ancestral city and the depoliticization of religion. But why does
this pattern persist, especially after a generation of political independence,
and a very fluid political scene in Nigeria, of which Yorubaland, no longer
administratively unified, is only a part? How does a model of hegemonic
control explain the persistence of social cleavages after the hegemon leaves
the scene? Must we invoke rational choice theory and assume that the
transition costs are too high?

I have already mentioned material and ideological forces that have
acted to sustain the present pattern of cleavages in Yorubaland. Let me first
examine the material forces. The structure of the modern Nigerian state
was built on the Lugardian system of regions based on a reactionary
analysis of tribal (and, in the north, religious) boundaries. Battles that
involved Igbos against Hausas, Yorubas against Igbos, minority tribes
against the regionally powerful tribes were all built on a foundation of
indirect rule. As Yoruba politics entered the federal realm, politicians
found that the idea of a "Yoruba" interest could most easily be articulated
on a foundation of sub-Yoruba (i.e. ancestral city) interests. The fact that
independent Nigerian politics was based on regions helped to sustain
colonial cleavage patterns in Yorubaland based on ancestral cities.

Furthermore, as we have seen, ancestral cities are still able to provide
valued goods such as protection to Yorubas escaping from troubled situations elsewhere and, through the kings, tracts of land. Until the 1978 Land
Decree, which appears to permit strangers to alienate land from chiefly
authorities, Yoruba kings could promise land to nonresident sons of the
town.

A third material factor focuses on the interests of the first generation of
political elites in independent Nigeria. Chief Awolowo, who developed
the earliest electoral strategies in Yorubaland, remains the dominant
political force in Yorubaland at the time of this writing. He is identified by
all Yorubas as an "Ijebu man" and by all Nigerians as a "Yoruba." As I
write this, he is past seventy years old. Many Nigerians argue that when he

passes from the scene, and when his elder, Azikiwe, the Igbo patriarch, leaves as well, there will be a new opportunity to change the basis of political coalitions in Nigeria. Those elites who gained power during an era of tribalism have an interest in sustaining its vocabulary.[58]

Other cases of ethnic opposition suggest that as long as the hegemonic coalition is not faltering economically, it is unlikely that the disadvantaged groups will turn their latent hostility into political action.[59] Only a long period of relative economic decline for the Yorubas vis-à-vis the rest of Nigeria would make it worthwhile for Yoruba Muslims to seek redistributions from their Christian counterparts. Only then would they begin to refocus their political identities.

However reasonable these explanations seem to be, they cannot do justice to the pattern of cleavages that presently exists in Yorubaland. Given the existence of a new land decree, the fact of Awolowo's advanced age, and the deep problems facing Nigeria in light of its budget cutbacks in the wake of declining oil revenues, a look only at the material forces would lead one to forecast a potential realignment toward religion in the near future. The discussion in chapter 6 on the nonpoliticization of religion in Yorubaland points out, however, that there is no Muslim revivalism on the Yoruba horizon. Ideological forces have combined with material forces to sustain colonial cleavage patterns: Yoruba towns have turned traditional religious rituals into a civic religion; wealthy businessmen living in Lagos are invited back their ancestral cities to recite the chants formerly reserved for priests; and the rituals have turned into public holidays.[60] Rituals act to sustain personal identification to towns even when the towns are less able to provide material resources to the individual. Stereotypes of people from other towns abound in Yoruba vocabulary, and this too sustains personal identification with one's ancestral city.

Most important, however, has been the creation of a "common sense" as the ideological force of hegemony. The idea that ancestral city represents "blood" while religion represents "choice" is so deeply embedded into commonsense thinking that experience and empirical data demonstrating otherwise fail to disabuse Yoruba people of this "truth." Rational choice theorists are correct when they point to the high transition costs involved in changes in one's political identity; but they are unable to grasp the nature of these costs. The model of hegemonic control gives an account of how commonsense frameworks delimit the range of identity-investment opportunities considered by political entrepreneurs. Primordial theories correctly point to the power of traditional identities; but these theories cannot make sense of the political (rather than biological) foundation of primordial identities, a historical factor that was identified in the model of hegemonic control. In the case of Yorubaland, the model of hegemonic control gives a plausible explanation of the way primordial identities become forged politically, and how, once forged, these identities become commonsensically real.

This discussion of indirect rule in Yorubaland focuses on an important social force missed by theories of primordial attachment and by theories of rational choice as well—the role of the hegemonic state. Colonial Britain is a special kind of hegemonic state, to be sure, but like all hegemons, Britain had an interest in efficient social control. The need for efficiency of social control led British administrators to create incentives for certain kinds of groups to form, and for other sorts of groups to disband or be repressed. In any state, but in colonized ones especially, the pattern to political organization which makes demands on the state is itself a function of state actions. While patterns of social stratification may be a function of a whole range of social and economic variables, the patterns of politicized cleavages may be better understood as largely a function of the strategies of political control by hegemonic states.

But two questions immediately arise: how broadly can we generalize from the case of hegemony in Yorubaland? And, is it possible to use this case study as a foundation for future work in comparative social theory? To help address these questions, and to show the broad explanatory power of the hegemony approach, two apparent anomalies to the theory of hegemony as presented here will be analyzed. One focuses on northern Nigeria and the other on Yoruba politics in the neighboring Republic of Benin. By choosing two cases from areas so closely related to Nigeria's Yorubaland, it will be possible to provide short vignettes, since the reader will already be acquainted with the basic historical facts.

Northern Nigeria: A Case of Transethnic Alliances in the Wake of Indirect Rule

As should be apparent to the reader from the discussion of the Sharia debate, religion is highly politicized in the northern states of Nigeria. Since Northern Nigeria and Yorubaland were both under the same system of British indirect rule, should not the theory of hegemony lead us to expect similar outcomes? Does the northern Nigeria case disconfirm the model of hegemony? Let us now look at the northern situation more carefully.

In northern Nigeria there were a number of cross-cutting cultural identities when the British were consolidating their protectorate in the early twentieth century. The principal ones were ancestral home (distinguishing among migrants from different outside areas); tribe (distinguishing the Hausa from other language groups such as the Fulani); clan (distinguishing lineages within a tribe such as the Fulani); and religion (distinguishing among Muslim and non-Muslim; also distinguishing among different Islamic brotherhoods).[61]

Of all these lines of cleavage, religion became a principal cultural marker for politics in the north. In the late colonial period and the first civilian government, the Northern Peoples' Congress (NPC) united an extremely diverse region under the flag of a single party. The symbolism of Islam was sufficiently strong to keep the north united. A united north served as the key ingredient that led to a northerner becoming Nigeria's first prime minister. The symbol of Islam uniting the north—despite its breakup into ten of Nigeria's nineteen states—explains the vociferous support that northerners (from the six states of the far north) gave to the state promotion of the Sharia courts, as described in chapter 1.

Opposition to that unity was also organized from a religious framework. The principal opposition party in the Northern Region to the NPC in the preindependence years was the Northern Elements Progressive Union (NEPU), whose ideology favored the rights of the common people over the royal families; so it is proper to consider NEPU an ideological or leftist alternative to the NPC. NEPU leaders nonetheless knew that ideology alone does not create a mass base. They had to appeal to people's attachment to cultural communities. One tack might have been to represent the common man as a true *Hausa* (a tribally based identity), who was displaced by Fulani overlords in the course of the Islamic jihad of the early nineteenth century. But this could not have been very successful, since the leader of the jihad, Uthman dan Fodio, a Fulani, was very popular among Hausas as well as Fulanis. Also, one of the leading lights of NEPU, Aminu Kano, was Fulani. Another tack was to split the north based on religious criteria. In fact, two leading analysts of northern politics have seen NEPU recruitment largely in terms of religious differentiation. "The most notable instance of a link between the party and sectarian . . . affinities," Whitaker reports, "was the connection between NEPU and the religious brotherhood called Tijaniyya." In fact, Whitaker writes of a "natural alliance" between the Tijaniyya religious order in opposition to the Qadiriyya order, which was prevalent among leaders of the NPC. And Paden reports that in the 1964 election campaign NEPU leader Amino Kano successfully exploited the religious issue by employing campaign posters with pictures of himself being blessed by the head of the Tijaniyya brotherhood. Paden emphasizes the acute divisions within the north based on religious differentiation and the ease with which these brotherhoods established a transethnic base. Political cohesion across tribes, political division across Islamic brotherhoods: this is a dominant image of northern politics as presented by Paden.[62]

When the north became divided into ten states, new political divisions emerged. The NPN (successor to the NPC) adjusted to this new structure by recruiting actively—with promises of patronage—the "minority tribes" throughout the federation. In 1979, NPN presidential candidate Shagari received over 50 percent of the vote in the eleven states with large minority populations. The GNPP, centered in a minority area of the north (among the Kanuris in Borno State) also attracted many votes among minorities. In the Second Republic, then, the Hausa-Fulani aristocracy allied with southern tribal minorities became the ruling coalition. Opposition parties, including the UPN (predominantly Yoruba) and the NPP (predominantly Igbo) suggest that tribe—the three major ones plus changing coalitions of minority tribes—was the primary cleavage line in Nigeria's Second Republic.[63]

Yet this does not mean that religion-based politics in the north was dormant. One faction of the old NEPU was reformed by Amino Kano as the Peoples' Redemption Party (PRP). Aminu was a Fulani (his mother, however, was from a minority group in the north) from Kano, well schooled in and a friend of the Tijaniyya brotherhood. Although he was a true Nigerian nationalist figure, the social basis of his electoral support in Kano and Kaduna (as it had when he was a NEPU leader in the First Republic) remained among the Tijaniyya "brothers."

Outside of party politics, the most significant popular political movement in the north opposing the NPC-NPN aristocracy has been a new Islamic movement known as the "Maitatsine." Mohammed Marwa (known as Maitatsine), the founder of the movement, migrated from Cameroun, organized a religious following among the poor in Kano, distributed free rice, and preached asceticism and Islamic purity. The movement's precise categorization is a subject of dispute, for its leader sometimes portrayed himself not as an Islamic purist but as a new prophet Given Maitatsine's religious challenge and his evident popularity among the urban poor, the political authorities feared the revolutionary potential of his movement and outlawed it. The movement continued to grow, however, and became prevalent in a number of Kano neighborhoods. In 1980 about 4,000 of Maitatsine's followers were killed by government authorities in Kano. Marwa himself was also killed; in 1985 over one hundred religious followers of Maitatsine were killed in a riot provoked by a police raid. Three policemen were killed and 100,000 rounds of ammunition were discovered in Maitatsine caches.[64]

The power of religion to sustain the development of transethnic political coalitions of northerners remains strong. To be sure, the military coup d' état in December 1983, which led to the overthrow of the Fulani aristocrat from Sokoto and President of Nigeria, Shehu Shagari, by Muhammad Buhari, another Fulani from Sokoto, suggests that many forms of opposition exist having nothing to do with religion or tribe. As we have seen, the GNPP is not a religiously based form of opposition. Yet NEPU, PRP, and

Maitatsine have all been strong *popular* movements against the political leadership in the far north, and all have relied heavily on religious symbols to recruit their political followings. Religion not only unites the far north against Nigeria's south but remains a source for intranorthern political mobilization.

To claim that religion has been the basis for most political recruitment in northern Nigeria is not startling. But to claim that virtually all political alignments in Nigeria's north are "transethnic"—which is the other side of the coin—is startling indeed. In northern political discourse, political coalitions welding together Fulanis, Hausas, Beriberis, and Kanuris require no explanation, just as the political alliance of Christians and Muslims in Yoruba parties appears to insiders as unproblematical.[65]

Religion (and not tribe), then, has become the leitmotif for northern politics as ancestral city (and not religion) has become in Yorubaland. Yorubas organize in terms of ancestral city for internal battle and tribe for Nigeria-wide politics; northerners organize in terms of religious brotherhoods for internal battle and world religious membership for Nigeria-wide politics. Within the terms of the model of hegemonic control, how can this (apparently different) outcome be explained?

To answer that question, one must examine the role of Uthman dan Fodio, and his early nineteenth-century jihad. He did an exemplary job in uniting diverse desert peoples under a common version of Islam.[66] It would also be important to examine the British strategy of indirect rule in the north and see how it differed from its counterpart in Yorubaland. Lord Lugard's initial strategy in the north tried to incite Hausa peasants against their Fulani overlords. But he was surprised when the emir of Kano, a Fulani, escaped to the east (in Islamic tradition, escape from the heathen, called *hijra*, is not only legitimate, but glorified). The emir was able to attract many Hausa followers into his *hijra*. Recognizing the solidarity in Islam, Lugard began to rely on the emirate system, designed by the Fulani Uthman dan Fodio, in which office was entrusted in (Muslim) emirs rather than in (tribal) chiefs. Lugard embellished the practical adjustment to northern political realities in his book *The Dual Mandate*. There, he differentiated peoples on the basis of their evolutionary progress. Believing that social organization by tribe was lower on the evolutionary ladder than organization by religion, he held that northern Nigeria was socially more advanced. The British found it necessary, then, to rely heavily on Uthman dan Fodio's lieutenants to define and delimit political authority in the north. Sokoto became the political center of the North—and the sultan of Sokoto the most royal native—just as Oyo became the center of Yorubaland, with the Alaafin the most royal native.[67]

The point of this discussion is not to establish why religion became the dominant mode of political organization in northern Nigeria but, rather, to demonstrate the plausibility of two propositions: (1) that there were many cultural cleavages in the north that could have become politicized; and (2) that religious adherence is the primary basis for political identification and mobilization.

Rational choice theory can only help us to understand the strategies of leadership and followership among such political organizations as the NPN, the PRP, and the Maitatsine. It can help us answer such questions as what recruitment strategies work and how collective benefits are attained. But rational choice theory is less able to address the question of why, in Nigeria's north, religiously based collective political movements are far more likely to form than tribally based ones. What is needed is an understanding of the institutions created by a hegemonic bloc. While the hegemonic bloc might have been the leaders of the Fulani jihad or the British administration (or both), it is clear that the framework of religious politics had to be fashioned by state builders. Once it was fashioned, individuals calculated their own advantages within the given structure.

Indirect rule as a hegemonic strategy does not predict the politicization of tribe and the depoliticization of religion among the colonial subjects.[68] Rather, it predicts that, in systems of indirect rule, a hegemonic elite will coopt legitimate cultural elites (from one cultural subsystem) and supply those elites with additional resources while at the same time protecting them from the "traditional" limits to their power when in fact they had real authority. A new hegemonic bloc, including at least the reinvigorated elites along with the imperial bureaucrats, will have a joint interest in enhancing the role of the chosen cultural subsystem as the framework of "tradition." Which cultural elites get chosen is a function of the degree of their legitimacy within the social structure and the perceptions of the hegemon about the society being ruled. Yorubaland and northern Nigeria were clearly different on both of these criteria. Therefore, the reification of ancestral city in Yorubaland and of religion in North Nigeria are both consistent with Britain's hegemonic strategy of indirect rule.

Benin: Western Yorubaland under French "Direct Rule"

French colonialism in Africa was marked by "direct rule." While the differences between the British and French were not in reality as great as in theory, the basic idea behind French hegemony was the "steady suppression of the great chiefs and the destruction of their authority until the village becomes an administrative unit."[69] French administration in West Africa was centralized from a governor-general in Dakar, governors in each colony, and then down to *cantons* and *circonscriptions* within the colonies, each level administered not by a native authority but by a *fonctionnaire*. With the intention of delegitimating traditional authority, French colonialism supported a policy of assimilation. Those Africans who had "evolved" (called *évolués*) into Frenchmen could become French citizens and participate in the governance of the territory. French direct rule also involved direct taxation of urban dwellers. This policy caused many Yorubas to abandon city life, live on their farms, or migrate to Nigeria. The very integrity of the Yoruba city was severely compromised by French colonial policies.[70] We can infer that direct rule, by the logic of the argument presented here, should have reduced the significance of ancestral city politics.

Benin (formerly Dahomey) makes for an interesting test case of the theory of hegemony. It has a population of about 300,000 Yorubas constituting some 14 percent of the total population. They can be categorized by membership in ancestral cities: Ketu, Sabe, Anago (the generic word for Yoruba in the Benin context, which is basically a congeries of subgroups including the Awori, Ohori, and Ifonyin). If the theory here is correct, we should not expect the politicization of ancestral city in the Benin context. If ancestral city were consequential in Benin-Yoruba politics, then we would have to conclude that ancestral city identification among Yoruba was strong enough to become a dominant political framework no matter what system of colonial administration was in operation.

At first blush, the post colonial political history of Benin suggests the outbreak of "tribalism" that has been associated with British indirect rule. The united nationalist movement broke up in the 1950s into three different parties, each led by a regional figure. In the southeast, Sourou-Migan Apithy led a coalition of Yorubas and Gouns. Apithy is a Goun, which is closely related in language and history to Yoruba. In the southwest and central areas, Justin Ahomadegbé won support from the Fon and Adja peoples. In the north, Hubert Maga, with his base of support among the Bariba peoples, became dominant. Their parties represented the three traditional kingdoms—Abomey (Fon), Porto Novo (Goun), and Bariba— that were originally consolidated in the French colony of Dahomey. Voting in Dahomey has reflected regional and even village unity, implying the importance of ancestral city in the Yoruba cantons. If this is the case, perhaps "tribe" as a political identification has been so deep in the wider Yoruba culture zone that a theory of hegemony is not necessary to explain its recrudescence in the postcolonial period in Benin or Nigeria. Primordial loyalties to ancestral city would be the explanatory variable explaining tribal politics.

Further inspection of the Benin case, however, demonstrates the power rather than the inadequacy of the model of hegemony to explain political divisions. Of great importance is to note that the French in Dahomey did not rule in the same way as they ruled in Senegal and other places in Africa in which direct rule was truly applied. To be sure, a French official in Dahomey wrote to Paris after an early victory over the Abomey forces that "we had only to punish the insolence and the villainy of a black king." This suggests that traditional authority would be eliminated. However, the chief commander of the French expeditionary army in Dahomey wrote that "the chiefs who submit immediately and in good faith . . . will keep their positions."[71] From the 1930s, especially, the principles of indirect rule were stressed in Dahomey, and in explicit differentiation with other areas of France's African empire. This is largely because Dahomey was considered too poor, too remote (bordered by a British colony on the east and a German one—until the end of World War I—on the west), and too unimportant for serious political control. With heavy uses of indirect rule principles, one should not be surprised about the politicization of tribe in Dahomey.

Of even greater importance to the theory of hegemony is the fact that "tribalism" is hardly the correct epithet to summarize the dynamics of postcolonial Dahomey politics. A different framework—one more commonly associated with direct rule—was equally present. The different framework is one in which the évolués were united as a homogeneous political class. From a Nigerian perspective, the common cultural framework of the political class in Benin is astonishing. Nearly all of them, including Apithy, Ahomadegbé, and Maga (who was born a Muslim), are at least nominally Catholics. Second, a large number of the leading figures in all three parties, including Ahomadegbé, Maga, and Emile Zinsou (who once served as Dahomey's president), are graduates of the prestigious Ecole William Ponty and therefore had a classic "French" education. Third, as Dahomey went back and forth from military to civilian rule, each of the leaders at different times was in coalition with each other. Yoruba politicians served well with patrons from all the parties. Alexandre Adandé and Louis Ignocio-Pinto were two Yorubas who were early supporters of Ahomadegbé. Assogba Oke, of a mixed Goun and Yoruba family, served as vice president under Hubert Maga, and in fact was arrested when he attempted to stage a coup in 1963 to restore Maga to power. Never in Dahomey, as occurred in Nigeria, were tribal supporters of a candidate from an outside party considered by other members of the political class to be ethnic traitors. The members of the territorial assemblies did not have strong local ties. Eighty-two percent of the members of the 1957 Territorial Assembly and 79 percent of the 1959 Legislative Assembly were *fonctionnaires*. Since writing French was a sine qua non for becoming a candidate, the évolué class dominated in the political center. The political class from all regions clearly saw themselves as *French Dahomeans*.[72]

Also in contrast to Nigeria, Yoruba ancestral cities in Dahomey have not been associated with a particular side of a political divide. In the subprefecture of Ketu—perhaps the most homogeneous Yoruba ancestral city electoral unit in Benin—the population has long split evenly between the party of Apithy and that of Ahomadegbé. In the 1957 election for the Territorial Assembly, Apithy's party defeated Ahomadegbé's by 58–42 percent. In the December 1960 elections for the presidency, Ahomadegbé received 54 percent and the Maga/Apithy coalition received only 46 percent in Ketu. In Nigeria's Yoruba cities there have often been divisions of this sort, but most of them have had an ideological core.[73]

Benin has differed from many other French postcolonial states in the fact of its elite disunity. Elsewhere in French colonial Africa, the évolués were able to assert themselves by supporting a single leader who could unite the new political class: Senghor in Senegal, Touré in Guinea; Houphouët-Boigny in Ivory Coast, and Keita in Mali. (Throughout French Africa, tribal identities are culturally consequential, but my point here is that they have not become frameworks for collective political action.) It is clear that a political class of évolués did develop in Dahomey, but could not, as elsewhere in French Africa, consolidate its rule. Various attempts at the creation of a *parti unique* failed. In 1972 an ingenious strategy of presidential rotation among the three parties was agreed to, but that experiment was aborted by a military coup two years later, shortly after the first peaceful transfer of power.

The case of Benin is one of "incomplete hegemony." Two frameworks existed side by side with equal legitimacy. First was the Benin of three historical kingdoms, each representing a separate nation. Second was the Benin of the French Dahomeans, a political class united to fulfill the task of representing and defending the interests of the masses of a united Benin. Neither one became dominant; each was suppressed somewhat by the legitimacy of the other. Because French rule in Dahomey was not fully "direct," tribal identities remained politically consequential. Because French rule in Dahomey had some elements of direct rule, an évolué class almost established hegemony.

Ilorin, a Yoruba city in Nigeria, is another case of incomplete hegemony. Since it was administered as part of the Northern Region, one should expect the exacerbation of religious politics. But since it was not fully incorporated into the northern system, the religious framework of the British never had great impact in Ilorin. In 1903, for example, the CMS sought to penetrate Ilorin by sending a doctor there, but the Resident denied them access for fear of a disturbance. At that time, Lugard was high commissioner for Northern Nigeria. This battle continued when Lugard assumed the role of governor of Nigeria. Making a concession to the fact that Ilorin was not part of the true north, he permitted the CMS in Ilorin only if the missionaries remained outside the town walls.[74] In Ilorin politics, then, one sees both the religious dimension and the ancestral city dimension operating at the same time. The hegemony established in the north and in Yorubaland both influenced subsequent politics in Ilorin.[75]

These vignettes of cultural divisions in Benin and northern Nigeria should allow us to specify more precisely the power and range of the model of hegemony. First, it should be emphasized that although hegemony involves the creation of a political market, such markets may have very different constituting principles. Thus, different strategies of indirect rule are possible, depending on the social structure of the masses and the perceptions of the elites. As we saw, indirect and direct rule are different hegemonic strategies of colonial control. From this, it follows that internal forms of hegemony, of the kinds that Gramsci wrote about, would have still different strategic implications.[76]

Second, politics can take place without the establishment of a hegemonic order. Sometimes its absence will result in a case like Benin, which has suffered from coups and countercoups, and the population subject to appeals on very different cultural dimensions. But absence of hegemony need not mean disorder. In the United States, it would be absurd to suggest that there has been the establishment of hegemony. One sees, for example, both ethnic and class politics existing side by side, each defusing the potential explosion of the other. Absence of hegemony in the US context seems to promote order. A preliminary hypothesis for future comparative assessment is that, in the absence of hegemony, rational choice theories are far more effective in explaining the political organization of culture.

CONCLUSION

This chapter has relied on a model of hegemonic control in order to make sense out of the nonpoliticization of the religious cleavage in Yoruba society. It demonstrated how an exogenous power, interested in creating order in a weak state, would be led to the compelling strategy of forming an alliance with elites that have high legitimacy in the society but declining resources to exert authority. The hegemon can then support the expansion of power and control by those elites but, through cooptation, control *them*. (In this sense, the policy is not "divide and rule," but "divide and recombine so that you can rule through a dominated but legitimate elite.") Taking this view, one sees the power of the reification of the primordial.

One also sees the importance of key historical periods. Unlike both social systems and rational choice theories, the model of hegemony assumes that hegemonic forging of political alignments occurs rarely, and is a function of historically peculiar circumstances. But once a hegemonic order is created, its consequences are long-lasting.

Hegemonic power, however, is not completely free to forge identities. The British strategy could not have been successful unless there was a real basis in the symbolic repertoire of the society for such a pattern of cleavage. In Yorubaland, the hegemonic rulers were successful in part because they reinfused with coercive resources political elites who were both poor and legitimate. Challenges to hegemonic power must then attempt a very difficult task—to delegitimate what their own society sees as obviously and eternally legitimate. The hegemonic state bought short-term control at low cost, and set long-term patterns of political cleavage by reifying traditional culture and getting that traditional culture spun into a web of significance that neither the hegemon nor the dominated society can easily escape.

My answer to non-relationship here:
I relc to political movements or
— no rel. auth & at either societal or
individual level.
— but why not get political mobilizah.
through vibrant rel. orgs.? Maybe that is present

8| Conclusion: Politics, Culture, and Hegemony

The systematic study of politics and culture is moribund. It merits revival. What is required is a careful elucidation of culture's two faces, and a suggestion of how both can be comprehended from a single theoretical vantage point. As we have seen, social systems theory and rational choice theory each focus on only one face of culture. The framework of hegemony provides a viewpoint from which both faces of culture can be carefully examined.

Toward the revival of the study of political culture, I shall show in the first section that there are no epistemological reasons for abjuring cultural variables to explain political outcomes, even if one is committed to the neopositivist tradition in the social sciences.[1] I shall then show, in the second section, how the model of hegemony can complement both social systems theory and rational choice theory to provide a better framework for constructing a theory relating politics to culture.

THEORIES OF CLASS AND CULTURE: NEOPOSITIVIST PERSPECTIVES

The "political culture" of a society can be thought of as a function of the "points of concern" embedded in the dominant cultural subsystem. Political elites in any society will act strategically and ideologically in the hope of defining and delimiting which strands of their society's culture should become dominant. Those who are successful in establishing a dominant cultural framework form a "hegemonic bloc." The dominant cultural subsystem, once chosen, spins political life into a "web of significance" which grasps elites and masses alike. Since the hegemonic bloc is more concerned with the efficiency of control than the secondary consequence of having altered the cultural framework for action, the new elites will themselves become (often unwilling) subjects of their own past cultural choices. In this way, cultural subsystems have an impact on the subsequent choices of both elites and masses. Consequently, social science needs to develop theories capable of isolating this power of culture to influence politics.

Theorists who have attempted to measure the impact of culture on society and polity have, however, faced considerable difficulties. This is especially true of those who adopt a neopositivist epistemology and therefore ask: How is it possible to be sensitive enough to the *particular* in order to understand the independent variable (the cultural subsystem) with sufficient clarity to satisfy the anthropological conscience while at the same time being sensitive enough to the *general* in order to formulate the variables in ways that can be applied in a comparative framework? If the independent variable is Christianity (or Islam), it is so broad that virtually no systematic propositions can be defended concerning its impact on society. Yet, if the independent variable is "Christianity (or Islam) as a practical religion of the converted in Yorubaland," how is it possible to invalidate theories of its impact? There will be as many variables as there are observations.

Here is where economic theories have an apparent advantage within the neopositivist tradition. To understand the role of the working class, one can define it so that it is identifiable in a multitude of research settings; there will therefore be far more observations than variables, making theory-testing possible. It is not some idea that "culture does not matter" that has brought research on political culture to a standstill. Rather, the systematic study of culture within the political science has been emasculated by the neopositivist tradition, which sets as a central methodological requirement that a theory must have general laws that can disconfirmed.

A second advantage of the economics paradigm is that its explanations are intimately intertwined with the interests and strategic calculations of actors.[2] Cultural dispositions to favor substantive over procedural debate, as we found in the Muslim Yoruba setting, can easily wash away if an aggrieved party is told he can easily regain his rightful possession by demonstrating to a court of law that his opponent secured that possession by illegal methods. And, as Geertz found, cultural dispositions to favor a model of authority based on a "theatre state" will wash away if the theatre state enacts policies that threaten the economic position of leading sectors of the society.[3] To the extent that political outcomes are largely a function of the real pressures people face in daily life, cultural theories focusing on values, or even points of concern, will be based on extremely weak independent variables.

The attractiveness of the rational choice approach is therefore understandable from the neopositivist perspective. By emphasizing the fact of sharing rather than the meaning of what is shared, rational choice theorists are able to formulate general laws that are subject to disconfirming evidence. Consider Abner Cohen's hypothesis that emigrant communities involved in long-distance trade in places where banking institutions are undeveloped will emphasize through ritual those characteristics that differentiate them from the host society.[4] This hypothesis is not only plausible but is capable of being upheld by supporting evidence or limited in its application by the presentation of disconfirming evidence. Much less capable of being disconfirmed is Geertz's proposition that the Balinese people become engrossed by cockfighting because fights between cocks remind them of their own potential for anarchic destructiveness, which is just below the surface in their extraordinarily calm society.[5]

I remain unconvinced, however, that economic theories are necessarily more powerful or more subject to empirical assessment than are cultural theories. The first challenge to theorists of culture is to embed their analysis more fully into the surrounding social and political realities. The cultural independent variable must be defined in a manner in which it relates to other social subsystems. In the study of language as a cultural subsystem, for example, the semantics of a particular language may be less relevant for a theory of political outcomes than its "pragmatics."[6] In the study of religion as a cultural subsystem, as was pointed out in chapter 2, the "practical religion of the converted" is more powerful for explaining political outcomes than "theological doctrine." The sociological embeddedness of cultural independent variables will make them more relevant to explain real world decisions than will a model of culture as pure values.

Second, theorists of culture and politics should recognize that economic approaches that attempt to find regularities in behavior by people from the "working class" or "landowners" have been less than successful. Good economic theories of political behavior have had to reduce the synchronic and diachronic scope of their independent variables. We now read of the interests of the "German wheat growers" or the "French petite bourgeoisie." Karl Marx's most scintillating political analysis rests on definitions of groups that can hardly be generalized beyond France. Certainly, his propositions could not be disconfirmed by finding a range of comparable cases.[7]

The intellectual challenge for political cultural research is to generate propositions about the cultural impact on political life that are as general as Marx's propositions in *Eighteenth Brumaire*. Consider the following matched propositions: Muslim Yorubas in the mosque environment see domination as legitimate when they respect the personal qualities of the leader, whereas Christian Yorubas in the church see domination as legitimate when they accept the procedures that brought the incumbent his role. These propositions have a cultural item as the independent variable and a political item as the dependent variable. They can be disconfirmed by future analysis of Yoruba religious and political life. My proposition concerning the hegemonic persistence of the ancestral city cleavage in Yorubaland is also subject to disconfirmation. If religious strife were to develop between Muslims and Christians in Yorubaland without being promoted by a strong and profoundly radical hegemonic elite, my argument in chapters 6 and 7 would be disconfirmed. These propositions can be broadened by examination of Islam and Christianity in other cultural milieus. They can be narrowed by further investigation of Christianity and Islam elsewhere in Yorubaland. The symbols embedded in cultural subsystems are as subject to social-scientific scrutiny as any other type of independent variable in the social sciences. Other examinations of the first face of culture will rarely lead to the evocative insights that Geertz has achieved. He is an artist. But even though eschewed by Geertz, there is nothing to hold back the development of a neopositivist examination of culture and politics.

The third challenge for theorists of culture is to hook their wagon to the newly reformulated theories of the state. Political science that was influenced by the behavioral revolution held "the state" to be a chimera, and merely a function of the aggregate political pressures coming autonomously from society.[8] A tide of scholarship, however, pounding away at the assumptions of the behavioralists, has rediscovered the state. Recent scholarship has begun to theorize in a comparative manner about the state's role in fashioning society.[9]

A good theory of political culture should be a constituent part of any theory of the state. Since any state must come to terms with the cultural commitments of the members of the society it attempts to govern, states can be compared on their overall stance in regard to culture. These stances generally transcend particular governments within a country; and therefore they are best conceived of as attributes of states. In this study, only one form of state manipulation of culture received extensive analysis—that of an external hegemon employing a strategy of indirect rule. Through the example of France's use of direct rule in Africa, I noted that external hegemons can employ other strategies, whereby different strands of culture become dominant. Furthermore I noted that strategies of *internal* elites seeking hegemony would necessarily be different, although in the context of this study, I could not elaborate on the differences between internal and external hegemony. Finally, I pointed out—using the republic of Benin as an example—that hegemony might not be established at all. In all these cases the actions of the state in attempting to pick out and support different strands of culture, and thereby seeking to make those strands the privileged loci of symbolic production—a form of cultural hegemony— have had important political consequences for the subsequent nature and style of collective political action. Any study of the impact of culture on politics that does not take into account privileged loci of symbolic production or the role of the state in channeling culture will therefore be beset with inconsistent or null findings.

In summary, the development of a theory of culture and politics that is consistent with a neopositivist epistemology will require the following methodological strictures: sociological embeddedness of cultural independent variables; the search for and testing of guarded generalizations based on these variables; and the specification of the role of the state in fashioning culture.

It is now possible more formally to combine elements in social systems and rational choice theories into a larger framework, which I have called the model of hegemony and culture.

Social Systems Theory and the First Face of Culture

Clifford Geertz, as I have pointed out throughout this study, self-consciously seeks to understand and interpret the first face of culture. His reliance on social systems theory led him to postulate a set of subsystems that together constitute a coherent social system. Social systems are not rigid. Subsystems have their own internal dynamics that influence the wider social system. Exogenous change puts pressures on different subsystems and ultimately the social system as well. Social systems are therefore adaptive; they accommodate change as subsystems mutually adjust their values so that there will be a homeostatic equilibrium in the society. To explain how the symbols of one subsystem impinge on the social relations in other subsystems within a larger social system constitutes the problematic of Geertz's book *The Interpretation of Cultures*.

To put the social systems framework to test—to see if it adequately conceptualizes the role of culture in society—I had to make certain adjustments to Geertz's conception of a social subsystem and its functions. I introduced the ideas of "points of concern" as more reflective of culture than mere values or preferences; of discordant subsystems rather than equilibrated ones; and a practical notion of the definition of a culture rather than a theoretical one. What I have attempted to demonstrate is that the symbolic structure of practical religion forms a dialectic, guiding the religious adherents not so much to a set of values as to certain "points of concern" that are worth worrying about. Cultural symbols, in large part due to their inherent ambiguity, cannot provide a unidirectional force on a society's values. Rather, a symbol system will provide a clue to what is worth fighting about and also to what is so commonsensical that attempts to change it seem pointless.

In the Muslim Yoruba context, for example, leadership of the community is clearly worth contesting; but it is obvious to all actors that standard procedures for determining the selection of new leaders are not of vital concern. Nothing in the practical religion of the Yoruba converts gives a signal to Muslims as to who should be their imam; nor could anything tell them exactly what qualities he should have. Within the Muslim tradition there are many conflicting values on these matters. However, there is a common "point of concern" as to whether any particular leader has the personal qualities to fulfill adequately the role of chief imam, no matter what the procedure is to appoint him. The symbolic structure of the practical religion cannot tell us who will win; it can tell us what is worth fighting about. Religions as cultural subsystems can provide their adherents with a diverse set of symbols that often give contradictory guides to action. At most, these sets of symbols will give an indication of what questions require an answer or what concerns cannot be ignored. This is somewhat less than Geertz's suggestion, quoted earlier, that religions provide a sense of "a general order of existence."

A related problem with Geertz's approach to religion is that he assumes, with Santayana, that the conception of the "really real" provided by one's religion "consists in its special and surprising message and in the bias which that revelation gives to life." And thus Geertz speaks of a "congruence" between "religious symbols" and "a particular style of life."[10] This vision is misleading. It misses the point that elites in all subsystems attempt to direct the flow of symbols. They have an interest in infusing other social subsystems with the symbolic content of their own, to make their subsystem the privileged locus of symbolic production in the society. Only privileged symbol systems will "color [people's] sense of the reasonable, the practical, the humane, and the moral . . . and in so doing sustain each [the cultural system and practical life] with the borrowed authority of the other."[11]

Because Geertz is wary of the power of disconfirmation, his interpretive findings cannot easily be delimited. Nonetheless, the material presented in chapters 3 and 4 does present anomalies to Geertz's formulations. In Yorubaland, despite the reality of socially distinct religious cultures, the symbolic structures of Islam and Christianity do not infuse the political subsystem. Consider the following: Yoruba Christians attach great importance to the procedure by which their vicar is chosen; they are prepared to submit themselves to the preaching of virtually any man who has earned the right to wear an Anglican pastor's robes. Yet, on a political question, my Christian respondents showed little concern for the procedural implications for the division of authority in secular Nigeria. The question of whether a governor has the right to limit the educational opportunities for children born in other states was decided by Yoruba Christians on substantive grounds—on whether the governor was making a prudent decision, not whether he had the right to decide. To make this point more strongly: in Nigerian political life Yoruba Christians and Muslims have both used procedural and constitutional arguments as a normal political tool. Recalling the battle for control over the central mosque in Ile-Ife (see chapter 3), it might be noted that both parties took their case to the courts, even though they were uncomfortable—qua Muslims—with procedural criteria for succession. The number of educated Yorubas (mostly Christians, who had a mission education and went on to London for professional training) who have become lawyers, and their success in Nigerian politics, attest to a popular and practical attachment by Yorubas to procedures.[12] So we find different roles of procedure and substance in the context of the world religions; similar roles for procedure and substance for Yorubas of both world religions in answers to formal questions and in practical life: this suggests the nonhegemonic position of the world religions in Yorubaland.

Lest this example be used to confirm the irrelevance of all cultural points of concern for political choice, it should be noted that elites from Yoruba "ancestral cities" have been able to retain a hegemonic position for symbol infusion in Yoruba society. Yoruba kings can make a claim that people who have been tilling local land for a few generations are really "strangers" to the town. This definition of the situation will hardly be questioned, even by the "strangers" themselves, who will counter the king by pointing out that strangers should have greater rights. Even after a century of living in the Modekeke ward of Ile-Ife, it would be astonishing for the descendants of the Oyo refugees that settled there to call themselves "ọmọ Ife" (sons of Ife town). Under the *Pax Britannica* and beyond, those people have been considered, and consider themselves, strangers. This point of concern— that ancestral city ties should be the point of view from which rights, privileges, and obligations should be debated—is a central framework in Yoruba politics. Ancestral city metaphors color Yoruba social reality. To understand how a social system operates it is therefore necessary to determine the arenas of symbolic production that have the power to infuse other subsystems and to restrict the relevance of symbolic structures embedded in potentially competing subsystems.

This example about ancestral city membership helps to make another qualification in social systems theory. Most previous theories of political culture assume that culture is "deeply rooted" in society and is therefore a stable point of reference amid a changing socioeconomic and political environment.[13] What this study has shown is that cultural subsystems are internally dynamic and politically embedded. In the early nineteenth century, ancestral city membership was fluid, especially among the vast number of refugees who lost their homes and farms in the civil war years. Slaves and even whole communities of refugees were symbolically incorporated into new cities. It took British colonial control to rigidify the ancestral city framework and to make a clear and almost unbridgeable distinction between natives and strangers. To speak, then, of an eternal Yoruba value upholding one's connection to an ancestral city is neither historically nor sociologically viable.[14]

Despite these many criticisms of social systems theory, I have found, with Geertz, that cultural subsystems do in fact create their own commonsensical visions of political reality and suggest for their members what political problems are worth fighting about. Thus culture is important for the creation of commonsense frameworks concerning political concepts even if it does not directly determine political values or is not an unchanging reality, or if it has restricted societal relevance. This insight must not be lost in the search for an alternate theory.

Rational Choice Theory and the Second Face of Culture

Abner Cohen's rational choice theory offers a powerful explanation for the role of culture in society, but, as we shall see, it disregards the single viable insight in social systems theory. For Cohen, culture is significant because it provides a set of markers that a large number of people share. That people eat the same food, speak the same language, worship the same god, have similar physical features, and appreciate the same art creates among them a sense of trust and permits easy communication. This trust and ease of communication becomes a resource for ambitious people to exploit. Traders, for instance, will emphasize their cultural sharing when they seek to borrow money from "kinsmen" in a strange city. When banking systems cannot give reliable credit ratings, the social fact of cultural sharing enables merchants to establish their credit with strangers who are members of the same cultural institution.[15] Political entrepreneurs, seeking power in a complex society, will find that their own cultural repertoires constitute a powerful mobilizing resource. The more they can demonstrate the sharing of culture with potential supporters, the more they can generate political trust. Since cultural sharing is such an obvious resource, it is bound to be exploited by many political entrepreneurs. The secondary consequence of the employment of cultural symbols in politics is the reification of culture in the society. Cultural stratification as a primary dividing point in politics is, then, the macrosociological outcome of rationally pursued strategies of political entrepreneurs and their followers.

To be sure, the rational choice perspective is limited in that it cannot address the first face of culture. The insight that culture is a powerful resource for political entrepreneurs tells us nothing about the substantive implications of cultural mobilization. From Cohen's point of view, Shi'ite Iranians and Baptist Americans would, given the same market conditions, respond in similar ways. While this view holds some truth—I suppose, all other things being equal, both would want to sell dear and buy cheap—it disregards too much about political life. It ignores the fact that all people have multifaceted goals and that these goals are sometimes in conflict. People therefore develop implicit preference functions, which differ. A student of the first face of culture would assume that dominant cultural symbols provide guidance concerning which problems demand remedy. In this sense it is possible to hypothesize group preference functions.

Rational choice theorists can get some grip on group preference functions. When they assume rational action and subsequently observe actual behavior, they are able to discern what goals are being pursued. Although this is an excellent strategy, how can the existence of those preferences then be confirmed theoretically? Since rational choice theorists also emphasize the high costs of information, it is entirely possible that people act in a certain way—for instance, go to war when they are inadequately prepared—not because they have a preference for losing but because they did not know about their own lack of preparation.

What is required is an independent source of data about the relation of cultural symbols to group preferences. The data must be collected in a way Geertz's work has exemplified and in which I have tried to emulate in chapter 3: by the direct study of the symbol systems themselves. Only then will it be possible to discern whether groups are acting rationally, irrationally, or under severe information restrictions. Rational choice theory cannot by itself adequately adduce the differential preference functions across cultures.

Rational choice theorists feel on firmer ground when they address culture's second face: the fact that the sharing of cultural characteristics provides a basis for political organization. Despite the plausibility of their view that people manipulate their cultural identities in order to pursue wealth and power, the rational choice perspective has been shown to have two major inadequacies. First, it is a theory of marginal decisions. It can be very powerful only in analyzing decisions about identity change within a limited range of possibilities. Granting the power of rational choice theory to address marginal decisions of individuals investing in their political identity, it is crucial to point out that not all politics concerns marginal decisions. We want to know why the range of calculated choices is far more restricted than the range of possible choices. In Yorubaland, there is an objective basis for a religious cleavage to become politicized. Yet virtually no Yorubas have responded to political entrepreneurs seeking to mobilize them on this basis. To make one's "tribal" identity subordinate to one's "religious" identity in Yorubaland is not a marginal decision. It might not even be a rational decision. Yet it is not a part of the calculus of rational actors in the Yoruba political environment. Why not? Here, rational choice theorists cannot provide a compelling answer.

Their best answer is to emphasize the "transition costs" moving from one political identity to another, and to point out that most people are "risk-averse" and do not want to induce greater uncertainty by upsetting the political framework in which they make their marginal decisions.[16] This riposte, however, creates an inconsistency in the rational choice argument. Since the argument was designed to explain the fluidity of cultural identities in order to counter the primordialists, rational choice theorists have emphasized the ease with which people can reinterpret their identities.[17] The theory then finds itself able to explain any outcome by invoking contradictory assumptions. If Yorubas from Owu can become Egbas, as many did when they settled in Abeokuta as refugees, identities must therefore be fluid. If *Yoruba* Muslims reject the opportunity to see themselves as Yoruba *Muslims*, transaction costs must therefore be high. If a theory is able to explain an outcome and its opposite equally well, another theory is needed to explain which outcome is more probable. To put it another way: we need a theory to tell us that Yoruba *Owus* becoming Yoruba *Egbas* is a marginal decision but *Yoruba* Muslims becoming Yoruba *Muslims* is a structural change. Here the rational choice perspective is inadequate to the task.

The second problem with the rational choice perspective in its attempt to address the second face of culture is that it tends to ignore the interests of the state to reorganize identities. While it is true that Ijebu Yorubas found it productive to act politically as "Ijebus," it is equally true and perhaps more important that a strategy of political control by a colonial elite found it very useful to encourage Ijebus to do so. Imperial elites faced a major problem of creating political quiescence in colonial territories. Powerless but legitimate indigenous elites were a potential resource for the imperial power: infusing these elites with the capacity for domination so that order could be maintained became a compelling strategy.

The secondary consequence of such a strategy was the reestablishment of the cultural groups in which these indigenous elites had been legitimate leaders. Hegemonic powers have the resources to ossify a pattern of social cleavages, and to infuse the society with the belief that these cleavages are more real than other cultural cleavages. They are thus able to create barriers to identity exploration. There need be no free market in identities.

The Model of Hegemony and Culture

The model of hegemony and culture developed in this study can now be elaborated more fully. It is built on the revisions of social systems theory and rational choice theory discussed above, as well as the specifications of hegemony discussed in chapters 4 and 5. In so doing, it provides a model that resolves the Janus-faced image of culture and politics.

1. Cultural subsystems have embedded in them commonsensical notions about practical life and political relationships. This will be most apparent at the level of agenda setting, as cultural subsystems suggest to their members what points of concern are worth addressing. An individual whose identity is in part defined by a cultural subsystem will, when acting as a member of that subsystem, see the special points of concern embedded in the subsystem as obviously important. My study has shown that Christian and Muslim subcultures in Ile-Ife are real, and that within their domains they pose very different points of concern about political relationships and action. This is a central insight from the Geertzian perspective and stands as a challenge to any rational choice model of politics and

culture. It is impossible to develop a theory of calculation unless one knows what it is that is worth fighting for.

2. Culture should not be thought of as having isolated symbol systems. Thus, the points of concern for adherents of a religion, the cultural subsystem that received attention in this book, cannot be comprehended only from an examination of the religion's founding doctrines. One must examine the "practical religion" of the adherents, understood in terms of the founding doctrines in dynamic interaction with the social conditions under which the religion was introduced to the society under study. Nothing in the New Testament would lead us to hypothesize that a major impact of Christianity in Yorubaland was to legitimate strangers as authorities if they met proper procedural criteria. A practical understanding of Christianity in Yorubaland would point to the model of evangelization provided by Paul's letters and the exigencies of missionary life in nineteenth-century Africa. This notion of practical culture is an important amendment to social systems theory since it embeds culture sociologically yet still seeks to see the independent impact of culture on wider society.

3. All societies are multicultural, and their various cultural subsystems are not necessarily in homeostatic equilibrium or congruent with each other. Models of authority coming from the "ancestral city" framework in Yorubaland are quite different from models of authority in either the Christian or Muslim framework. Although ancestral city as a cultural subsystem has not received direct attention in this volume, its gerontocratic values and its assignation of particular lineages as noble ones with the right to provide incumbents for kingship have few parallels with the world religions. Yet Yoruba society can persist, and has persisted, despite cultural subsystems with incongruent models of authority. Where hegemony has been established, nonprivileged cultural subsystems do not necessarily threaten the political order. They are seen as obviously unrelated to political conflict. Those individuals who rely on a nonprivileged subsystem to inform their political commitments are viewed as misdirected or fanatic. This point directly challenges one of the major premises of social systems theory, which has seen social stability to result from the natural equilibration of the various social subsystems.

4. Under certain conditions the political relationships that are commonsensical within a single cultural subsystem will have a broader relevance and will provide a model for political action in the wider society. When such conditions are met, that cultural subsystem can be conceived of as hegemonic and as providing the privileged locus of symbolic production in the society. There are a number of ways in which certain cultural subsystems become privileged loci in society. Political foundings appear to enshrine certain cultural sybsystems as the privileged locus of symbolic production, and external hegemony in the context of indirect rule is one

form of political founding. In such a situation, the hegemon will seek out legitimate cultural elites who have only limited power and coopt them as allies to form a historic bloc. If an alliance is made, the cultural subsystem of one set of local elites will be reinforced, and its commonsensical notions of political relationships will infuse the political arena. Other strategies of hegemony are possible, though they have not been fully articulated in the context of this case study. The argument here—because it focuses on the use of state power to create a cultural framework in a society—goes beyond social systems theory (which sees the state as merely a subsystem in equilibrium with other subsystems) and beyond rational choice theory (which can postulate the interests of a ruling elite but can get no handle on the boundaries beyond which calculation is abjured).

5. Political divisions within a society will be a function of the conflicts within the framework of the privileged cultural subsystem. If "tribal" membership is hegemonic, political organizations will recruit on the basis of tribe; if "religious" membership is hegemonic, political organizations will recruit on the basis of religious adherence. Members of the society will see these cultural divisions as the natural and obvious ones for collective political action. This is not to postulate that non-elites suffer from "false consciousness"; it should be made clear that the model of hegemony need not predict political action within a cultural framework if there are no payoffs for organizing along those lines. People will act collectively along the preferred framework if there are benefits to be accrued for so doing.

6. With the constraints set by hegemons, rational choice analysis is a powerful tool for understanding the politics of culture. First, it can analyze the choices of elites in periods of political founding, to see which lines of cleavage are most advantageously exploited. The British choice to establish "ancestral city" in Yorubaland but "religion" in northern Nigeria is tractable from a rational choice perspective. Second, within any chosen cultural framework, it is useful to conceive of people acting from a rational choice perspective.[18] Once the British reified the idea of the Yoruba ancestral city, it became rational for kings of small towns to use (or fabricate) ancient "texts" to demonstrate their high position in the ancestral city framework. Third, as was hypothesized at the conclusion of chapter 7, in situations of "incomplete hegemony," where no line of cultural cleavage is dominant, the rational choice perspective should be extremely powerful in understanding the shifting cultural bases of political organization.

7. Nonprivileged cultural subsystems are capable, given changed power relations, of infusing recombined segments of a population. Any postulation of a complex social system involves, then, the postulation of a variety of "counterhegemonies." This is the central point of Gramsci's analysis of hegemony, with his postulation of a "contradictory conscious-

ness." It remains a challenge to social systems theory in that it identifies the ideological bases of potential political disequilibrium; and it remains a challenge to rational choice theory in that it differentiates strategies of collective political action theoretically between those coming from within the hegemonic framework and those coming from outside that framework.

SUMMARY

In chapter 1, hegemony was defined as *the political forging—whether through coercion or elite bargaining—and institutionalization of a pattern of group activity in a state and the concurrent idealization of that schema into a dominant symbolic framework that reigns as common sense.* Throughout this book, this definition has been elucidated. We have seen how ancestral city politics, and not world religion, works as a "pattern of group activity" and serves as the "dominant symbolic framework" in Yorubaland. Thus political calculations based on ancestral city attachments are "common-sensical" in the Yoruba context while calculations based on religious adherence are considered fanatic, irrelevant, or out of the realm of calculation. Meanwhile, cultural subsystems such as ancestral city or religion help define preference functions or points of concern to those whose identity is connected with the subsystem. We have seen how the British colonial administration was able to "forge," through "coercion" and "elite bargaining" (cooptation of ancestral city kings), and to "institutionalize" the ancestral city framework in Yorubaland. This single case has illustrated how hegemony can work.

More specifically, this book has concentrated on a case where the structure of externally imposed hegemony became the decisive factor concerning the format of the politicization of culture. Hegemonic power created in Yorubaland a privileged categorization of identity. The chosen categorization, that of "ancestral city," itself provided to Yorubas a symbolic repertoire concerning the nature of political relations, and this repertoire infused the wider social system. Another possible categorization of identity—that by identification with a world religion—has remained politically irrelevant in Yorubaland. But in the practical religions of Christianity and Islam one can see symbolic structures supporting very different ideologies of commonsensical political relations. Not only were the practical religions of Islam and Christianity different from each other; they also differed from the world view of the "ancestral city" categorization. Therefore, within the Yoruba social system, there exist noncongruent and nonpreferred (by the hegemonic order) cultural subsystems that hold within themselves the sources for counterhegemony. Hegemony can create a dominant subsystem; it cannot create a congruent and harmonious social system. Inherent in all hegemonic structures, then, is the possibility for nonmarginal affronts to the commonsensical order.

- critical + empirical aspects of
  book are very good
- the constructive theory, however, is
  weak -- wavers between tautology
  + ad hoc path dependency (i.e. the
  Brits did it).

- the best of aspect of book is its
  posing of the question: when are
  rul. identities mobilized + when
  not?

Appendix: Research Methodology

From a reading of Yoruba history, students of the first face of culture can raise some important questions about cultural preferences and values. They are likely to inquire rather carefully about the symbol of Ile-Ife as the religious womb to which all Yorubas trace their origins. Does the model of ancestral cities, each founded by one of Oduduwa's offspring, provide a commonsense framework for authority relations in all Yoruba cities? What does the symbol of Oduduwa mean, and how does it affect the day-to-day life of a modern Yoruba trader in Ijebu-Ode, a city far from Ile-Ife? If Christianity and Islam brought new symbols into Yoruba social life, have these symbols yielded any changes in the way Yorubas talk about authority or attempt to legitimate it? To address questions of this sort, the student of culture must interpret social life, attempting to sort out preferences and values from actual behavior. In Geertz's terms, "cultural analysis [becomes] guessing at meanings, assessing the guesses, and drawing explanatory conclusions from the better guesses."[1] From this enterprise, we should get a better appreciation of how cultural symbols shape social and political preferences.

Meanwhile, students seeking a better appreciation of culture's second face can raise some very different questions. How did the imperial rulers of Oyo so successfully exploit the Oduduwa myth in order to get political compliance from their subject cities? Why were the Ibadan political elites unable totally to discredit the defunct kings who lost their power base amid the nineteenth-century civil wars? With what resources did these kings maintain their authority vis-à-vis the new Christian and Muslim elites in the early twentieth century? To answer questions of this sort, anthropologists like Cohen seek to understand how cultural symbols are "manipulated" by elites in order to garner or sustain power. This task requires not symbolic interpretations of meaning but the systematic enumeration of political resources (of which symbolic repertoires constitute one of many) available to different actors.

My attempt to construct a viewpoint from which both faces of culture could be adequately examined meant engaging in two methodological enterprises that are often held to be distinct. I sought from my informants an understanding of what goals were worth pursuing and what they really wanted. But I also pressed them on their political strategies, assuming they wanted power and wealth. To get reliable answers to both sorts of inquiry required some finesse in the field. Not only was I reconciling two different methodological approaches in a single study, but I was also identifying myself as a participant in two different religious subcommunities in the same town. It is no wonder I was forced into some difficult dilemmas. Because my findings present a challenge to both the "social systems" and the "rational choice" perspectives, my research methodology will undoubtedly be put under question. It is therefore prudent for me to explain how I collected data, and how I was viewed by those I was attempting to study.

WHY NIGERIA? WHY YORUBALAND?

Political science lacks a compelling theory of the impact of cultural change on politics. In an earlier attempt to develop such a theory, I examined the impact of language change in Somalia on political thought and action. Amid that research, I was unable to differentiate the impact of the Arabic language from the impact of the Muslim religion on Somali life. Since religiosity seemed to correlate well with knowledge of the Arabic language, it was methodologically difficult to factor out the different sorts of impact religion and language might have on Somali society. Furthermore, messages from my informants seemed inherently contradictory. Somali informants would tell me that Islam forms the fundamental basis for all their values; yet they would confide to me that they could not understand very many words in the Qur'an, and that the *hadith* (the traditions of the prophet) provided little guidance for them. Religion seemed to matter both too much and too little.

My research in Somalia nonetheless provided confirmation of a fundamental tenet of Geertz's social systems theory. Indeed, a single cultural system (the Somali language) influenced behavior in the wider social system. I was most anxious to see if those findings might be generalized for another "cultural system," such as religion.[2] Intrigued yet bothered by the contradictory evidence I had heard concerning religion, and impressed by the popular conception that religious values are often determinative of political action, I decided to examine religious change in Africa so that I could better isolate its impact. Such a study would provide a better understanding of the symbolic interpenetration of social subsystems.

Field research in Somalia led me to raise the question of the independent impact of religious change on politics; but further field research in Somalia would not have allowed me to address that question systematically. How is one to measure the impact of Islam on a society where everyone is a Muslim? Everyone there also speaks Somali. Nearly everyone shares a nomadic heritage. Nearly every Somali has been exposed to the same poetic tradition. Any common orientation toward action could be attributed to the Somalis' poetic or nomadic or linguistic traditions rather than their religious tradition. I needed to find a research site where I could better isolate the religious variable. Ideally, I wanted a society with a population which differed according to religion but whose population was similar on other social, economic, and cultural variables.

I wanted, then, to do a study which overcame the major methodological problem in Max Weber's seminal study of the differential economic impact of Protestantism and Catholicism. In *The Protestant Ethic and the Spirit of Capitalism*, Weber attempted to demonstrate that a specific style of economic behavior—the capitalist spirit—was (inadvertently) induced by Protestant teachings and doctrines. But without demonstrating that there were no significant differences between those who left the Catholic church (to become Protestants) and those who stayed, Weber and his followers could not answer one objection that was raised to their thesis: namely, that the Europeans who already had an interest in breaking the bonds of the precapitalist spirit might well have left the church precisely for that purpose. In other words, the economic interests of certain groups could be seen as inducing the development of the protestant ethic. Without a better controlled study, Weber's line of causation could be turned the other way.[3]

Nigeria, being evenly split between Muslims and Christians, would at first glance appear attractive as a site for replicating Weber's tests. But to use Nigeria as a unit of analysis would subject one to the same criticisms leveled at Weber's study. In Nigeria, the dominant centers of Islam are in the northern states, which have had centuries of direct contact with the Islamic world, a history of Islamic state structures antedating British colonial rule, and a memory of a revivalist jihad in the early nineteenth century which unified a large area under orthodox Islamic doctrine. The dominant centers of Christianity are in the southern states and fringe areas of the north. Although these areas had sporadic contact with the Christian world for centuries, it was not until the late nineteenth century that Christian communities took root. Here, mission schools brought Western education, and capitalist entrepreneurs encouraged the people to plant cash crops and to become increasingly associated with the world capitalist economy.

In attempting to discern the differential impact of Christianity and Islam on Nigeria, then, how could one control for the differences in nationality, or in economy, or in the number of generations exposed to a world religion, or in the motivations for conversion, or in ecology—all of which are different in Muslim and Christian strongholds? While some overall differences between Islamic and Christian communities in Nigeria could be catalogued, it would not be reasonable to attribute any of those differences to the specific impact of religion.

Between Nigeria's coastal forest and inland desert, however, both Christian and Muslim evangelists sought converts—with relatively equal success—in the nineteenth century. From this vast savannah area in Nigeria (and in other countries on the Guinea coast) it is indeed possible to isolate the religious impact on social and political life. I chose to focus my research on Yorubaland because its history has been brilliantly documented. Not only do scholars have the incomparable *History of the Yorubas* by Samuel Johnson at their disposal, a manuscript that was lost twice and then painstakingly rewritten from notes by the author's brother; but they also have the work of a generation of historians, edcuated at the University of Ibadan, that has followed in the Johnson tradition to make the historiography of the Yoruba perhaps the richest in sub-Saharan Africa. High-quality historiography is the secret weapon of good social science.

The historical record of Yorubaland makes it a useful case—a crucial experiment—to develop a theory of the impact of religious change in particular on society and polity. Christianity and Islam made great strides in Yorubaland at about the same time, were attractive to similar social groups, and attained relatively similar levels of success. Since a single nationality now includes adherents to each of the world religions, one can compare the two subcultures—Muslim Yorubas and Christian Yorubas—without the "noise" of nationality differences interfering. My initial goal—to show how cultural meanings translate into political and economic behavior, and to develop a theory of the first face of culture—could be fulfilled through a study of Yoruba converts.

WHY THE COMPARATIVE METHOD?

Still the comparative method itself must be justified. Its disadvantages are obvious: studying two religious limits one's *depth* of exploration so that one's judgments about their impacts are less sound than if one concentrated attention on a single religion. (Max Weber, in self-deprecating jest, quotes Goethe: "dilettantes compare");[4] studying only two religions in a single society doesn't give one the *breadth* of data necessary to isolate variables statistically, as would be possible if I had studied the impact of the two religions on a number of societies.

The comparative method is most useful when a small number of cases share a great number of key attributes. When similarities abound and differences are subtle, it is possible to isolate those subtle differences in order to observe their impact on society.[5] Should one compare the effects of colonialism and desertification on Africa, one would gain nothing from the comparative method. These two forces, one political the other climatic, are so different that it is impossible to learn about one by sorting out the effects of the other.

Perhaps the most persistent line of criticism I received from scholars who have worked in African studies is that Christianity and Islam, although both thought of as "religions," are so different that comparing them can only give false insight. Christianity and Islam, these critics would contend, may not be as different as colonialism and desertification but are different enough to vitiate the possibilities of controlled comparison.

Since the bulk of my analysis concerned the differences between these two religions, I should point out the broad similarities between them to justify my use of the comparative method. Both Christianity and Islam are "world religions" in that they have gathered "multitudes of confessors" from a variety of culture zones to join their ranks.[6] The idea that the individual stands alone before God and must make a confession of faith to God characterizes a world religion ideologically; the fact that evangelists of these religions see the whole world as their stage of operation in the search for converts characterizes a world religion organizationally. Both

Christian and Muslim religious virtuosos proselytized in Yorubaland to induce Yorubas to make confessions of faith to a new God.

This new God, in both religions, makes judgments on the moral qualities of the convert's life. This was clearly understood by the religious elders I interviewed. Among them, 62 percent of the Christians and 83 percent of the Muslims, asked what would happen if they violated some religious injunction, answered that "God will judge." That this is new to Yoruba modes of thought is suggested by J. S. Mbiti, who argues that in African philosophy there is no clear theory of the future. While there are myths about the past, there are no myths about the "end of the world, since time has no end. African peoples expect human history to continue forever."[7] Islam and Christianity both infused into Yoruba society an ideology of the future and a theory of the consequences of sin.

From the point of view of the potential converts, Christianity and Islam had yet another ideological similarity. Due to their commitment to find converts everywhere, the evangelists of both religions did not try to restrict entry into the religious shrines. While the Yoruba traditional religion involved many secret ceremonies and private shrines, the world religions welcomed strangers as well as members. Unlike the middle-of-the-night traditional ceremonies, orthodox Christian and Muslim ceremonies were primarily midday affairs. Regular daily and weekly services were known to all.[8]

While most people would grant those similarities, many critics have argued that Christianity was a real threat to African society whereas Islam melded with local culture. It is widely believed that Christianity in Africa was a conflictual social force while Islam was more accommodative, more "African." One historian, concerned with Islam's successes in East Africa, writes: "Most obviously, Islam was here as elsewhere more easily assimilated than Christianity because of its inherent attributes." He quotes the great Islamic scholar von Grunebaum to the effect that "the minimum demands of Muslim theology" are much lower than in Christianity, which has "greatly facilitated the transcultural effectiveness of the Muslim mission."[9]

Among the Christians in Ile-Ife, where I did my field research, that myth lives despite all evidence to the contrary. The vicar of the church I attended emphasized to me how few were the demands on the converts in the Muslim mission: "All you have to do is learn one prayer and get washed and you're a Muslim."[10] One leading church member emphasized the same theme moments after introducing me to his third wife!

In fact, the demands made by Muslims on the new converts were substantial, comparable to demands on converts by the Christian mission. Studies of the Christian mission are filled with material on Christian opposition to polygyny and to slavery, whereas, the different strategic injunctions of Muslim evangelists are not mentioned. In Yorubaland, Muslims made selective assaults on Yoruba customs. They detested Yoruba burial rituals, sought to limit the use of facial markings, restricted the Yoruba diet by proscribing pork and alcohol, opposed the secret societies (*ogboni*), and still oppose ostentation in dress and general expenditure for celebrations of family milestones. They even tried to decrease the effectiveness of the lineage as a social unit.[11] Muslim evangelists were often no less kind to Yoruba traditional religion. Some called the Yoruba gods "helpless effigies," and ceremonies honoring Egungun and Ṣango were scorned. Muslims fought against traditional sacrifices, and imams often found themselves in professional conflict with traditional priests.[12]

Meanwhile, the Christians had to make at least as many concessions to local culture as the Muslims did, or as St. Paul had done in an earlier time. Very few Victorian Englishman actually served abroad. The CMS had great trouble recruiting, funding, and keeping alive its missionaries. Malaria made it impossible to keep regular personnel in many posts. And the political situation inland was no help. Rebellions against foreigners such as the one in Abeokuta in 1867 consigned missionaries to the coast. The real burden of evangelical work, for Christians as well as Muslims, fell on local personnel.[13]

These personnel were able to put the Christian message in the local idiom. Whereas English Protestants had long ago abjured magic, the head of the CMS hierarchy in the Ile-Ife area in the early century wrote in his diaries about using his magic lantern to attract converts in each town he visited. If the local people committed themselves to gods based on their reputed magical powers, then it was important for Christian missionaries to demonstrate their hold over magic. In the church hymnal, too, the local idiom was exploited by the missionaries. In one hymn, the line "Ṣango [God of thunder] could not save a rat" is repeated. And, part of the charm of Christianity in Ile-Ife, as we saw in chapter 3, was the local fame garnered by the Reverend Adejumo, who was not only a traditional healer but a reputed polygynist as well. It can hardly be held that Christians rigidly confronted all Yoruba customs.[14]

Even the Catholics had to reinterpret their theology to make it comprehensible to foreigners. One Catholic priest in Ibadan told me that the Yoruba concept of many divinities in a religion with a High God is very similar to the Christian concept of the Trinity, and is thus consonant with Yoruba values. The result is that Christianity, not wholly unlike Islam, was quietly assimilated into the local tradition. In Dr. B. Hallen's interviews with Yoruba *oniṣegun* (indigenous healers),—many of the answers contained references to Jesus. Hallen urged his informants to talk about matters before the coming of Christianity, but few did, since they saw Christianity as a link in the chain of their own tradition.[15] The historical data allow us to conclude that Christian and Muslim evangelists both made limited thrusts at the Yoruba tradition: the tradition was able to incorporate the new gods, most of the evangelists were a part of the tradition, and their resources were limited.

To a considerable extent, then, Islam and Christianity looked very similar to potential converts in early twentieth-century Yorubaland. Conversion to either religion was perceived as a similar sort of personal investment opportunity. CMS missionaries in southern Nigeria were invited by local kings to fight their own battles, just as Afonja invited a Fulani Muslim to challenge Oyo's supremacy. The anti traditional religious paraphernalia that accompanied these missionaries were seen by the kings as a small price to pay.[16]

While the kings were investing in their continued power, ordinary individuals were making investments in their own identities. Most converts to both religions reported to me that they saw a world religion as a progressive, powerful, and civilized force that appeared to be riding the wave of the future. Muslims as well as Christians were impressed by how much more modern the education, the prayers, and the medicine appeared in the Christian and Muslim communities. In both religions, converts were making an investment in their future.[17]

I asked my sample of Christian and Muslim elders what changes their religion had brought to Yorubaland. There were some differences. Christians associated their religion with modern education; Muslims associated theirs with cleanliness, peace, moral actions, and community. But despite these differences, in this open-ended question 45 percent of the Christians and 37 percent of the Muslims mentioned "civilization," and 54 percent of the Christians and 43 percent of the Muslims mentioned the "end of bad customs." "Civilization" suggested to these people liberation from local control and ever new opportunities for wealth and health. It was for this civilization that most Yorubas converted to both world religions.[18]

To be sure, there were major differences in the social milieus in which the two religions appeared in Yorubaland. For example, Peel has found that a higher percentage of Muslims converted as migrants; Christians were more effective in recruiting people who were never refugees. My data support Peel. When I inquired about the conditions under which my respondents' first relative converted to his world religion, 32.4 percent of the Muslims but only 3.1 percent of the Christians mentioned that the convert was then living outside his ancestral city.[19] Despite this difference, and others, there were sufficient similarities between Islam and Christianity as they attracted new converts in Yorubaland to allow a productive comparison of the two religions and their impacts.

BEHOLDING CULTURE'S SECOND FACE

If Yorubaland provided a reasonable controlled "laboratory" to examine the differential impact of two world religions on a single nationality, preliminary fieldwork in a number of cities in Yorubaland compelled me to examine culture's second face. From the point of view of an outsider whose expectations concerning social life derive from the European experience, the most striking aspect of religious differentiation in Yorubaland was its "unnatural" toleration. I met countless Yorubas who spent inordinate hours in church or mosque affairs and a high percentage of their disposable income contributing to church or mosque. Yet these same people would not think of voting on the basis of their religion, or organizing a political party or a political protest movement to further the interests of their religious community. On Sundays, in every Yoruba town I visited, churches would attract "standing room only" crowds; on Friday afternoons, the march to a town's central mosque had an aura of a Chaucerian pilgrimage. Yet, however zealous these religions are in their attempts to win the full allegiance of their members, Yoruba adherents found it virtually impossible to see Yoruba members of the other world religion as adversaries. I asked myself why adherence to the two world religions did not provide opportunities for new forms of political mobilization. Any answer to my questions about the cultural impact of religion on Yoruba political values would be inadequate if it did not also help answer the question of why religion had not become politicized in Yorubaland.

The demands of controlled comparison brought me to Yorubaland. In Yorubaland it was possible to isolate religious change in order to assess its impact on the social and political systems. But once my research began, the issue of the sources of religious toleration presented itself as requiring explanation. These problematics were clearly interrelated, and I now see them as addressing the two faces of political culture.

WHY ILE-IFE?

Ile-Ife provided a particularly good research site to examine the two faces of political culture. First, the percentages of Christians and Muslims, while not exactly equal, are comparable. Ile-Ife is somewhat west of the main nineteenth-century European trading route amid the civil war years, and therefore did not become a Christian stronghold. Being somewhat east of Ibadan, and less welcoming of Oyo refugees, it did not become a Muslim stronghold either. In the most recent and comprehensive survey, conducted by the Oyo State Statistical Department, Christians and Muslims are shown to constitute a 58–42 ratio in Ife.[20]

Not Ife proper, but Modakeke ward, an Oyo refugee center, provided the fertile soil for the early Christian and Muslim communities in Ile-Ife. Both the Christians and Muslims had viable operations going in Modakeke by the end of the nineteenth century. In the early twentieth century, the Reverend Kayode for the Christians and Kaseem Adeosun for the Muslims, both of whom were Ife men (ọmọ Ife), used their congregations in Modakeke as springboards for diving into Ile-Ife's center.[21] Despite Modakeke's important historical role, I did not engage in field research there. I concentrated on the people who consider themselves ọmọ Ife (i.e. having Ile-Ife as their ancestral cities). I did this because Yorubas who come from the eastern cities are often associated with Christianity; those who come from Oyo (like the Modakeke people) are more likely to be associated with Islam. People who are ọmọ Ife have neither association among other Yorubas. Religion is divorced from identification with one's ancestral city. In Ife proper, where religion cross-cuts ancestral city in popular consciousness as well as in statistical tables, the examination of culture's second face—when I ask why my respondents organized collective political action in terms of ancestral city rather than religion—can be done with greater clarity.

Viable Christian and Muslim subcultures among people of the same ancestral city; Christianity and Islam both developing at about the same time and attracting adherents for the same apparent reasons; and an "unnatural" history of religious amity: Ile-Ife was a microcosm of the existential situation in Yorubaland and thus a desirable research site for my purposes. As I walked through the town for the first time and saw the central mosque and an imposing Angelican church on two sides of the king's palace, I was satisfied that the two world religions could be productively compared in Ile-Ife.

WHY ONLY ONE CHURCH? WHY ONLY THE CENTRAL MOSQUE?

The Christian community in Ile-Ife is by no means unified. Among missionary-created establishments. Catholics, Baptists, Methodists, and Seventh Day Adventists compete with the Anglicans. And, as mentioned, the growing and dynamic religious establishments in Ile-Ife and in Yorubaland are the indigenously organized Aladura churches. Why concentrate on the Anglicans, and on only one of the five Anglican churches in Ife town, not to mention the plethora of Anglican establishments in Ife Division?

I chose the Anglican church because it is most closely identified with the British colonial experience. More than any other Christian denomination, the Anglicans defined Christianity in Yorubaland. In Ife, Anglicans account for 36 percent of the Christian population. Anglicanism is accurately described by Parratt as "fashionable" and as having considerable influence.[22] While other Christian denominations have had flurries of influence in Yorubaland, Anglicanism provided the standard and most influential missionary church in Yorubaland.

To concentrate attention on the Anglicans instead of the Aladuras also required a critical choice. But, for my research purposes, the aladuras represented a very important spin-off from missionary Christianity rather than an organization which required a more central focus. The original aladura converts, as Peel so carefully demonstrates, were the urban clerks, brought up in missionary churches, who then migrated away from their home cities.[23] The Aladura churches moved Christianity away from some of the Victorian values with which it came to Africa. The Christianity that introduced itself in the nineteenth century is therefore better understood through an examination of the impact of missionary Christianity—although the fact that missionary Christianity spawned independent churches is crucial to an overall understanding of that religion in Africa.

A similar issue is raised in regard to the choice of studying only the central mosque of Ile-Ife. Although virtually all Muslims in Yorubaland are Sunnis following the Malaki school of law, there are a number of Sufi orders. There is also a splinter movement called the Ahmadiyyas. Like the Aladuras in Christianity, the Ahmadiyya movement among the Muslims represented to a certain extent a dialectical response to conventional Islam. The Ahmadiyyas, impressed by the success of the Christians, attempted to use proselytizing methods similar to the Church Missionary Society. Other doctrines and practices were also introduced, so that the Saudis excluded the Ahmadiyyas from participation in the pilgrimage to

Mecca. Like the Aladuras, the Ahmadiyya mosques were seen as important internal responses to Islam, but were not examined directly.

For purposes of controlled comparison, one unfortunate element in my choice of church and mosque was the fact that members of St. Paul's Anglican Church were far better off economically than members of Enuwa Mosque. I chose these two institutions in large part because they were, in local context, unexceptional. Christians, as we have seen in chapter 6, have done better economically than have Muslims in Yorubaland. So it is possible that the differences in "practical religion of the converted," adduced in chapter 3, were the result of economic rather than cultural forces. I doubt that this is the case, since the differences are so closely connected with differences at the level of "practical religion" and seem to have no obvious economic basis. But I cannot rule out an economic reinterpretation of those data.

I was reasonably certain, in light of my visits to churches and mosques in Ibadan, Oyo, and Ilorin and discussions with informants, that the church and mosque that I chose were not extraordinary or obviously different from the Yoruba norm. In any event, the research environment in Yorubaland compelled me to make a virtue out of the standard anthropological procedure of giving a very small society a great deal of scrutiny. By "research environment" I am referring primarily to the value Yorubas place on information.

The Social Role of Information

Like the exact location of water holes in the Somali desert, or the specifics of a personal stock portfolio of an American businessman, information about the social relations within a Yoruba compound is carefully guarded from strangers. Amid my first week in Yorubaland, I watched a woman berating the ticket seller at the University of Ibadan zoo for having the effrontery to ask her the age of her children. She was aware, she admitted, that under a certain age they could enter free; but she would still not consent to reveal their ages. Once my research began, I was again and again confronted by this same reality. Once, after participating in an Anglican church service, I asked a wealthy businessman to explain to me what the message of the sermon was. He would not tell me, and I subsequently learned that I would have to get information even of that sort by my own wits. While visiting a member of the mosque, I once asked if there were any Christians in the compound. "No, we are all Muslims here," he responded. On my next visit (on a Sunday) I met a few members of his compound returning from church. More significant, as I began doing formal interviewing, I found that whenever I interviewed someone I had not met many times previously, I would face great reluctance to reveal anything. This was especially the case when I tried to interview within the Ahmadiyya mosque without having first developed a regular social relationship with those whom I interviewed. When I considered handing out questionnaires to schoolchildren, a young informant wisely reminded me that I would not get truthful information. His mother had once told him that he should reveal nothing about his family on any occasion at school. It was a very rare event indeed, either for me or for other researchers in Yorubaland, when vital information was offered gratuitously.

Yorubas are not unaware of this aspect of their culture. In one revealing sermon, the vicar of the Anglican church retold the Samson and Delilah story. His sermons were usually met with a calm indifference (especially the time when he waxed eloquent in discussing Julian Huxley's theological views), cynical laughter (among the lawyers and businessmen wishing he would finish up so they could get home), and expectant religiosity (parishioners waiting for a cue to shout out their "hallelujahs"). But this time there was an intense interest usually reserved for those sermons in which the vicar told of miraculous recoveries from illness. The message the vicar drew—that you should put your trust in nobody but Jesus—instantly resonated. A tenet for survival in Yoruba society is to give no one, not even a relative, the ammunition to destroy you.

Once, when I was a guest at a celebration given by a lecturer at the University of Ife, I learned that, although very young, he had a second wife. He urged me to keep this quiet, as he did not want many of his colleagues to know about it. He cited to me the Yoruba proverb, *Gbogbo aṣo ki a a ṣe e ṣa ni oorun*, "Not all clothes need be displayed." Wearing good clothes is one of the main mechanisms of displaying wealth in Yoruba society, and having more than one wife represents wealth.

Yoruba secrecy provided both a constraint and an opportunity. It was a constraint because I could not expand the range of my observations without paying heavy costs in terms of the quality of information procured. That was why I limited myself to one church and one mosque in a single city. (Compensating for the limited empirical focus is the very rich and detailed literature on churches and mosques in other Yoruba cities, enabling me to assess the generality of the phenomena I have observed.) The opportunity took me longer to appreciate. Once I had ceased lamenting the difficulty of collecting cultural data in Yorubaland, I recognized that my confrontation with Yoruba secrecy was teaching me something important about Yoruba culture. Indeed, I began to learn that a considerable part of the cultural challenge of the world religions was their public and open rituals.

FIELD METHODS

My governing idea was to enter into the Christian and Muslim subcultures through regular attendance at religious services. This idea turned out to be strategically sound. In my first trip to Yorubaland in 1977, my main goal was to see whether I could engage in participant observation within the Christian and Muslim subcultures. I visited churches and mosques in Ibadan, Oyo, and Ilorin, and found that my idea was feasible. By 1979–80, the year in which I returned to complete my research, I was confident that I would be welcome in Yoruba churches and mosques. My first visit to St. Paul's Anglican Church in Ile-Ife was uneventful. I sat alone, and only an usher paid much attention to me, even though I was the only non-African in the church. He gave me a hymnal, the day's program in mimeographed form, and showed me the book of prayer, making sure that I understood what was going on. He found out that I was living at the university. At the end of the service, he asked me to pay for the hymnal. I then left quietly, no one else approaching me.

The central mosque evoked more anxiety, however. If I had made some faux pas in the church, there were a number of other Anglican churches in the same town I could have attended. But since I had settled my family in Ile-Ife, a major error in the mosque would have been catastrophic—it was *the* central mosque for the town. The first week, when I had expected the mosque hawkers to abound so that I could purchase a proper hat for prayer, was unusually quiet, and I could find no hat peddlers. Afraid to enter the mosque hatless, I watched from the outside. The following week, properly attired, I entered and was immediately approached by a large, well-dressed man. When I asked, "May I pray, serve God, here?" he answered, "Yes, are you a Muslim?" Not listening to my equivocal answer, he led me to the (scarce) water for ablutions. (I had answered, in English, "I am a believer." This is how the Prophet classified the Jews; but it is also the literal translation for Christian in the Yoruba language. I don't know how he interpreted my answer, if he was indeed listening to it. In the next few weeks, all who cared would learn the precise truth.) I was assigned a prayer mat, made to feel welcome, but had no further conversations and left as quietly as I had left the church.

I wanted to use regular attendance at these services as a springboard for jumping into the two subcultures. But by the end of two months I could report only minuscule progress. Although I was welcome in both church and mosque and was making acquaintances, I had visited the homes of only about ten worshipers. On my third visit to the mosque, as I walked on the main road from the bus stop, I was gently redirected through one residential area right up to the back entrance of the mosque. A month later, a member of St. Paul's Church saw me at the bus stop on Friday afternoon, and offered to give me a lift to the mosque. Each week at both church and mosque, more members would approach me, give me their address, and invite me to their compounds.

In this early period of weekly attendance, I kept careful records of what I thought I saw. I noted that the church had open portals, which invited entrance, while the mosque had a closed passageway, making each entry significant. As Christians entered the church, many crossed themselves, but no visible change of behavior occurred, and conversations continued. Entry into the mosque changed behavior radically. All of a sudden, uncharacteristic for Yorubas, the Muslims became quiet and reserved.

In the church, regular participation in song and dance by the congregation was expected; but in the mosque, worshipers spent most of their time sitting quietly. In the church there was a clear distinction in dress between the official robes of the leaders, the European dress of the ushers, and the sparkling robes of the more affluent worshipers; while in the mosque there were hardly any distinctions in dress, and worshipers tended to dress less ostentatiously than in the church. (Muslims showed *their* good choice in cloth by bringing their own private prayer mats.)

For Christians, literacy, and the concomitant ability to read hymns and psalms, brought status; for Muslims, only the imam had a Qur'an, and so there was no way for ordinary participants to demonstrate literacy. On Sundays there was a special service for Christian children; on Fridays, no provision was made for young Muslims. In the church, Yoruba-language greetings were the norm; the mosque replaced these with Arabic greetings. In the church, there was a careful and specialized accounting of all monies collected. In the mosque, accounts were kept in a school notebook, and monies distributed informally, on the floor, with all those claiming a share sitting around a circle. In the church I saw a number of carefully differentiated tasks, with different people performing each task. In the mosque, tasks were not clearly specified and some people performed a wide variety of jobs. I duly recorded these differences but at first found very little significance in them. Later, however, I wove some of these observational strands into more discernibly political patterns (see chapter 3 above).

As informants began to accept me in their compounds, and as my language abilities increased (they never became good enough to hold an extensive conversation, but only to elicit specific information or to capture the gist of a sermon or a conversation), I began to feel as if I was living in two interrelated worlds. Going to the church was for me like observing a progressive school in the United States. The vicar spoke quietly, and tried to teach his congregation about issues its members had rarely considered. I came to appreciate the various constituencies he had to serve. To the bishop in Ibadan he had to show that he would improve the material condition of the church. (He did, and after completing a marble floor job for the church at the cost of 26,000 nairas, he duly received a promotion and a new posting to Ibadan.) To the market women he had to provide the expectation of relief for their multifarious worldly anxieties over money and health. He feared losing them to the Aladura priests, who ministered more meticulously to worldly pain and suffering. To the businessmen and lawyers he had to provide an environment where they could display their wealth and success to the outside world. This complex array of needs was addressed every Sunday.

At the mosque my experience was different. Mosque officials insisted I sit up close to the imam, and I was brought into what might be described as an inner club. Every Friday, the service was characterized by its sameness, its simplicity, and its solidarity. The most touching part of the ceremony was during the final ritual. The muezzin would chant the commands with the aid of a microphone while the imam alternated with him in a nonamplified monody. The absolute attention, the symmetrical prostrations, and the choral chanting created a mood of quiet contemplation which has no parallel in Yoruba society.

Through my stay, Christians would see me with the Muslim elite, and Muslims would see me with the Christian officials. I did not conceal the nature of my research strategy, which most townspeople found rather quaint. Some thought I was commendably religious, and no amount of protestations about my agnosticism could change their minds. No one was outraged by my apparent bireligiosity. Within two months in Ile-Ife, I had faced many problems. But I was developing some appreciation of the subcultures of the Ife Christian and Muslim communities. In my visits to the compounds of my newly acquired acquaintances, I held informal interviews, which made me a visible face around town, thereby reducing distrust of me and giving me new sources of hypotheses about the role of religion in Yoruba society.

In fact, I have rarely learned anything new from formal interviews in Africa; I have used them only to confirm or disconfirm insights I have derived from visiting and talking. Consider the following insights from these informal encounters. The first is from my site planning visit in 1977. I was in Ilorin, and met a young Muslim civil servant collecting money, house to house, for a new central mosque. He was a devout Muslim, yet showed no inclination, as I walked and chatted with him, to differentiate himself from Christians, although I invited him to do so. Shortly thereafter I met a Christian soldier in a bar. I asked him, amid a long and rambling conversation, what it was like to be a Christian in a city in which Muslims were so dominant. He said it didn't matter. He had once been sued and fined in a Sharia court. Yet he praised the Muslim courts for their efficiency and fairness. The second problematic of this study—explaining why religion has not become politicized in Yorubaland—became defined for me in these chance encounters.

My second illustration is from Ile-Ife. I was driving a key senior official of the church to the local bank, and I stopped to buy gasoline. Right behind me in line was one of my regular hosts, a young man I had met in the mosque. He walked over to my car and gave an extended greeting, not to me, as I had expected, but to my passenger. Long as traditional Yoruba greetings often take, this one took even longer. The respect to the elder man by the young alhaji was exemplary, even obsequious. Business done, and on the road to the bank, I asked my passenger what was happening, because the greeting looked terribly formal. He explained that his daughter, as a secondary school student, had been having an affair with this alhaji, after school. She became pregnant, and her father faced a grave dilemma. If his daughter had the child out of wedlock (as the vicar recommended), she would be a pariah in Yoruba society. If she married the alhaji, she would be lost to the church. Considerable negotiations ensued, with alternatives discussed, such as marriage to an elder Christian in search of a young second wife. Eventually the young girl married the alhaji, but relations between families became strained. The highly formalized greetings reflected a public display of harmony to smooth over those private strains. I had interviewed both of these men about Christian/ Muslim relations, and neither had mentioned this case to me. I had met the young wife and her child. She knew I was an acquaintance of her father. Yet no one informed me. It is here where I learned better about both the sources of toleration, but also the tensions which exist between Muslim and Christian Yorubas.

The obverse of these illustrations is the fact that on formal prescheduled interviews I often found potential informants to be cautious and suspicious. Sometimes interviewees would invite friends and relatives to an interview. Rather than attempting to control the environment, I permitted the environment to define the interview. Watching respected elders perform in front of their entourage usually provided grist for my theoretical mill. It became clear that the compoundwide dramas which are performed for investigators often provide more reliable guides to cultural values than answers to formal questions that appear on interview schedules. These dramas provide the independent data on cultural preferences that should complement theories of rational action. Without data of this sort, as I pointed out in chapter 8, rational actor explanations become circular.

THE FORMAL SURVEY

Once I felt established in Ile-Ife, I attempted to supplement my impressions from systematic observations and informal encounters with a set of formal interviews. First, I sought data concerning the social, economic, and familial roles of the core Christian and Muslim communities I was studying. I had already hypothesized that Christians and Muslims came from the same socioeconomic groups in the early twentieth century; that Christians had done better economically; that the lack of Christian-Muslim social differentiation was more myth than reality; and that the sources of toleration had to be sought elsewhere. Second, I wanted to pursue hypotheses concerning the differential political impact of church and mosque on their religious adherents. I therefore formulated political questions that could tap the differences I had already observed in the religious subsystem.

I interviewed thirty-five Christians and thirty-five Muslims, all of whom were deeply identified with their respective religions. For the toleration problematic, I felt that I would best capture both the sources of toleration and any emerging enmity from those who were most devout. If there were any political differences due to differential religious exposure, such differences should appear among this very group. The data elicited from those questionnaires were analyzed in chapters 4 and 7.

I pursued the following strategy in search of a sample. I cultivated a senior member of the church and a senior member of the mosque, each of whom would escort me to the homes of thirty-four other members of his religious community (each escort himself was also interviewed). This person would explain the purpose of my research—emphasizing that I was studying the religious and other views of Yoruba Christians and Muslims— and then sit with the interviewee while my translator, a young man who was studying for his secondary school examinations, administered the interview and recorded the open-ended questions on tape. (My translator was from a Christian family from a different quarter of town from the worshipers of St. Paul's. He claimed to have no close family connections with any of the respondents. The main focus of the respondents, in my judgment, was on me and my escort, not on the translator.)

For an escort to the Christian community, through the intervention of the vicar, I relied on a semiretired businessman who had been a force in Ife politics since the 1950s. With major battles behind him, he was able to procure interviews for me with virtually anyone I asked for. That I proved a willing ear to his stories about his political career endeared me to him. I also helped his son pursue some educational opportunities, and that was his compensation. In the mosque, a semiretired *alhaji* performed the equivalent role. I occasionally gave him small gifts, but I believe his principal compensation for escorting me was that he was fascinated by this foreigner who took such an interest in his mosque. My association with the University of Ife, he believed, conferred considerable status on his compound, which I regularly visited, and he was not beyond political ambition in city politics. Both my escorts fully understood my research program, and quite often intervened in an interview to remind the interviewee that he hadn't revealed information about his third wife or some other matter. These escorts proved most useful in ensuring a higher degree of honesty by the interviewees.

The Christian community was interviewed first. This was because I succeeded there first in getting an escort, and also because I needed to interview a set of mosque elders on the history of Islam in Ile-Ife (written histories of Christianity were already available) before I administered the formal interview. The Muslim community was pleased to have me record its history, and my performance of the role of scribe enhanced my status when the time came for the standardized interview. Slow to start those interviews with the Muslims, however, I was twice approached by members of the mosque who saw me interviewing Christians and asked when it would be their turn. Because I was a regular participant in services, nearly every man I interviewed had seen me a dozen or so times before, and I had some acquaintance with many of them. The first ten or fifteen minutes of every interview were usually given to a discussion between me and the interviewee over small matters. Most of those interviewed were therefore not suspicious of what might be my deeper intentions. Some expected compensation. I took the advice of my escorts, both of whom encouraged me to give a naira or two to the poorest of the interviewees.

I relied completely on the judgment of my escorts to choose senior male interviewees who were well respected in their religious institution. The restriction on sex requires some discussion, especially because women play such a dominant role in the construction of Yoruba culture. Since women had their own societies and their own cults, I became convinced, early in my field research, that time would not permit scrutiny of the differential religious impact of Christianity and Islam on Yoruba female culture. (My vignette on sexual equality is based on observations of women while I was interviewing and sitting among men. The impact on Yoruba women of conversion to the world religions deserves careful study, which remains to be done.) Outside of these few guidelines, I imposed no further restrictions on my escorts' choice of respondents.

The interviews took place over a six-week period; so it was possible for those interviewed to pass on questions to those not yet interviewed. (I don't think this happened, for the answers did not get more sophisticated or more ritualized in the later interviews. This could have been Yoruba secrecy working in my favor; more likely it was my irrelevance in the community.) Without formally attempting to make the two samples commensurate, I managed to tap a similar set in church and mosque, (see table A.1). In age, in association with Ile-Ife as their ancestral city, and in percentage of converts as opposed to those born into their world religion, the Christian and Muslim samples are broadly similar.

WHO "I" WAS

Who was it that these Yoruba Christians and Muslims saw interviewing them? I told them of my Jewish background and the fact that my grandparents had emigrated from Russia in the late nineteenth century because of religious pogroms there. Strife based on religious affiliation, I added, had plagued the western world for a long time, and there is therefore an expectation among sociologists from my culture that religious differentiation would automatically induce suspicion and eventually conflict. I cited the case of Christian-Jewish enmity for two millennia, culminating in the Hitlerian holocaust; the Muslim-Jewish enmity from the pogrom in Medina through the present problems in the Middle East; the Christian-Muslim battles in Lebanon; the Catholic-Protestant wars from the Reformation and still hot today in Northern Ireland; and the Hindu-Muslim conflict in the Indian subcontinent. I told my Yoruba acquaintances that from my perspective, although there have been long periods of peace among religious groups in the West, religious conflict is seen as normal. Therefore the Yoruba case of religious differentiation coinciding with religious harmony was a theoretical anomaly. I also told some of my interviewees that I wanted to know whether, after eighty years of religious differentiation among the Yorubas, Christians and Muslims had become in any significant ways different.

But what I told them about myself is different still from what they saw. When members of the Muslim community found out that I was not a

TABLE A.1

Demographic Characteristics of the Samples	Respondents	
	Christians	Muslims
Mean age	65.4	65.5
Standard deviation	2.340	1.888
Percentage who consider Ile-Ife their ancestral city	100	87.9
Percentage born into traditional religion	42.9	31.4

Muslim, they learned that I was flattered by their urging me to convert. I was attracted by the ascetic ideal of the Muslim ceremonies, which brought a quiet solemnity to an otherwise boisterous Yoruba audience. And so, even though I made friends faster among the better-educated Christians, I did not feel the same rush of pride when they proselytized to me. The educated Christians were perplexed by my empathy for the Muslims, and one educated Christian asked me why I would want to pray like a crocodile.

If I felt more flattered to be courted into the Muslim milieu, I was less competent to participate in it. I had to be taught the proper way to cleanse myself before prayer, and I had found it intimidating to cross the threshold into the mosque for the first time. Yet I had no fears about walking straight through the open doors of the church, nor any difficulties in making sense out of their service. The vicar, on my second visit, called me into his vestry and, after talking with me, introduced me to the church elite. With them I could explain my research as if I were in the womb of my own university.

Members of the wider community were not blind to all this. It was not until the third week of my mosque attendance that someone there asked me why I hadn't entered that first week. And one of my regular informants—the alhaji who married the church official's daughter—did not introduce himself until after the fourth service I attended. During my second visit to his home, he asked me why I did not enter the mosque on that first visit. Whether I was in church or mosque, in the market, or just visiting around town, I was an object for scrutiny.

And also mockery. My ears never really heard the differentiated tones of the Yoruba language, and my linguistic errors would be repeated to me in different parts of town. When I successfully "pasted" a host at a celebration—placing money on his forehead while dancing—word of it traveled fast, and I heard many versions of it. The women who sold bushmeat (smoked game) in the market adjacent to the mosque took delight in calling me "alhaji," especially when I was moving around with members of the Christian community. Research in Africa continued to intrigue me because so much of the time one's subjects seem to be holding up amusement-park mirrors in front of them, so a great deal of what one sees is grotesque images of oneself. In fact, one purpose of this extended discussion of research methods is to dispel any belief that remains in the social sciences that the researcher can remain distinct from the subject.

LOCAL ANSWERS TO MY QUESTIONS

As I explained my purposes to Yoruba intellectuals, religious elites, and other interested parties, I received a coherent set of responses to the two research problematics. These answers were compelling and provided an excellent foil for my development of a vision different from theirs.

The problem of religious toleration received the greatest attention. Nearly everyone with whom I spoke about my research believed that toleration was due to Yorubas' sharing a common culture. The central premise the Ibadan-trained historian T. G. O. Gbadamosi's *The Growth of*

Islam among the Yoruba is that despite the important inroads of Islam, there is an overarching unity to Yoruba culture. Gbadamosi suggests that "the single most important factor in Yoruba life, important because of its pervasive and determinant quality, was the body of Yoruba traditional beliefs and worship."[24] Many Yorubas emphasize not the common religious beliefs, but the fact of common ancestry, conjoined with the belief that one's ancestors define who one is. Common ancestry between Yoruba Christians and Muslims, it is held, assures cultural unity. Others mentioned common language, common urban peasant culture, and similar political institutions. In line with this, the role of the Yoruba king is crucial. He is the king of an entire city-state, and must accommodate the needs of all religious communities. The vicar of the then king of Ife's church insisted to me that the king should and would enter the mosque if there was a need for his authority. Indeed, Yoruba informants would cite the proverb, *Qba oni gbogbo ẹsin*, "The king, patron of all religions." Most of my informants stressed that "we are all one," and that there is no real difference to cause conflict.

Yoruba informants also argued that cross-cutting cleavages among the Yoruba people moderated conflict. When family cross-cuts religion, it was pointed out to me by a variety of Yorubas, religious conflict will inevitably recede. A university scholar brought up a case of an emerging Muslim-Christian difficulty in Abeokuta, but a negotiated settlement was assured since the bishop and the chief imam were of the same family. In an academic conference, one Yoruba wrote that there were reasons for conflict, "but the structure of society in Nigeria does not permit the full translation of the attitude of antagonism into practical realization . . . These mutual and reciprocal dealings go to show that in Nigeria, whatever may be the official attitude of the adherents of the three religions (Christianity, Islam and traditional religion) in practical terms, it is not possible to keep them apart from one another."[25] And the vicar of the church I regularly attended pointed out to me that although Christians and Muslims might be "poles part" on many matters, differences must be "repressed" to maintain "peace" in the multireligious family compound.

There was a supplemental argument related to the first two. Many Yorubas felt that their own religion was "deep," while Christianity and Islam were "shallow." One alhaji, just returned from Mecca, responded to my question about the relevance of the Sharia court system to Nigeria. He hardly knew the word, but once it had been explained to him, he responded, "In Saudi Arabia they can go by the Qur'an, but here we have to go by the law."[26] A Yoruba scholar recited for me a Yoruba song: "Christianity [or Islam] doesn't hold a Yoruba man from observing custom." By this argument, the source of religious toleration is in the practical irrelevance of the two world religions.

A point often made by my informants, was that Yorubas are naturally tolerant people. Gbadamosi argues in his study that Yoruba culture "discountenances extremism."[27] The chief imam in Ile-Ife could not believe that any religious man would fight over religion, and claimed that those who do must know nothing about religion. A writer to the editor to the Lagos *Daily Times* expressed incredulity that Asians in Nigeria were suspicious of each other because of religion. "I am appealing to the Asians concerned," he wrote, "and the Saudis in particular to please learn to tolerate others' beliefs as is common with all Nigerians."[28]

Many of my informants, even those who made eloquent statements on one of these points, were not fully satisfied with the responses they gave me. One informant, after speaking lyrically about Yoruba toleration, walked me to my car. Out in front of the car an Aladura ceremony was taking place, and he was quick to mock their "primitive" rituals. Another senior member of the church, who also pointed out the fact of unity within Yorubaland, disputed my contention that Christians were better off economically. At the same time he implicitly agreed with me when he claimed that Muslim failure was due to "fatalism" and the fact that they "don't recognize that God isn't going to come down and help us with our problems." Stereotyped views of members of the other religious subcultures were just beneath the surface and at times belied protestations of cultural unity. Other data (presented in chapter 7), and well known by many of my informants, also contradict the general tenor of their answers.

Nonetheless, there was, among my informants, a pervasive belief in the unity of Yorubas which transcended membership in world religions. This belief of course is a social fact, which has had its own effects on social relations. As students of religious history know, early converts to Christianity and Islam were asked to break ties with their families and to realign their identities to fit a new religious reality. To say that family transcends religion in Yorubaland begs the question of why Yorubas have not adjusted their visions of their ancestry to create religious homogeneity. (The data presented in part 2 show that families have in fact moved toward such homogeneity.) Accepting that there is some merit to the Yoruba perspective, but being skeptical of it all the same I have called their view "the premise of natural religious harmony."

Responses to questions concerning my other research problematic—whether after three generations of differential religious experience, Christian and Muslim Yorubas have developed different "cultures"—were less assured. An Anglican vicar, who expressed deep shock that I had married a woman of a different faith and could not believe that a Christian-Muslim marriage in Yorubaland could have a "real" basis, told me later that there were indeed considerable differences between Yoruba Christians and Muslims. When I asked him to elaborate, he began discussing ideas of Christian fellowship and mutual support. But then he said, "I guess it is the same with the Muslims." He then revealed that he could not tell whether a Yoruba man is a Christian or Muslim unless it comes up in conversation. I had a similar experience with a Muslim scholar, who claimed that Islam affects the way one walks, talks, eats, and does everything. But on further reflection he acknowledged that when he meets another Yoruba he can tell (by dialect) where his ancestral city is but cannot immediately tell his religion. If asked to reflect on the matter, most

Yorubas will agree that the differential impact of Christianity and Islam on their culture has been minimal. Again, without claiming accuracy, I call this belief "the premise of no difference."

CONCLUSION

Yorubaland was a remarkable field site for a "natural experiment" comparing the differential impact of Christianity and Islam on political values and behavior. The existential situation was ideal: viable subcommunities of Christians and Muslims; conversion at about the same time for the same reasons; and converts coming from the same social groups. But formidable practical and theoretical problems had to be faced. How does a participant observer develop rapport with two "rival" elites? How does a foreigner penetrate the secrecy so firmly embedded in the local culture? How does an investigator develop independent data bases for religious and political values?

This appendix should serve two purposes. First, the explicit details of my research choices should challenge critics to link my findings to my methodology. If any critic were able to show a systematic bias in my data based on my field methods, my conclusions would be discredited. Second, this appendix addresses social science field methods in general. Social science should confront the "big questions" armed with general concepts such as "religion," "Islam," and "Christianity" that transcend any one research site. Yet these general concepts must be examined differently in different research environments. Social science should seek general propositions about, say, the relationship between Christianity or Islam and political authority. But the way it collects data to support any proposition must be sensitive to, and suggested by, the particular environment in which the research is carried out.[29]

Notes

PREFACE

1. Particularly culpable is Adda B. Bozeman's *Conflict in Africa* (Princeton: Princeton University Press, 1976). But Clifford Geertz's "The Integrative Revolution," in *Interpretation of Cultures* (New York: Basic Books, 1973), and Aristide Zolberg's "The Structure of Political Conflict in the New States of Tropical Africa," *American Political Science Review* 62, no. 1 (March 1968), both emphasize the high levels of conflict (and not toleration) among cultural groups in Africa.

2. See Alvin Rabushka and Kenneth Shepsle, *Politics in Plural Societies: A Theory of Democratic Instability* (Columbus, Ohio: Charles E. Merrill, 1972). See also Robert Melson and Howard Wolpe, "Modernization and the Politics of Communalism: A Theoretical Perspective," *American Political Science Review* 64, no. 4 (December 1970).

3. J. D. Y. Peel *Ijeshas and Nigerians* (Cambridge: The University Press, 1983).

4. In fact, many Yoruba scholars have provided explanations, but they are ad hoc generalizations about Yoruba culture rather than research findings based on the question of the nonpoliticization of religion as a dependent variable. This issue is discussed in the Appendix to this volume, under the heading "Local Answers to My Questions."

CHAPTER 1

1. Fuller details on the Sharia debate are available in David Laitin "The Sharia Debate and the Origins of Nigeria's Second Republic," *Journal of Modern African Studies* 20, no. 3 (1982), from which the following section draws heavily. The basic document for the subsequent analysis is Federal Republic of Nigeria, *Proceedings of the Constituent Assembly: Official Report* (Lagos, 1977). All references to this volume will be referred to in the text with "c," denoting column. When a speaker is identified in the text, the state he represents (within Nigeria's present federal system) will be noted in parentheses.

2. See Martin J. Dent, "Dangers of Polarity in Religious Matters," *West Africa* (London), 24 April 1978; Margery Perham, *Native Administration in Nigeria* (London, 1937); and "What You Need to Know about the Sharia Court of Appeal," *New Nigerian* (Kaduna), 12 August 1977.

3. Federal Republic of Nigeria, *Reports of the Constitution Drafting Committee* (Lagos, 1976), 2:24.

4. Ibid., vol. 1, which contains the entire Draft Constitution.

5. A classic statement of the politics in plural societies is that of J. S. Furnivall, *Colonial Policy and Practice* (Cambridge: Cambridge University Press, 1948) Furnivall's position is developed in Alvin Rabushka and Kenneth Shepsle, *Politics*

in Plural Societies: A Theory of Democratic Instability (Columbus, Ohio: Merrill, 1972).

6. D. N. Wambutda, "Towards a Peaceful Religious Co-existence in Nigeria: From a Christian Perspective," in I. A. B. Balogun (ed.), *Religious Understanding and Co-operation in Nigeria*, Proceedings of a Seminar Organized by the Department of Religions, University of Ilorin, 7–11 August 1978, p. 87.

7. Reported in the *New Nigerian*, 8 May 1977.

8. The role of appeals in Sharia is discussed in Martin Shapiro, *Courts: A Comparative and Political Analysis* (Chicago: University of Chicago Press, 1981), chap. 5.

9. James S. Coleman, *Nigeria: Background to Nationalism* (Berkeley: University of California Press, 1958), p. 18.

10. J. S. Eades, *The Yoruba Today* (Cambridge: Cambridge University Press, 1980), p. 2.

11. J. D. Y. Peel, *Ijeshas and Nigerians* (Cambridge: Cambridge University Press, 1983), p. 162.

12. Coleman (n. 9), p. 15.

13. Ibid., p. 361.

14. As I argued in Laitin (n. 1), the compromise was accepted because the military leaders were unified and adamant that the MCAs should come to an agreement on this issue. Here I am arguing that it was the Yoruba delegates who made compromise easier.

15. Clifford Geertz, *The Interpretation of Cultures* (New York: Basic Books, 1973); Abner Cohen, *Two-Dimensional Man: An Essay on the Anthropology of Power and Symbolism in Complex Society* (Berkeley: University of California Press, 1974). Hereafter, references to these volumes, in the text and the notes, will be by the abbreviations *IC* and *TDM*. I develop this comparison more fully in "Rational Choice and Culture: A Thick Description of Abner Cohen's Hausa Migrants," in Fred Eidlin (ed.), *Constitutional Democracy: Essays in Comparative Politics: A Festschrift for Henry W. Ehrmann* (Boulder, Colo.: Westview, 1983). The subsequent discussion has drawn heavily from that article.

16. This is largely my own set of criteria. Criterion "c," however, is directly derived from Geertz's discussion in "Religion as a Cultural System," reprinted in *IC*. By it, he means the nonprogrammed elements in a species' search for survival. That human beings seek shelter is not a cultural fact; that some human beings build wood frames and others brick structures is cultural.

17. Abner Cohen, *Custom and Politics in Urban Africa: A Study of Hausa Migrants in Yoruba Towns* (Berkeley: University of California Press, 1969), pp. 212–13.

18. Cohen has distanced himself methodologically from "action theorists" in social anthropology, who, he feels, ignore sociocultural realities in their statements of rational action. Action theorists operate fully from a rational choice perspective (*TDM*, pp. 40–43). Nonetheless, Cohen appears to accept the general approach of these theorists.

Cohen might nonetheless defend himself from my categorization of his methodological position by arguing that his "Two Dimensions" are parallel with my "Two Faces." He would be partly correct. But in applying his theory, Cohen has emphasized the notion that a symbolic repertoire is a resource for political entrepreneurs. He has largely ignored the other direction of causation: the implications of the meanings within the symbolic repertoire for agenda setting by political entrepreneurs. I discuss this point in "Rational Choice and Culture" (n. 15).

19. Graham Allison, *Essence of Decision* (Boston: Little, Brown, 1971). See especially "Model I," chaps. 1–2.

20. P. C. Lloyd, in J. L. Gibbs, *Peoples of Africa* (New York: Holt, Rinehart & Winston, 1966), p. 551, has listed over fifty city-kingdoms in Yorubaland, all tracing their origins to Oduduwa. Among them are Ile-Ife, Oyo, Ondo, and Ijebu. However, the complexity and diversity of Yoruba society do not easily allow for such clear-cut dimensions of cleavage. "Subtribe" or "ethnic group" is often used to capture the differences between the peoples of these city-kingdoms. But the language of tribe and ethnicity do not capture the people's connection with city-kingdoms that is so basic to Yoruba discourse about their identities. City kings may no longer be sovereigns, but kingship and other chiefly titles confer considerable status today on the incumbents. Cosmopolitan men will often return to their ancestral cities to assume these offices. Despite the usefulness of the concept of "ancestral city" to describe a principal line of cleavage among the Yorubas, it has its own problems: some Yoruba groups (e.g. the Egba) were too decentralized to be called city-kingdoms, yet they play roles in contemporary Yoruba politics similar to those groups (e.g. the Ijebu or Ile-Ife) that have unequivocal connection to an ancient centralized kingdom. For a good statement of the diversity among Yoruba cities, see R. J. Clarke, "Agricultural Production in a Rural Yoruba Community" (Ph.D. diss., University of London, 1979), esp. p. 71. Nonetheless, I do not think that my simplification in describing a primary Yoruba cleavage line as one of "ancestral city" will do a disservice to Yoruba studies. More important, this simplification will allow me to highlight for the nonspecialist the sociological significance of the pattern of cultural politics in Yorubaland.

21. See Harry Eckstein, *Division and Cohesion in Democracy* (Princeton: Princeton University Press, 1966), for a full exposition of congruence theory. To be sure, it is possible to accept the systems framework without accepting that congruence yields health. But in American social science in the 1950s, where these ideas were developed, most researchers considered that orderly adjustment of social subsystems exemplified a healthy social system. Even Daniel Bell, who has distanced himself intellectually from social systems theory, accepts the congruence idea. "What we have today," he argues in *The Cultural Contradictions of Capitalism* (New York: Basic Books, 1976), p. 53, "is a radical disjunction of culture and social structure, and it is such disjunctions which historically have paved the way for more direct social revolutions."

22. Laitin, *Politics, Language, and Thought* (Chicago: University of Chicago Press, 1977), chaps. 6–8.

23. Marshall Sahlins, *Culture and Practical Reason* (Chicago: University of Chicago Press, 1976), p. 211.

24. See Quintin Hoare and Geoffrey Nowell-Smith, eds., *Selections from the Prison Notebooks*, (London: Laurence & Wishart, 1971), for an English translation of A. Gramsci's relevant works. The principal secondary sources on which I ⁓relied include Perry Anderson, "The Antinomies of Antonio Gramsci," *New Left*

Review 100 (November 1976–January 1977); Walter L. Adamson, *Hegemony and Revolution: Antonio Gramsci's Political and Cultural Theory* (Berkeley: University of California Press, 1980); and Raymond Williams, *Marxism and Literature* (Oxford: Oxford University Press, 1977).

CHAPTER 2

1. Montesquieu, *The Spirit of the Laws*, bk. 24, sec. 3.

2. Clifford Geertz, *Islam Observed* (Chicago: University of Chicago Press, 1968).

3. See my review of Geertz's *Islam Observed* in David Laitin, "Religion, Political Culture and the Weberian Tradition," *World Politics* 30, no. 4 (July 1978). The notion of "family resemblances" is from L. Wittgenstein, *Philosophical Investigations*, 3d ed., trans. G. E. M. Anscombe (New York: Macmillan, 1968); see, e.g., paragraph 67.

4. This quotation, from Santayana's *Reason in Religion*, forms the epigraph for Geertz's "Religion as a Cultural System" in *The Interpretation of Cultures* (New York: Basic Books, 1973). Geertz first published this essay in 1966, two years before *Islam Observed* was published.

5. Geertz, *The Interpretation of Cultures*, p. 90.

6. Max Weber, *Sociology of Religion*, trans. Ephraim Fischoff (Boston: Beacon, 1963) (hereafter cited in the text as *SR*), and Max Weber, *The Protestant Ethic and the Spirit of Capitalism*, trans. Talcott Parsons (New York: Scribner's 1958) (hereafter cited in the text as *PE*), provide the fundamental theoretical apparatus for the subsequent discussion. In my "Religion, Political Culture and the Weberian Tradition" (n. 3), I provide fuller details on the structure of Weber's argument. But a caveat: my discussion of the "Weberian tradition" in this book emphasizes one strand in Weber's work, one that was picked out and rewoven (along with strands from the work of Emile Durkheim) by T. Parsons, C. Geertz, and H. Eckstein. Any reading of Weber's *Economy and Society* would demonstrate the master's keen insight that culture, to be influential, must be carried by a well-endowed social group. This is hardly different from, but less well specified than, my model of hegemony. Despite my highlighting only one strand in Weber's work, it is nonetheless fair to differentiate the Weberian tradition (focusing on social and cultural *groups*) from the Benthamite tradition (focusing on *individual* calculation) as I do throughout this book.

7. *Persian Letters* (1721), trans. C. J. Betts (Harmondsworth, Eng.: Penguin, 1973), letter 97.

8. For further discussion of Christian-Muslim doctrinal differences, see J. D. Y. Peel *Aladura: A Religious Movement Among the Yoruba* (London: Oxford, 1968), pp. 46–47; and the Reverend Obayan (Permanent Secretary, Kwara State Ministry of Education, and Chaplain, University of Ilorin Christian Community), Keynote Address to the Proceedings of a Seminar Organized by the Department of Religions, University of Ilorin (7–11 August 1978), in I. A. B. Balogun, ed., *Religious Understanding and Cooperation in Nigeria* (Ilorin, Nigeria), p. 41. I discussed the subject in an interview with Alhaji M. A. Omotoso, Ilorin, Nigeria, 23 August, 1977.

9. Joseph Schacht, *An Introduction to Islamic Law* (Oxford: Clarendon, 1964),

p. 5. See Martin Shapiro, *Courts* (Chicago: University of Chicago Press, 1981), who challenges this conventional view of Islamic law.

10. See David Laitin, "Religion, Political Culture and the Weberian Tradition" (n. 3), pp. 578, 582. See also M. A. Shaban, *Islamic History A. D. 600–750 (A.H. 132): A New Interpretation* (Cambridge: The University Press, 1971), 1: 8–9.

11. Edward W. Said, *Orientalism* (New York: Pantheon, 1978). Said is by no means against comparisons, just against caricatures.

12. Emile Durkheim, *The Rules of the Sociological Method* (New York: Free Press, 1964), chap. 1.

13. The empirical refutations of Weber's thesis about Protestantism are numerous. See S. N. Eisenstadt, "The Protestant Ethic Thesis in Analytical and Comparative Context," *Diogenes* 59 (1967), for a good summary of them.

14. Maxime Rodinson, *Islam and Capitalism*, trans. Brian Pearce (New York: Pantheon, 1974), chap. 5.

15. Weber's "The Social Psychology of the World Religions," in H. H. Gerth and C. Wright Mills, eds., *From Max Weber* (New York: Oxford University Press, 1946), pp. 284–85.

16. Geertz, "Religion as a Cultural System" (n. 4), p. 90; my emphasis.

17. Humphrey J. Fisher, "Conversion Reconsidered: Some Historical Aspects of Religious Conversion in Black Africa," *Africa* (London) 43, no. 1 (1973). See also Geertz, *Islam Observed* (n. 2), chap. 3, "The Scripturalist Interlude."

18. K. Thomas, *Religion and the Decline of Magic* (New York: Scribner's, 1971), pp. 68, 363ff.

19. James C. Scott, "Protest and Profanation: Agrarian Revolt and the Little Tradition," *Theory and Society* 4, no. 1 (1977): 33. See also William M. J. van Binsbergen, "Popular and Formal Islam, and Supra-local Relations: The Highlands of North-western Tunisia, 1800–1970," *Middle Eastern Studies* 16 (January 1980) for another example.

20. Thomas Metzger, *Escape from Predicament* (New York: Columbia University Press, 1977), p. 14.

21. Fazlur Rahman, "The Sources and Meaning of Islamic Socialism" in Donald E. Smith, ed. *Religion and Political Modernization* (New Haven: Yale University Press, 1974), p. 250.

22. Henry Bienen, "Religion and Economic Change in Nigeria," unpublished manuscript, Princeton, N.J.

23. For a fuller discussion of similarities, see M. G. S. Hodgson, *The Venture of Islam* (Chicago: University of Chicago Press, 1974), vol. 1, esp., p. 125. On this point, see 2: 336–38. Hodgson, a devout Christian with a deep and long-standing respect for Islam, has been an incomparable source for my study.

24. ibid., 2: 336.

25. For a sympathetic view of the communism of early Christianity, see Karl Kautsky, *Foundations of Christianity* (New York: Monthly Review Press, 1972). On the various strands of theorizing about equality in the Christian tradition, see S. A. Lakoff, "Christianity and Equality," in J. R. Pennock and J. W. Chapman, eds., *Equality* NOMOS IX, (New York: Atherton, 1967). The quotation in the text and my interpretation of equality in Islam is from M. A. Shaban (n. 10), 1:9.

26. Hodgson (n. 23) vol. 2, chap. 7. Some of these differences are encompassed

in Gellner's inventive "pendulum swing" theory of Islam. He sees in world religions a natural oscillation between two poles: the first around a "syndrome of characteristics" encompassing strict monotheism, puritanism, scriptural revelation, egalitarianism, and sobriety; the second around a syndrome encompassing hierarchy, ritual specialization, mysticism, and excess. Religions oscillate between these poles, but only at one pole is there a stable equilibrium. For Islam it is at the first pole; for Christianity, the second. Gellner attributes the difference to the social conditions at the early stages of the religion—the fact that the peripheral areas in Islam were tribal and decentralized while Christianity spread amid a well-controlled empire. E. Gellner, "A Pendulum Theory of Islam," *Annales de Sociologie*, 1968. Gellner's "syndromes," however, are not completely congruent with my differentiation. He finds, for instance, rules and processes central to the Islamic tradition. This goes completely against my analysis. He provides no evidence to support the claim, so I cannot properly evaluate its merits.

27. Hodgson, (n. 23), 2:344.

28. Ibid., 2:346

29. Daniel H. Levine, *Religion and Politics in Latin America* (Princeton: Princeton University Press, 1981), p. 146.

30. Shaban (n. 10), chaps. 2–4.

31. Hodgson (n. 23), 2: 352–53.

32. Recent studies on English separatism include Murray Tolmie, *The Triumph of the Saints: The Separate Churches of London, 1616–1649* (London: Cambridge University Press, 1977); and B. R. White, *The English Separatist Tradition* (Oxford: Oxford University Press, 1971). In these works, the differences between Catholicism and Protestantism on the dimension of hierarchy take on some significance. But in my analysis, in large part because I am studying Anglicanism, those differences are not central.

33. Hodgson (n. 23), 2:360.

34. For the *hijra* and its relevance to Northern Nigeria, see R. A. Adeleye, *Power and Diplomacy in Northern Nigeria, 1804–1906: The Sokoto Caliphate and its Enemies* (London: Longmans, 1971), p. 291.

35. Hodgson (n. 23), 2:338.

36. For this section, the principal sources include E. Bolaji Idowu *Olodumare: God in Yoruba Belief* (London: Longman, 1962); 'Wande Abimbola, *Ifa: An Exposition of Ifa Literary Corpus* (Ibadan: Oxford University Press, 1976); and W. Bascom, *Ifa Divination: Communication between Gods and Men in West Africa* (Bloomington: Indiana University Press, 1969). I should note that I am uncomfortable with the terminology. "Traditional" connotes that (a) the beliefs and institutions are static and unchanging, and (b) the religion is theologically less sophisticated than "modern" religion. In my judgment, neither of these connotations can be sustained in the case at hand. For Nigerian students of comparative religion, the term "traditional religion" in a step forward from the previously common "animism" or "ancestor worship," which were used to describe the indigenous religious institutions and beliefs. *Orita*, the Ibadan-based journal of comparative religion, recommends the use of the term "traditional religion" for this reason. I will therefore use it in this study, accepting the guidelines of Nigerian researchers, so as not to add to the terminological confusion.

37. N. A. Fadipe. *The Sociology of the Yoruba* (Ibadan: Ibadan University Press, 1970) uses *olorun* to name the supreme being. Idowu (n. 36) calls him *olodumare*. Both agree, however, on the strong monotheistic bent to Yoruba religion.

38. See W. Bascom, "Yoruba Concepts of the Soul," in A. F. C. Wallace, ed., *Men and Cultures* (Philadelphia: University of Pennsylvania Press, 1960), p. 401. In chap. 7, I shall elaborate on the Yoruba concept of *emi*.

39. On *ifa* divination, see Abimbola (n. 36) and Bascom (n. 36).

40. And this is why there is virtually no atheism in traditional religion—it would be commensurate with renunciation of nationality. Thus, one is amused when Geertz writes in *The Interpretation of Cultures* (n. 4), p. 109: "If the anthropological study of religious commitment is underdeveloped, the anthropological study of religious noncommitment is nonexistent. The anthropology of religion will have come of age when some more subtle Malinowski writes a book called 'Belief and Unbelief' (or even 'Faith and Hypocrisy') in a Savage Society.'"

41. See K. Barber, "How Man Makes God in West Africa," *Africa* 51, no. 3 (1981); and J. S. Eades, *The Yoruba Today* (Cambridge: The University Press, 1980), pp. 123–24.

42. H. Keyssar, "Comments" on J. Pemberton, "Sacred Kingship and the Violent God: The Worship of Ogun Among the Yoruba," *Berkshire Review* 14 (1979): 108.

43. E. A. Ayandele, *The Missionary Impact on Modern Nigeria, 1842–1914: A Political and Social Analysis* (New York: Humanities Press, 1967), chap. 8.

44. An excellent example of this phenomenon is in S. O. Babayemi's brilliantly researched and profound dissertation, "The Fall and Rise of Oyo c. 1760–1905: A Study in the Traditional Culture of an African Polity" (Ph.D. diss., University of Birmingham, 1979). Although he gives lucid explanations of Yoruba power arrangements, he constantly refers to Yoruba religious and political institutions as "complex," implying that only a restricted audience will ever appreciate the lessons of Yoruba cosmology. It would be astonishing to read a modern Yoruba intellectual describe his religious culture as simple, and as a model for others. But cf. B. Maupoil, *La géomancie à l'ancienne Côte des Eclaves*, Travaux et mémoires de l'Institut d'Ethnologie, 42 (1943), who shows that Yoruba baba'lawo brought Ifa divination to the (foreign) court of Abomey. Thus Yoruba religion was not exclusivist. But entry costs were too high for Yoruba religion to be considered similar to the world religions whose missionaries deliberately made entry costs low.

45. The intellectualists, then, systematically search for gaps in "traditional" religion which are then "filled" by the world religions. On these putative gaps, see J. Mbiti, *African Religions and Philosophy* (New York: Praeger, 1969), who wavers on the issue. See also R. Gray, "Christianity and Religious Change in Africa," *African Affairs* 77, no. 306 (January 1978), for a critique of the intellectualist position.

46. The by now seminal piece is R. Horton, "African Conversion," *Africa* (London) 41, no. 2 (April 1971).

47. J. Peel, "Conversion and Tradition in Two African societies: Ijebu and Buganda," *Past and Present* 77 (November 1977): 124.

48. See J. D. Y. Peel, *Ijeshas and Nigerians* (Cambridge: The University Press, 1983), pp. 152–59, on the *osomaalo* system.

49. See Peel, *Ijeshas and Nigerians*. In his interviews, Peel reports that "in very many cases the fact of migration was mentioned as if it was a sufficient explanation of conversion" (p. 167). See also Peel, "Religious Change in Yorubaland," *Africa* (London) 37, no. 3 (July 1967).

50. G. O. Gbadamosi, "Patterns and Developments in Lagos Religious History," in A. B. Aderibigbe, ed., *Lagos: The Development of an African City* (Nigeria: Longman, 1975), pp. 183–84. On Christianity as "fashion" in Lagos, see Kristan Mann, "The Dangers of Dependence: Christian Marriage among the Elite Women in Lagos Colony, 1880–1915," *Journal of African History* 24, no. 1 (1983).

51. Peel, *Ijesas and Nigerians* (n. 48), p. 167.

52. J. D. Y. Peel, "*Olaju*: A Yoruba Concept of Development," *Journal of Development Studies* 14, no. 2 (January 1978).

53. H. J. Fisher, Conversion Reconsidered: Some Historical Aspects of Religious Conversion in Black Africa," *Africa* (London) 43, no. 1 (1973); and A. D. Nock, *Conversion* (London: Oxford University Press, 1933).

54. For a general picture, consult J. Spencer Trimingham, *History of Islam in West Africa* (London: Oxford University Press, 1962). The best sources on the growth of Islam among the Yoruba are G. O. Gbadamosi, *The Growth of Islam among the Yoruba, 1841–1908* (Atlantic Highlands, N.J.: Humanities Press, 1978); M. O. A. Abdul, "Islam in Ijebu Ode' (M.A. thesis, Institute of Islamic Studies, McGill University, 1967); E. D. Adelowo, "Islam in Oyo and Its Districts in the Nineteenth Century" (Ph.D. thesis, Department of Religious Studies, University of Ibadan, 1978); and R. J. Ryan, *Imale: Yoruba Participation in the Muslim Tradition* (Missoula, Mont.: Scholar's Press, 1978).

55. On military aid from Borgu, see S. O. Babayemi (n. 44), pp. 105–6. On dignity, see Edward W. Blyden, of West Indian birth and West African ancestry, who was a Presbyterian pastor, Liberian government minister, British colonial civil servant in Sierra Leone, and intellectual. In his *Christianity, Islam, and the Negro Race* (1887; reprinted Edinburgh: Edinburgh University Press, 1967), he makes the idea of "dignity" a leitmotif in his discussion of African Islam. He refers approvingly to Bosworth Smith (*Mohammed and Mohammedanism*, Lectures delivered at the Royal Institution of Great Britain, 1874), who remarked, "Christian travelers, with every wish to think otherwise, have remarked that the Negro who accepts Mohammedanism acquires at once a sense of dignity of human nature not commonly found even among those who have been brought to accept Christianity." Blyden, pp. 9–10.

56. See Gbadamosi, in Aderibigbe (n. 50). See also Razak 'Deremi Abubakre "The contribution of the Yorubas to Arabic Literature" (Ph.D. diss., University of London, 1980) who emphasizes the integrity and independent development of Islam in southern Yorubaland. See p. 172.

57. B. Awe, "The Northern Factor in the Oyo-Yoruba Resurgence of the Nineteenth Century," paper presented at the Institute of African Studies, University of Ibadan (May 1980), p. 12. My account of Islam in Oyo relies on Adelowo (n. 54).

58. B. Awe, "The Northern Factor" (n. 57), p. 12. Major sources on Ibadan are Gbadamosi, *Growth of Islam* (n. 54), and Ryan, *Imale* (n. 54). See W. O. A. Nasiru, "The Advent and Development of Islam in Ibadan" (unpublished ms., Ibadan, 1979) for a slightly different account. Chiefly titles in this period of Ibadan's history were in flux. Precise translations of *Baṣọrun* and *Balẹ* will be provided in chapter 6, as they are not necessary at this point.

59. See Gbadamosi, *Growth of Islam* (n. 54), pp. 96–97. My account of Ijebu relied heavily on Abdul (n. 54), and Peel, "Conversion and Tradition" (n. 47).

60. G. O. Gbadamosi, "The Imamate Question among Yoruba Muslims," *Journal of the Historical Society of Nigeria* 6, no. 2 (December 1972).

61. Gbadamosi, *Growth of Islam* (n. 54) pp. 56–57.

62. Ibid., pp. 161–63, and Gbadamosi, "The Imamate Question" (n. 60).

63. An excellent example is given in A. Cohen, *Custom and Politics in Urban Africa* (Berkeley: University of California Press, 1969), chap. 4.

64. H. J. Fisher, "The Ahmadiyya Movement in Nigeria," in K. Kirkwood (ed.), *African Affairs*, St. Anthony's Papers no. 10 (London: Chatto & Windus, 1961).

65. Ryan (n. 54) argues that Yoruba Islam is just now entering the stage of reform.

66. The literature on Christian expansion is vast. The seminal works are J. F. Ade Ajayi, *Christian Missions in Nigeria, 1841–1891: The Making of a New Elite* (Evanston: Northwestern University Press, 1965); Ayandele, *The Missionary Impact* (n. 43). On the independent churches, see H. Turner, *History of an African Independent Church* (Oxford: Clarendon Press, 1967); Peel, *Aladura* (n. 8); and J. A. Omoyajowo, "Cherubim and Seraphim Church in Nigeria" (Ph.D. diss., University of Ibadan, 1971).

67. Obafemi Awolowo, *Awo* (Cambridge: The University Press, 1960), p. 20. Cf. note 40 above.

68. Peel, "Conversion and Tradition" (n. 47), p. 137.

69. J. D. Y. Peel, "Religious Change in Yorubaland," *Africa* (London) 37, no. 3 (July 1967).

70. In his preface to *The Missionary Impact* (n. 43), p. xvii, Ayandele remarks, "As far as the Nigerian peoples were concerned, the administrator and the European missionary were birds of the same feather and they saw them really flocking together." But the data, especially those uncovered by Ayandele himself, suggest a far more complex picture.

71. Professor J. Kofi Fynn of the University of Ghana emphasized this point to me when I presented these ideas at the University of Ife in May 1980.

72. The quotation is reproduced in J. H. Kopytoff, *A Preface to modern Nigeria* (Madison: University of Wisconsin Press, 1965), p. 120. For background, see S. O. Biobaku, *The Egba and their Neighbours, 1842–1872* (Oxford: Clarendon Press, 1965), chap. 5.

73. See the CMS Archives (Birmingham) (G3A2/0/1917–1928) for regular correspondence on the bookshop. In G3A2/0/1926/4 there was discussion of a bookshop for Ile-Ife, but the Executive Committee felt there was not enough "European staff" and it feared embezzlement.

74. J. F. Ade Ajayi, *Christian Missions* (n. 66), pp. 60–61.

75. S. A. Akintoye, *Revolution and Power Politics in Yorubaland, 1840–1893: Ibadan Expansion and the Rise of the Ekitiparapo* (New York: Humanities Press, 1971), p. 6.

76. J. A. Atanda, *The New Oyo Empire: Indirect Rule and Change in Western Nigeria, 1894–1934* (London: Longmans, 1973), chap. 2.

77. Nigerian National Archives (Ibadan), CMS (Y), Rev. C. Phillips's diaries, entries of January 1900.

78. E. A. Ayandele, "The Colonial Church Question in Lagos Politics, 1905–1911," *Odu*, University of Ife, Journal of African Studies, 4, no. 2 (January 1968): 56.

79. Ayandele, *Missionary Impact* (n. 43), pp. 150–51.

80. Phillips's diaries (n. 77), 10 August 1904.

81. Ayandele, *Missionary Impact* (n. 43), p. 67.

82. Ikime, *The Fall of Nigeria: The British Conquest* (London: Heinemann, 1977), p. 10.

83. Ayandele, *Missionary Impact* (n. 43), pp. 64ff. For another account, see Peel, "Conversion and Tradition" (n. 47).

84. David B. Abernethy, *The Political Dilemma of Popular Education* (Stanford: Stanford University Press, 1969), p. 64.

85. From the Report by Sir F. D. Lugard on the Amalgamation of Northern and Southern Nigeria and Administration, 1912–1919. Presented to Parliament by Command of His Majesty, December, 1919. Reprinted in A. H. M. Kirk-Greene, ed., *Lugard and the Amalgamation of Nigeria* (London: Frank Cass, 1968), p. 150.

86. A. G. Hopkins, "Property Rights and Empire Building: Britain's Annexation of Lagos, 1861," *Journal of Economic History* 40, no. 4 (December 1980): 792–93.

87. Abubakre (n. 56) is interesting on this point. A partisan of Arabic culture in Yorubaland, he points to the startling presence of Arabic phrases and words in popular culture and poetry. But in his exhaustive bibliography of Yoruba manuscripts written in Arabic, he has only seventy-six titles, most unpublished and half of them by a single author, Sheikh Adam al-'Iluri, Ādam 'Abdullāh. But, more important, and a credit to his scholarship, Abubakre points out that, unlike English, Arabic never developed a pidginized form among the Yorubas. This surely reflects the fact that few Yorubas tried to make that language their own. Literacy in Arabic never reached the level that English did in Yorubaland. Early trends were of course accelerated by the imposition of British administration.

88. Ajayi, *Christian Missions* (n. 66), p. 255.

89. Turner, *History*, (n. 66), 2: 365–67.

90. Daniel N. Wambutda, "A Study of Conversion among the Angas of Plateau State of Nigeria with Emphasis on Christianity" (Ph.D. diss., University of Ife, 1978).

91. Pierre Fatunbi Verger, "The Status of Yoruba Religion in Brazil," *Kiabara*, Journal of the Humanities, University of Port Harcourt (Nigeria), 2 (1978). This research was carried out in Bahia, Brazil.

92. J. A. T. Robinson, *Honest to God* (Philadelphia: Westminister Press, 1963). After I finished my Nigerian field work, I traveled to England to peruse the

CMS archives. At Westminster Abbey I had the opportunity to observe Anglican-ism at its center. The dean of Westminster, in his sermon on the modern predica-ment, employed nearly as many academic footnotes as are contained in this chapter.

93. Reuven Kahane, "Religious Diffusion and Modernization," *Archives européennes de sociologie* 21 (1980): 132–33. See also Geertz, *Islam Observed* (n. 2), p. 13.

94. Fisher, "The Ahmadiyya Movement" (n. 64).

95. This is the thesis in J. Scott, "Protest and Profanation" (n. 19), and in his "Revolution in the Revolution: Peasants and Commissars," *Theory and Society* 7, nos. 1–2 (1979).

96. E. Bolaji Idowu, *Olodumare: God in Yoruba Belief* (London: Longmans, 1962), chap. 9.

97. Dan R. Aronson, "Cultural Stability and Social Change among the Modern Ijebu Yoruba" (Ph.D. diss., University of Chicago, 1970), pp. 123–24.

CHAPTER 3

1. See the Appendix for a full description of field techniques employed in this study. It should be noted here that in the context of my field observations, "now" denotes 1979–80. Subsequent to my field research, the Ọọni of Ife died, the vicar of St. Paul's Anglican church received a big promotion, and various other changes took place.

2. The history in this section was compiled from interviews in Ile-Ife with Chief Imam Y. A. Balogun, Alhaji "Taosir," Alhaji Akintola, Alhaji Omisore, Idris Fatunmise, and Ibrahim Areago, held in February, March, and April 1980. Alhaji Ake was instrumental in getting me appointments with these mosque elders.

3. O. Oyediran, "Political Change in a Nigerian Urban Community" (Ph.D. diss., University of Pittsburgh, 1971).

4. From Oshogbo High Court, Bello Asani v. Yusuf Adeosun (mimeo), 1967, p. 36.

5. This section relies heavily on M. A. Fabunmi, *Ẹsin Kristi ni Ile-Ifẹ ati Agbegbe* (Ile-Ife: Kosalabaro Press, 1970).

6. This account is from S. Johnson, *The History of the Yorubas* (London: Routledge & Kegan Paul, 1921), pp. 230–31, 525, and 646-48.

7. Church Missionary Society (CMS) Archives, Birmingham, England (G3A2/O/1903/138) "Life of E. A. Kayode."

8. Nigerian National Archives (hereafter abbreviated NNA), (CMS 'Y' 1/3/9), Phillips's diaries, 1900.

9. NNA (CMS 'Y' 1/3/8), Phillips's diaries, 1898.

10. In my scrutiny of Phillips' diaries, I did not see a reference to arriving in "Ife" until November 1904, when the church at Ayetoro—the first church in Ife proper—had already opened. In all previous visits, he noted in his diary that he had "arrived in Modakeke."

11. NNA (CMS 'Y' 1/3/9) Phillips's diaries, 1899, entry of 13 February.

12. Ibid., entry of 23 May.

13. Phillips's diaries, 1900 (n. 8), entry of 26 January.

14. Phillips's diaries, 1899 (n. 11), entry of 4 June.

15. CMS, *Extracts from the Annual Letters of the Missionaries for the Year 1905* (London, 1906), CMS Archives.

16. NNA (CMS 'Y' 1/3/9) Phillips's diary, 1904, entry of 25 November.

17. NNA (CMS 'Y' 1/5/19), Letters (local) to the Secretary, Yoruba Mission 1923–1933, letter of 24 July 1925 to Archdeacon McKay from F. Melville Jones. I found no documentary evidence in CMS files of Adejumo's polygyny. However, many of my informants in Ile-Ife volunteered that he was a "bigamist" and they enumerated his "wives."

18. CMS Archives, Birmingham, F. Harding's Report on the Yoruba Executive Committee of 28 January–3 February 1902 (G3.A2/0/1902/50); Letter from Phillips to Executive Committee, 7 January 1902, p. 4; see also CMS Archives, Birmingham (G3.A2/0/1905/21). Minutes of Executive Committee, 17–26 January 1905, where Mr. Kayode's Ordination on 4 December was reported. After hearing Bishop Phillips's report on the "revengeful and oppressive conduct of the Native Ruler," the Secretary to the Executive Committee minuted that "much sympathy was expressed with the catechist" (p. 11).

19. CMS Archives Birmingham (G3.A2/0/1903/59), F. Melville Jones, Secretary, Minutes of E.C. Meeting 28 January–6 February, 1903, Lagos, pp. 7–8.

20. This distinction goes back to the work of Ferdinand Tönnies. I use this conceptualization despite the fact that I don't accept the evolutionary theory that lies behind it in the classical tradition.

21. NNA, CMS Papers, Yoruba Mission Letters from the Secretary CMS London to the Secretary, Yoruba Mission, Lagos, March 1903–August 1905 (CMS Y 1/1/13), 30 April 1903.

22. CMS Archives, London (G3.A2/0/1902/51), p. 4; (G3.A2/0/1903/59), F. Melville Jones, Secretary, Minutes of E.C. Meeting, 28 January–6 February 1903, in Lagos, pp. 7–8; (G3.A2/0/1904/41), Minutes of Executive Committee, January 1904.

23. CMS Archives, Birmingham (G3.A2/0/1902/48), F. Harding's Report on the Yoruba Executive Committee of 28 January–3 February 1902, p. 12.

24. CMS, *Extracts from the Annual Letters of the Missionaries* (London, 1904), p. 216.

25. CMS Archives, Birmingham (G3.A2/0/1918/48), Minutes of CMS Executive Committee, Lagos, 14–20 May 1918, p. 9.

26. CMS Archives, Birmingham, (G3.A2/0/1923/64), Remainder of Minutes of E.C. of 14–19 May 1923.

27. One of the lecturers read an early draft of this chapter and commented on the accuracy of its observations.

28. E. D. Adelowo, "Islam in Oyo and its Districts in the Nineteenth Century" (Ph.D. diss., University of Ibadan, July 1978), p. 142.

29. Ibid., pp. 426–29.

30. On the Parakoyi, see ibid., p. 112; Adelowo documents a Hausa line of succession to the chief imamship in Oyo. In Ilorin, a Yoruba-ized Fulani family controls the chief imamship. These appear to be exceptions to the more general pattern of local control over the central mosques.

31. From Oshogbo High Court, Bello Asani v. Yusuf Adeosun, 1967, p. 36.

32. Ibid., p. 39.

33. Ibid., pp. 29b ff.

34. Adeosun v. Oke et al., Heard in the Court of Appeal, Western State of Nigeria, Ibadan, 7 March 1968, p. 5.

35. Ibid., p. 8.

36. John N. Paden, in *Religion and Political Culture in Kano* (Berkeley: University of California Press, 1973), describes the Muslim battles for emirate succession in northern Nigeria in terms very similar to what I saw in battles for the imamship in Muslim Ile-Ife.

37. Sermon at St. Paul's, 25 May 1980.

38. Sermons at Enuwa Mosque, 25 April and 16 May 1980.

39. To be sure, if I were to argue that Jesus' love transcends any bargaining relationship, a scholar with the skill of Steven Brams could demonstrate that all I was describing was a different form of bargain. See his insightful *Biblical Games: A Strategic Analysis of Stories in the Old Testament* (Cambridge: MIT Press, 1980), esp. chap. 3.

40. Max Weber's categorization does not allow him to distinguish "authority" from "domination"; his *Herrschaft* conflates the two. See Max Weber, *Economy and Society*, ed. G. Roth and C. Wittich (Berkeley: University of California Press, 1978), esp. 1:61–62, n. 31 by Roth. On authority and credit ratings, see F. G. Bailey, *Strategems and Spoils* (Oxford: Blackwell, 1969), pp. 43–44. Bailey distinguishes the moral leader with a high credit rating from the contractual leader (of, say, a band of mercenaries) with a low credit rating. Domination, it seems to me, is the primary mode of contractual leadership in long-standing organizations.

41. P. C. Lloyd, the doyen of the nonindigenous sociologists of Yoruba society, has made a similar observation in *Power and Independence: Urban Africans' Perception of Social Inequality* (London: Routledge & Kegan Paul, 1974), p. 130.

42. H. W. Turner, *History of an African Independent Church* (Oxford: Clarendon Press, 1967), 2:39.

43. Here I am relying on the categories of A. Hirschman, *Exit, Voice, and Loyalty* (Cambridge: Harvard University Press, 1970).

44. The data on farm size and polygyny was from a survey conducted by I. H. Van den Driesen, who kindly supplied me with some of the data. Since the Christian sample was wealthier, and wealth also correlates with number of wives, it could be concluded from that survey that Christian membership might have had a marginal impact on richer men to have fewer wives than their wealth would justify.

45. Turner (n. 42), 2:43–44.

46. M. G. S. Hodgson, *The Venture of Islam* (Chicago: University of Chicago Press, 1974), 1:182.

CHAPTER 4

1. On the psychological push for congruence between religion and other aspects of life, see the images presented by Clifford Geertz in *Islam Observed* (Chicago: The University of Chicago Press, 1968), pp. 116–17. The congruence hypothesis has been most fully developed by Harry Eckstein. See his *Division and Cohesion in Democracy* (Princeton: Princeton University Press, 1966).

2. For the classic statement about the crisis of identity in the wake of incon-

gruent values, see Lucian W. Pye, *Politics, Personality, and Nation Building* (New Haven: Yale University Press, 1962).

3. I owe a considerable dept to Donald Morrison for sharing with me these data before he has had the opportunity to analyze them. I have culled together responses from the following questions in his questionnaire: 13, 16, 19, 20, 21, 22, 180, and 182. An interesting discussion on Yoruba views on development and change is presented by J. D. Y. Peel, "*Ọlaju*: A Yoruba Concept of Development,' *Journal of Development Studies* 14, no. 2 (January 1978).

4. Morrison, questions 8, 9, 11, 36, 37, 40, 154.

5. P. C. Lloyd, *Power and Independence*, (London: Routledge & Kegan Paul, 1974), pp. 160–61.

6. Christian respondents were given code numbers C1–35, and Muslims M1–35.

7. Geertz, *Islam Observed* (n. 1).

8. M. O. A. Abdul, "Yoruba Divination and Islam," *Orita* (Ibadan) 4, no. 1 (June 1970): 3.

9. A. R. I. Doi, "An Aspect of Islamic Syncretism in Yorubaland," *Orita* (Ibadan) 5, no. 1 (June 1971).

10. Patrick J. Ryan, *Imale: Yoruba Participation in the Muslim Tradition: A Study of Clerical Piety* (Missoula, Mont.: Scholars Press, 1978), p. 160, recorded this song in a Yoruba mosque: Money makes a young man a hero; . . . / God the Ruler is the Ruler who has the money at his side / He can make it for every one of us . . . / God is the Ruler who has shilling-money; / The path I will take to seek help is the hand of my Lord the King.

11. Samuel Johnson, *The History of the Yorubas* (London: Routledge, 1921). See also E. B. Idowu, *Olodumare: God in Yoruba Belief* (London: Longmans, 1962).

12. J. S. Eades, *The Yoruba Today* (Cambridge: The University Press, 1980), p. 134.

13. See T. G. O. Gbadamosi, *The Growth of Islam among the Yoruba, 1841–1908* (Atlantic Highlands, N.J.: Humanities Press, 1978), p. 104.

14. Ibid., pp. 145–46.

15. Akbar Muhammad, "Islam and National Integration through Education in Nigeria," in J. L. Esposito (ed.), *Islam and Development* (Syracuse: Syracuse University Press, 1980), p. 195.

16. Fascinating material on this unusual man is available from the *Sunday Times* (Lagos), 21 August 1977; and the *Daily Times* (Lagos), 1 January 1980.

17. J. S. Trimingham, *The Christian Church and Islam in West Africa* (London: SCM Press, 1955), p. 18.

18. J. F. A. Ajayi, *Christian Missions in Nigeria 1841–1891: The Making of a New Elite* (Evanston: Northwestern University Press, 1965), p. 23.

19. Among historians, there is consensus on this point. See Gbadamosi (n. 13), p. 156, n. 159, for references to Ajayi, Ayandele, and Webster.

20. J. H. Kopytoff, *A Preface to Modern Nigeria* (Madison: University of Wisconsin Press, 1965), pp. 248–49.

21. Humphrey J. Fisher, "Independency and Islam: The Nigerian Aladuras and Some Muslim Comparisons," *Journal of African History* 11, no. 2 (1970). See also A. R. I. Doi, "The Yoruba Mahdi," *Journal of Religion in Africa* (Leiden) 4, no. 2 (1971): 136, n. 34.

22. The *Ibadan Ecclesia Anglicana*, no. 25, Fourth Quarter, 1979, pp. 7–8, noted and responded to "the desire and interest of our members in the Cathedral to go on holy pilgrimage" by contracting with a group known as the "Inter Church Travels Agency." Chief Awolowo (a Christian) legitimated his world tour in the spring of 1980 to the Middle East, Europe, and the U.S. by calling it a religious pilgrimage. See the *Daily Times* (Lagos), 13 May 1980.

23. P. R. McKenzie "Samuel Crowther's Attitude to other Faiths During the Early Period," *Orita* (Ibadan) 5, no. 1 (June 1971).

24. The classical formulation here is that of A. D. Nock, *Conversion* (Oxford: Oxford University Press, 1933). See also P. Ryan (n. 10) and C. Geertz (n. 1).

25. See E. T. Donaldson, ed., *Beowulf* (New York: Norton, 1966), p. 55. I am relying on Daniel McCarthy's undergraduate paper prepared in spring 1979 for my course on political culture, University of California, San Diego.

26. One sees this tension just beneath the surface in the volume edited by I. A. B. Balogun, *Religious Understanding and Co-operation in Nigeria*, Proceedings of a Seminar Organized by the Department of Religions, University of Ilorin, 7–11 August, 1978.

27. Pierre Van den Berghe, *Power and Privilege at an African University* (Cambridge, Mass.: Schenkman, 1973), p. 211.

28. A good example to refute the religious evolutionary perspective is presented by C. Benard and Z. Khalilzad, "Secularization, Industrialization and Khomeini's Islamic Republic," *Political Science Quarterly* 94, no. 2 (Summer 1979).

29. Maxime Rodinson, *Islam and Capitalism*, trans. B. Pearce (New York: Pantheon, 1973), p. 75.

30. In his study of peasant revolts, James Scott comes to a similar conclusion. Scott, "Protest and Profanation," part 2, *Theory and Society* 4, no. 2 (1977): 225. I criticize Rodinson on this point in David Laitin, "Religion, Political Culture and the Weberian Tradition," *World Politics*, July 1978, pp. 578–83.

31. Discussed by M. Aronoff, "Conceptualizing the Role of Culture in Political Change," in Aronoff (ed.) *Political Anthropology Yearbook*, vol. 2 (New Brunswick, N.J.: Transaction, 1982).

32. M. Spiro, *Burmese Supernaturalism* (Englewood Cliffs, N.J.: Prentice Hall, 1967), demonstrates the complexity of symbolic structures within Buddhism and the potential societal relevance as well.

33. Systems of symbols are potential resources for the creation of utopian programs; only then does the question of congruence arise. Paul Brass, in *Language, Religion and Politics in North India* (Cambridge: The University Press, 1974) sees the forging of "symbolic congruence" as a strategy by a political elite to consolidate control over a "nation" whose boundaries had been defined by that elite in order to serve its own political interests.

34. K. Mannheim, *Ideology and Utopia* (London: Routledge, 1936).

35. Aristide Zolberg, "Moments of Madness," *Politics and Society*, Winter 1972, esp. pp. 205–6.

36. On the origins of the Maitatsine movement, see *New York Times*, 12 January 1981; *New Nigerian* (Kaduna) issues throughout January and February 1981; M. Z. Kano, "The Maitatsine Movement: An examination of a Micro-Religious Community's Challenge to Power in Kano," presented at the 1981

meeting of the African Studies Association, Bloomington, Indiana; P. Lubeck, "Islam and Resistance in Northern Nigeria," in W. Goldfrank (ed.), *World System of Capitalism* (Beverly Hills, Cal.: Sage, 1979); and Edmund Burke III and Paul Lubeck, "Islam, Oil and Nationalism," paper prepared for the conference on Global Crises and Social Movements, Santa Cruz, California, 1981. See *West Africa* (8 November 1982) and Alan Cowell's report of 16 November, 1982 in the *New York Times* for the continuing saga as the movement spread to Borno state. See also *West Africa* (6 May 1985) for a report on renewed Maitatsine-related violence in Bauchi state.

CHAPTER 5

1. The model study for the social systems perspective is Max Weber's *The Protestant Ethic and the Spirit of Capitalism*, trans. Talcott Parsons, (New York: Scribner's, 1958). Contemporary sociologists writing in this tradition have been equally influenced by Emile Durkheim's classic *Elementary Forms of Religious Life* (New York: Collier, 1961). I focus more on Weber than Durkheim in this book because my interest in the implications of cultural change is more closely connected with Weber's dependent variable in *The Protestant Ethic*, viz., subsystemic adaptation, than with Durkheim's dependent variable, viz., social solidarity. For the first attempt to bring the Durkheim/Weber social systems perspective into American social science, see Talcott Parsons and Edward Shils (eds.), *Towards a General Theory of Action* (Cambridge: Harvard University Press, 1951). The functional or homeostatic view of society is developed in Marion J. Levy, Jr., *The Structure of Society* (Princeton: Princeton University Press, 1952).

2. Clifford Geertz, "The Integrative Revolution," in his *The Interpretation of Cultures* (New York: Basic Books, 1973), pp. 260–61.

3. Joseph Gusfield codified some of those findings in his "Tradition and Modernity: Misplaced Polarities in the Study of Social Change," *American Journal of Sociology* 72 (January 1967). See also Lloyd I. Rudolph and Susanne Hoeber Rudolph, *The Modernity of Tradition* (Chicago: University of Chicago Press, 1967).

4. M. C. Young *Politics in the Congo* (Princeton: Princeton University Press, 1965).

5. See Myron Weiner, *Sons of the Soil: Migration and Ethnic Conflict in India* (Princeton: Princeton University Press, 1978); Mary F. Katzenstein, *Ethnicity and Equality: The Shiv Sena Party and Preferential Policies in Bombay* (Ithaca: Cornell University Press, 1979); and Paul Brass "Class, Ethnic Group, and Party in Indian Politics," *World Politics* 33, no. 3 (April 1981).

6. The classic statement of this position is by Mancur Olson, *The Logic of Collective Action* (Cambridge: Harvard University Press, 1965).

7. This is only one of a set of plausible propositions in Robert Melson and Howard Wolpe, "Modernization and the Politics of Communalism," *American Political Science Review* 64, no. 4 (December 1970).

8. Alvin Rabushka and Kenneth Shepsle, *Politics in Plural Societies: A Theory of Democratic Instability* (Columbus: Merrill, 1972).

9. This is the preliminary statement by Ronald Rogowski in "Understanding Nationalism: The Possible Contributions of a General Theory of Political Cleav-

age," unpublished manuscript, University of California, Los Angeles, September 1980.

10. Stanley Hoffmann, "Obstinate or Obsolete? The Fate of the Nation-State and the Case of Western Europe," in J.S. Nye (ed.), *International Regionalism* (Boston: Little, Brown, 1968), pp. 200–01.

11. This is from a paper by Robert Bates, "Modernization, Ethnic Competition, and the Rationality of Politics in Contemporary Africa," in Donald Rothchild and Victor Olorunsola (eds.), *Ethnicity, State Coherence, and Public Policy: African Dilemmas* (Boulder: Westview, 1983), p. 161.

12. Brian Barry "Ethnicity and the State," in D. J. R. Bruckner (ed.), *Politics and Language: Spanish and English in the United States* (Chicago: University of Chicago, Center for Policy Study, 1978), p. 46.

13. See Abner Cohen, *Custom and Politics in Urban Africa* (Berkeley: University of California Press, 1969).

14. I owe my colleague Samuel Popkin a great debt for teaching me to respect this approach and for listening to me trying to rebut it. See his *The Rational Peasant* (Berkeley: University of California Press, 1979), pp. 259–66. The "Olson problem" is raised in Olson (n. 6).

15. Michael Hechter, *Internal Colonialism* (Berkeley: University of California Press, 1975); also his "Group Formation and the Cultural Division of Labor" *American Journal of Sociology* 84, no. 2 (1978).

16. Peter Gourevitch, "The Reemergence of 'Peripheral Nationalisms': Some Comparative Speculations on the Spatial Distribution of Political Leadership and Economic Growth," *Comparative Studies in Society and History* 21, no. 3 (July 1979): 306.

17. Michael Hechter is a convert to the microeconomic perspective to explain group solidarity. Yet he is sufficiently sensitive to historical reality to acknowledge that "an analysis of group solidarity begun by considering the action of individuals leads inexorably to a conclusion emphasizing the primacy of state policies." See his "A Theory of Group Solidarity" in *Choice Models for Buyer Behavior*, Supplement 1, ed. Leigh McAlister (Greenwich, Conn.: JAI Press, 1982), pp. 294, 321 n. 15.

18. Walker Connor's work suggests that however strong states are, repressive policies in regard to nationalities often yield greater assertions of nationalism. See his "Self-Determination: The New Phase" *World Politics* 20, no. 1 (October 1967), and "Nation-Building or Nation-Destroying," *World Politics* 24, no. 3 (April 1972).

19. This is the thrust of the literature on "nation-building." See Karl Deutsch and William Foltz, *Nation-Building* (New York: Atherton Press, 1963). The importance of state action to overcome parochialism remains a common theme. See R. S. Milne, *Government and Politics in Malaysia* (Boston: Houghton Mifflin, 1967). A classic study of the manipulation of culture in order to create a nation is that of Eugen Weber, *Peasants into Frenchmen* (Stanford: Stanford University Press, 1976).

20. Steven Lukes, *Power: A Radical View* (London: Macmillan, 1974); John Gaventa, *Power and Powerlessness: Quiescence and Rebellion in an Appalachian Valley* (Urbana: University of Illinois Press, 1980).

21. The connection between pluralism and economic theory is fully developed in Robert Dahl and Charles Lindblom, *Politics, Economics, and Welfare* (New York: Harper, 1953).

22. See E. E. Schattschneider, *The Semi-Sovereign People* (New York: Holt, Rinehart & Winston, 1960), p. 71. This point was developed by Peter Bachrach and Morton Baratz, "The Two Faces of Power," *American Political Science Review* 56 (1962).

23. Gaventa (n. 20), p. 15.

24. Ibid., p. 13.

25. Gwyn Williams, quoted in Joseph Femia, "Hegemony and Consciousness in the Thought of Antonio Gramsci" *Political Studies* 23, no. 1 (March 1975): 30–31.

26. Gramsci, *Il materialismo storico e la filosofia di Benedetto Croce*, quoted in Femia (n. 25), p. 33.

27. Femia (n. 25), p. 34.

28. Gramsci, *Il materialismo storico e la filosofia di Benedetto Croce*, quoted in Femia (n. 25), p. 33.

29. Perry Anderson, "The Antinomies of Antonio Gramsci," *New Left Review* 100 (November 1976–January 1977): 29, for a summary statement of the role of hegemony in political society.

30. James Scott, "Hegemony and the Peasantry," *Politics and Society* 7, no. 3 (1977): 284.

31. Gramsci did not hold to this distinction rigidly, nor did Anderson (n. 29) claim that Gramsci did. But Anderson focuses on Gramsci's inability, despite many reformulations, to fight himself out of that rigid dichotomy between civil and political society.

32. See A. Przeworski and M. Wallerstein, "The Structure of Class Conflict in Democratic Capitalist Societies," *American Political Science Review* June 1982, for a bargaining approach to class compromise.

33. See David J. Cheal, "Hegemony, Ideology and Contradictory Consciousness," *Sociological Quarterly* 20, no. 1 (Winter 1979), who devises an interesting test for the notion of "contradictory consciousness" and finds support for the Gramscian formulation.

34. See chapter 1 of Paul Brass, *Language, Religion, and Politics in North India* (Cambridge: Cambridge University Press, 1974) for a sophisticated presentation of the idea of multiple cultural identities.

CHAPTER 6

1. See Arend Lijphart, "The Comparable-Case Strategy in Comparative Research," *Comparative Political Studies* 8 (July 1975).

2. P. C. Lloyd, *Yoruba Land Law* (London: Oxford University Press, 1962), chap. 3.

3. J. D. Y. Peel, *Ijeshas and Nigerians* (Cambridge: Cambridge University Press, 1983), p. 223, discusses with great sociological sophistication the changing formulation of *ilu* identity.

4. Samuel Johnson, *The History of the Yorubas* (London: Routledge & Kegan Paul, 1921), p. 3. This account is considered to have a pro-Oyo bias. It was

influential, for British administrators relied on Johnson's perspective in their attempt to refashion the tradition.

5. Ibid. See also J. A. MacKenzie, District Officer, "Extracts from a Report on Native Organization of the Ife Division," mimeo: n.d., written after 1931 but before 1934.

6. R. Law, *The Oyo Empire c. 1600–c. 1836* (Oxford: Clarendon Press, 1977), pp. 28–29.

7. Professor R. Armstrong, Institute of African Studies, University of Ibadan, personal correspondence; and I. Olomola, "Eastern Yorubaland Before Oduduwa," in I. A. Akinjogbin and G. O. Edemode (eds.), *The Proceedings of the Conference on Yoruba Civilization*, University of Ife, Nigeria July 1976, vol. 1.

8. Olomola (n. 7), p. 59.

9. See 'Biodun Adediran, "From 'city-states' to Kingdom: Political Centralization among the Sabe Sub-group of Western Yorubaland," Seminar paper, Institute of African Studies, University of Ife, March, 1979), p. 9, for an explanation of motives for peripheral cities to link up with Ife. On this point in general, see A. I. Asiwaju, "Political Motivation and Oral Historical Traditions in Africa: The Case of Yoruba Crowns, 1900–1960," *Africa* (London) 46, no. 2 (1976).

10. R. Horton, "Ancient Ife: A Reassessment," University of Ife (Spring, 1976). Cf. Robin Law, "Making Sense of a Traditional Narrative: Political Disintegration in the Kingdom of Oyo," *Cahiers d'études africaines* 22, nos. 3–4 (87–88), (1982).

11. The subsequent discussion is derived from Law (n. 6); S. O. Babayemi, "The Fall and Rise of Oyo c. 1760–1905: A Study in The Traditional Culture of an African Polity" (Ph.D. diss., University of Birmingham, 1979); P. Morton-Williams, "The Oyo Yoruba and the Atlantic Trade, 1670–1830." *Journal of the Historical Society of Nigeria* 3, no. 1 (1964); I. A. Akinjogbin, "The Expansion of Oyo and the Rise of Dahomey 1600–1800," in J. F. A. Ajayi and M. Crowder (eds.), *History of West Africa* (New York: Columbia University Press, 1972), v. 1; and A. Mabogunje and J. D. Omer-Cooper, *Owu in Yoruba History* (Ibadan: Ibadan University Press, 1971).

12. The major sources for this section include C. S. Whitaker, *The Politics of Tradition* (Princeton, N.J.: Princeton University Press, 1970); S. A. Akintoye, *Revolution and Power Politics in Yorubaland* (New York: Humanities Press, 1971); B. Awe, "The Rise of Ibadan as a Yoruba Power 1851–1893" (Ph.D. diss., Oxford University, 1965); and G. O. Oguntomisin, "Political Change and Adaptation in Yorubaland in the Nineteenth Century, *Canadian Journal of African Studies* 15, no. 2 (1981). On the politics of chiefly titles in Ibadan, see K. W. J. Post and G. D. Jenkins, *The Price of Liberty* (Cambridge: The University Press, 1973), chap. 1.

13. Oyeleye Oyediran's work is the best source for contemporary Ife politics. The most complete teatment of Ife politics is in his dissertation, "Political Change in a Nigerian Urban Community," University of Pittsburgh, 1971.

14. S. A. Akintoye (n. 12), pp. 122–23.

15. Akin Mabogunje and J. D. Omer-Cooper, *Owu in Yoruba History* (Ibadan: Ibadan University Press, 1971), p. 84.

16. Akintoye (n. 12), pp. viii–xix; see also Dan R. Aronson, "Cultural Stability and Social Change among the Modern Ijebu Yoruba" (Ph.D. diss., University of

Chicago, 1970), chap. 4; S. Johnson (n. 4), pp. 567–68; and G. O. Oguntomisin, "Political Change and Adaptation in Yorubaland in the Nineteenth Century," *Canadian Journal of African Studies* 15, no. 2 (1981).

17. See Akintoye (n. 12), pp. 69–72. The Ibadan system appears to be similar to the method of "direct rule" as employed by the French colonialists in Africa. See my discussion of direct rule in Dahomey (today's Benin), chap. 7.

18. See O. Oroge, "The Institution of Slavery in Yorubaland with Particular Reference to the Nineteenth Century" (Ph.D. diss., University of Birmingham, 1971). See also J. Clarke, "Households and the Political Economy of Small-Scale Cash Crop Production in South-Western Nigeria," *Africa* 51, no. 4 (1981). Parallel to Ibadan's changes are the large institutional changes taking place in new Oyo— not to preserve tradition but to regain lost power. See Babayemi (n. 11), chap. 3.

19. See Anthony Hopkins, *An Economic History of West Africa* (New York: Columbia University Press, 1973), pp. 125–26. See also Clarke (n. 18) for a rebuttal. Clarke argues that the emergence of small traders did not occur in Yoruba-land until the Pax Britannica. His data seem to support Hopkins's argument, however, on the following point: the war chiefs who operated so successfully as trading units in the Ibadan quasi empire were less subject to centralized state control than were the satellite cities in the Oyo Empire, whose kings were more directly controlled by Oyo. Thus, my point—that reconsolidation of central authority under legitimate trade would have been easier if the slave trade had not been constrained by the British blockade—is not disconfirmed by Clarke's analysis. In David D. Laitin, "Capitalism and Hegemony: Yorubaland and the International Economy," *International Organization* 36, no. 4 (Autumn 1982), I develop this point, but without the benefit of having read Clarke's work.

20. Elsewhere I have reinterpreted the socioeconomic conditions that led to British imperialism. See Laitin (n. 19).

21. See Obafemi Awolowo, *Awo* (Cambridge: The University Press, 1960), p. 20.

22. J. A. Atanda *The New Oyo Empire: Indirect Rule and Change in Western Nigeria, 1894–1934* (London: Longmans, 1973), pp. 228–33.

23. S. Johnson (n. 4), pp. 571–72.

24. Professor Robert Armstrong was kind enough to remind me of this point time and again. On the manipulation of descent, see Robin Law, "The Northern Factor in Yoruba History," in I. A. Akinjogbin and G. O. Ekemode (eds.), *The Proceedings of the Conference on Yoruba Civilization Held at the University of Ife, Nigeria, 26th–31st July, 1976*; and Isola Olomola, "How Realistic are the Historical Claims of Affinity among the Yoruba," paper delivered at the University of Ife, Institute of African Studies, March 1979.

25. J. S. Eades, *The Yoruba Today* (Cambridge: Cambridge University Press, 1980), p. 47. See also Akintoye (n. 12), pp. 80 and 95, as he demonstrates how fusion occurs among groups, given political necessity. This theme will be put into a more theoretical framework in chapter 7.

26. Mabogunje and Omer-Cooper (n. 15), p. 83.

27. P. C. Lloyd, *Power and Independence: Urban Africans' Perception of Social Equality* (London: Routledge & Kegan Paul, 1974), p. 121.

28. Aronson (n. 16), p. 208–9. To be sure a number of Ibadans, especially Christians, became part of Awolowo's *Ẹgbẹ* and later joined the Action Group.

29. Post and Jenkins (n. 12).

30. For a different interpretation, cf. R. Sklar, "The Ordeal of Chief Awolowo," in G. Carter (ed.), *Politics in Africa: Seven Cases* (New York Harcourt, Brace & World, 1966).

31. Peel (n. 3), p. 249.

32. Akinade Olumuyiwa Sanda, "The Dynamics of Ethnicity among the Yoruba" (Ph.D. diss., UCLA, 1974), p. 139; see also Aronson (n. 16), pp. 218–19.

33. Peter Koehn, "Prelude to Civilian Rule: The Nigerian Elections of 1979," *Africa Today* 28, no. 1 (1981): p. 37. Awolowo won 92.6 percent in Ogun and 94.5 percent in Ondo, the two other homogeneous Yoruba states.

34. To be sure, other "strangers" than Oyos have been involved in this dispute. For a fuller discussion of the economics of *isakole* and rent, see I. H. Van den Driesen, "Patterns of Land Holdings and Land Distribution in the Ife Division of Western Nigeria," *Africa* (London) 41, no. 1 (January 1971).

35. University of Ibadan, Nigerian National Archives (hereafter NNA), Ife Div 3/9, Annual Report, 1949.

36. O. Oyediran, "Local Influence and Traditional Leadership: The Politics of the Ife Forest Reserve," *Odu* (Ife), n.s. no. 7 (April 1972).

37. O. Oyediran, "In search of the Power Structure in a Nigerian Community," *Nigerian Journal of Economic and Social Studies* 14, no. 1 (July 1972).

38. C. E. F. Beer, *The Politics of Peasant Groups in Western Nigeria*, (Ibadan: Ibadan University Press, 1976), chap. 3.

39. *West Africa* (London), 22 August 1983, pp. 1927–28.

40. Pierre L. Van den Berghe, *Power and Privilege at an African University* (Cambridge, Mass.: Schenkman, 1973), p. 232.

41. Lloyd (n. 27), p. 171, for the quotation; pp. 169, 141, for supporting data. See also Sanda (n. 32), pp. 186–91.

42. G. O. Gbadamosi, "The Establishment of Western Education among Muslims in Nigeria, 1896–1926," *Journal of the Historical Society of Nigeria* 4, no. 1 (December 1967). On the data from Ile-Ife, I. H. Van den Driesen kindly supplied me with some of the data available from his research. The full sample, unfortunately, was not available. A complete discussion of the data base is in his "Patterns of Land Holding and Land Distribution in the Ife Division of Western Nigeria," *Africa* (London) 41, no. 1 (January 1971).

43. *Darul-Salam*, Islamic Youth League of Nigeria (Ibadan Branch), first issue (September 1966). Cf. *The Christian Student*, published by the Student Christian Movement, University of Ibadan; vol. 1 is from 1955. The University of Ibadan stores all ephemeral publications of registered groups. On the deficiencies of Muslim education in Lagos, see Sonia F. Graham, *Government and Mission Education in Northern Nigeria, 1900–1919, with Special Reference to the Work of Hanns Vischer* (Ibadan: Ibadan University Press, 1966), p. 73.

44. A. B. Fafunwa, *History of Education in Nigeria* (London: Allen & Unwin, 1974), p. 72; see also Van den Berghe (n. 40).

45. Richard Sklar, *Nigerian Political Parties* (Princeton: Princeton University Press, 1963), p. 285. On the differential performance of Ijebu Christians and Muslims, see also Aronson (n. 16). A Yoruba proverb, "Eyi ko-to-ofo, eyi-ko-to-ofo, fila Imale ku pereki" (Repeated refusal to attach importance to losses makes the Muslim's cap small; i.e., he can't afford a bigger one), gives cultural expression

to this differential economic performance. This proverb is reported in J. O. Ajibola, *Owe Yoruba* (Ibadan: Oxford University Press, 1947), no. 396.

46. Van den Driesen's data (n. 34) for land ownership. See also C. E. F. Beer, *The Politics of Peasant Groups in Western Nigeria* (Ibadan: Ibadan University Press, 1976); and S. S. Berry, "Christianity and the Rise of Cocoa-Growing in Ibadan and Ondo," *Journal of the Historical Society of Nigeria* 4, no. 3 (December 1968).

47. Aronson (n. 16), p. 285. Interestingly, and to jump ahead of the argument, Aronson shows that the Ibadan people, who are themselves predominantly Muslim, interpreted their relative poverty by reference to the *Ijebu* Christians rather than to the Ijebu *Christians*. For data on the percentage of Muslims in Ijebu, see M. O. A. Abdul, "Islam in Ijebu Ode" (M.A. thesis, McGill University, 1967).

48. On these data, I compared Muslim Yoruba respondents with Yoruba Protestants. Morrison also had responses from Catholic and "Independent Christian" Yorubas. The results would not have been markedly different if I had included the latter two groups along with the Protestants. I wish to thank Professor Morrison for his willingness to provide me with these data.

49. Sklar (n. 45), pp. 248–49.

50. David D. Laitin, "The Sharia Debate and the Origins of Nigeria's Second Republic," *Journal of Modern African Studies* 20, no. 3 (1982).

51. O. Oyediran, "Political Change in a Nigerian Urban Community" (Ph.D. diss., University of Pittsburgh, 1971).

52. Emmanuel Dada Adelowo, "Islam in Oyo and Its Districts in the Nineteenth Century" (Ph.D. diss., University of Ibadan, 1978), pp. 213–48. See also David B. Abernethy, *The Political Dilemma of Popular Education* (Stanford: Stanford University Press, 1969), p. 239. In my interviews, a number of Muslims told me stories of pressures they faced to convert when they attended mission schools.

53. See, e.g., *New Nigerian* (Kaduna), 18 August 1977; 19 August 1977; 29 August 1977; 1 June 1978; and 5 December 1979. *Daily Times* (Lagos) 22 November 1979; 6 November, 1979.

54. See, e.g., *Daily Times* (Lagos), 14 November 1979; 7 December 1979; 30 December 1979; 25 March 1980; 25 June 1980.

55. Van den Berghe (n. 40). My informant for my site planning visit agreed to find me Christian and Muslim men who would describe for me their religious life. She contacted only Christian men. It was only after I pressed her that she described her fear in contacting an elder of the Muslim community.

56. University of Ife, Circular No. 13/1979, "Posting of Notices on the Main Gate of the University," signed by E. O. Adetunji, Registrar.

57. Friday, 18 January 1980.

58. See, e.g., R. A. Shittu, *Islamic Ideology: Path to Democratic Socialism in Nigeria* (Shaki, Oyo State: Arowojeka Press, 1979[?]). Shittu is a Muslim Yoruba who has earned a degree in law. He has tied his political ambitions to an Islamic movement within Yorubaland. On the Christian side, in Yorubaland and elsewhere in Africa, church authorities often find themselves in opposition to political authorities who are particularly repressive (Amin in Uganda; Mobutu in Zaire; and Nguema in Equatorial Guinea) or who neglect poverty in backward areas where

there are mission outposts. Conflict between church and state in these matters has already occurred in a number of African settings. In Yorubaland, the role of the church in education was questioned by Governor Jakande in 1980. The Catholic archbishop, Olubunmi Okogie, was outraged; but he diplomatically worked out an accommodation. See *Daily Times* (Lagos), 25 June, 1980. Religious leaders with political ambition abound; but, as I shall argue in the next section, it is the public demand for religiously defined political leadership that is lacking in Yorubaland.

59. Robin Law cites a number of writers who have imagined a Muslim onslaught onto a Christian and pagan Yorubaland. See his *The Oyo Empire c. 1600–c. 1836: A West African Imperialism in the Era of the Atlantic Slave Trade* (Oxford: Clarendon Press, 1977), pp. 297ff.

60. Ibid., pp. 35–37; and Babayemi, (n. 11), p. 275. See also Johnson (n. 4), p. 194.

61. See C. S. Whitaker, Jr., *The Politics of Tradition: Continuity and Change in Northern Nigeria*, 1946–66 (Princeton: Princeton University Press, 1970), chap. 3, for an excellent background to Ilorin politics.

62. Abernethy (n. 52), pp. 153–54.

63. James Coleman, *Nigeria: Background to Nationalism* (Berkeley: University of California Press, 1958), pp. 364–66; Post and Jenkins (n. 12), p. 397; and John Paden, *Religion and Political Culture in Kano* (Berkeley: University of California Press, 1973), pp. 204–10.

64. *West Africa* (London), 22 August 1983, pp. 1927–28.

65. John A. A. Ayoade, "Electoral Politics in Western Nigeria" (Ph.D. diss., University of Ibadan, 1971).

66. See, e.g., Joane Nagel, "Politics and the Organization of Collective Action: The Case of Nigeria, 1960–1975," *Political Behavior* 3, no. 2 (1981); and Lloyd (n. 27), pp. 53–54.

67. O. Oyediran, "In Search of the Power Structure in a Nigerian Community," *Nigerian Journal of Economic and Social Studies* 14, no. 2 (July 1972); see also Western State of Nigeria, "Report of the Commission of Inquiry into the Civil Disturbances which occurred in certain parts of the Western State of Nigeria in the month of December 1968, and other matters incidental thereto or connected therewith," Lagos, 1969.

68. Morrison (n. 48), question nos. 002, 006, 007, 012, 034, 159, 176, 185, 186, and 201. On two questions, 010 and 060, the Christians showed greater satisfaction in feeling competent to get a civil servant to do his job properly and in influencing government in general.

69. The literature on the Nigerian civil war is vast. The most complete chronicle is that of A. H. M. Kirk-Greene, *Crisis and Conflict in Nigeria: A Documentary Sourcebook, 1966–1970*, 2 vols. (London: Oxford University Press, 1971).

70. John N. Paden, "Communal Competition, Conflict, and Violence in Kano," in Robert Melson and Howard Wolpe (eds.), *Nigeria: Modernization and the Politics of Communalism* (East Lansing: Michigan State University Press, 1971).

71. See John J. Stremlau, *The International Politics of the Nigerian Civil War, 1967–1970* (Princeton: Princeton University Press, 1977), for a discussion on the manipulation of world opinion.

72. See the willingness of the northern representative to the Aburi Conference ("Meeting of the Nigerian Military Leaders held at Peduase Lodge, Aburi, Ghana," Nigerian Federal Ministry of Information, Lagos, 1967) to allow the East to secede.

73. See Awolowo's talk reported in the *Daily Times* (Lagos), 2 May 1967. His reasoning is discussed in John Stremlau (n. 71), pp. 52–53.

74. A major premise of Robert Melson and Howard Wolpe, *Nigeria: Modernization and the Politics of Communalism* (East Lansing: Michigan State University Press, 1971), is that communal action, such as the massacres of the Igbos in the north or the Igbo secession, can be explained by a rational choice model. But even if the model could explain those two things, it is inadequate when asked to explain such things as the "failure" of a southern Christian alliance of Yorubas and Igbos, which would have divided Yorubaland based on religion.

CHAPTER 7

1. There is a third, nontheoretical one: many scholars, as mentioned in the Appendix, feel that Yorubas are naturally tolerant people. See, e.g., Geoffrey Parrinder, *Religion in Africa* (Baltimore: Penguin, 1969), p. 235, who makes this claim for Africans in general; and T. G. O. Gbadamosi, *The Growth of Islam among the Yoruba, 1841–1908* (Atlantic Highlands, N.J.: Humanities Press, 1978), p. 12, for the Yorubas in particular. In the present context, this claim avoids the sociological question of why Yorubas appear to be tolerant with respect to religion and less tolerant of strangers from different ancestral cities.

2. John S. Mbiti, *African Religions and Philosophy* (New York: Praeger, 1969), pp. 3, 263.

3. On Yoruba names, see Samuel Johnson, *A History of the Yorubas* (London: Routledge & Kegan Paul, 1921), chap. 5. For their contemporary significance, see Karin Barber, "The Challenge of Yoruba Oriki to Literary Criticism," paper delivered to the African Studies Association, Bloomington, Indiana, 1981.

4. See, e.g., Gbadamosi (n. 1), p. 127.

5. See Joseph Omosade Awolalu, "Sacrifice in the Religion of the Yoruba" (Ph.D. diss., University of Ibadan, 1970), esp. p. 369.

6. See chapter 4, where I discuss my theoretical objections to the concept of syncretism.

7. The following observations are my own. But other expatriates who have no interest in whether the Yorubas are doctrinally sound are often astonished by the apparent devoutness of Yorubas in their practice of Islam and Christianity. See J. S. Eades, *The Yoruba Today* (Cambridge: The University Press, 1980), p. 134; see also "Nigerian Tribal Leader Wields Great Influence in Business and Politics," *Wall Street Journal*, 30 October 1979: "A tall white wooden cross stands in the back garden and is a testament to the chief's devout Christianity. He leads his family in worship and religious songs daily at 5:30 a.m."

8. A. Babs Fafunwa, *History of Education in Nigeria* (London: Allen & Unwin, 1974), p. 58.

9. H. W. Turner, *History of An African Independent Church* (Oxford: Clarendon Press, 1967). See esp. vol. 2, *The Life and Faith of the Church of the Lord (Aladura)*, where Turner demonstrates beyond doubt a rich independent and

Christian theological tradition in Yorubaland. Turner's thesis is corroborated by data provided in J. D. Y. Peel, *Aladura: A Religious Movement among the Yoruba* (London: Oxford University Press, 1968), and in J. B. Webster, *The African Churches among the Yoruba, 1888–1922* (London: Oxford University Press, 1964).

10. The *Nigerian Islamic Review* (Lagos) reported in its second number that the first issue sold out its 5,000 copies in Lagos alone in twenty-four hours. Extra printings were ordered.

11. Pierre L. van den Berghe, *Power and Privilege at an African University* (Cambridge, Mass.: Schenkman, 1973), p. 209.

12. David Kidd, *Factors Affecting Farmers' Response to Extension in Western Nigeria*, Report no. 30 (East Lansing: Consortium for the Study of Nigerian Rural Development, 1968).

13. A few Yorubas told me that they had converted because they "heard the word of God." A small number told me of their visions in colorful detail. Although I did not actively seek such testimony, my feeling is that deep religious experiences were not part of the early conversion experience. Too many of my interviewees could hardly remember the exact circumstances of their decisions to convert. Ecstatic religious experiences were generally associated more with the aladura converts in the 1920s and later.

14. I owe Barry Hallen a great debt for allowing me to inspect his raw interview data. His research, in collaboration with J. O. Sodipo, seeks to demonstrate the epistemological foundations of a genuine Yoruba philosophical tradition. See their paper, "An African Epistemology: The Knowledge/Belief Distinction and Yoruba Thought," delivered to the African Studies Association, Bloomington, Indiana, 1981.

15. See S. M. Lipset, *Political Man* (New York: Doubleday, 1960), p. 77.

16. Professor A. I. Asiwaju, University of Lagos, personal communication.

17. K. W. J. Post and G. D. Jenkins, *The Price of Liberty: Personality and Politics in Colonial Nigeria* (Cambridge: The University Press, 1973), p. 34.

18. Obafemi Awolowo, *Awo* (Cambridge: The University Press, 1960), p. 11. For data on Awolowo's sister, see the obituary notice for their mother, *Sunday Times* (Lagos), Feburary 1980.

19. See, e.g., M. G. S. Hodgson, *The Venture of Islam* (Chicago: University of Chicago Press, 1974), 1:173. Or from the New Testament, see, e.g., Matthew 8:21: "Another man, one of his disciples, said to him, 'Lord, let me go and bury my father first.' Jesus replied, 'Follow me, and leave the dead to bury their dead.'"

20. There is a bias in my sample that must be acknowledged. Since I interviewed church and mosque elders, I have a self-selected group of people for whom religion is important. Therefore my data will overemphasize the social cohesion of co-religionists. However, since I chose my church and mosque from the center of the town, and almost all the men interviewed were sons of Ile-Ife, solidarity based on ancestral city will also be overemphasized. So there should not be a systematic bias in either direction.

21. Since I was interested in the social construction of the family, I did not specify which sister should be described. If I were inteested in analysing changes in the "traditional" family structure, I would clearly have had to specify the sister.

22. Muslim exogamy overall is greater. This reflects an aspect of Yoruba

Muslim culture that I have not discussed in this volume. I treat it in "Conversion and Political Change: A Study of (Anglican) Christianity and Islam among the Yorubas in Ile-Ife," in M. J. Aronoff (ed.), *Political Anthropology Yearbook* (New Brunswick, N.J.: Transaction, 1982).

23. See M. C. Young, *Politics in the Congo* (Princeton: Princeton University Press, 1965), especially his discussion of the Bangala people, pp. 242–46; Robert Bates, "Ethnic Competition and Modernization in Contemporary Africa," *Comparative Political Studies* 6, no. 4 (January 1974); Nelson Kasfir, "Explaining Ethnic Political Participation," *World Politics* 31, no. 3 (April 1979); Abner Cohen, *Custom and Politics in Urban Africa* (Berkeley: University of California Press, 1969); and Joseph Gusfield, "The Social Construction of Tradition: An Interactionist View of Social Change," in J. D. Legge (ed.), *Traditional Attitudes and Modern Styles in Political Leadership* (Melbourne: Angus & Robertson, 1973).

24. Saburi O. Biobaku, *The Egba and their Neighbours, 1842–1872* (Oxford: Clarendon Press, 1965), p. 3.

25. A. I. Asiwaju, "Political Motivation and Oral Historical Traditions in Africa: The Case of Yoruba Crowns, 1900–1960," *Africa* (London) 46, no. 2.

26. T. Chappel, "The Yoruba Cult of Twins in Historical Perspective," *Africa* (London) 44, no. 3 (1974). Chappel's study concentrates on the historical timing. He offers no causal theory for change. Obviously both ideas and demographic changes had some influence. The point here is that "tradition" is not a static but a dynamic reality.

27. P. C. Lloyd, *Power and Independence: Urban Africans' Perception of Social Inequality* (London: Routledge & Kegan Paul, 1974), and Van den Berghe (n. 11), both writing in the socialist tradition, use this evidence to help to explain the lack of working-class consciousness in Yorubaland.

28. Eades (n. 7), p. 63.

29. On the relevance of India to twentieth-century African political thought, see *Awo* (n. 18), pp. 160–62, and Ali A. Mazrui, "Mahatma Gandhi and Black Nationalism," in *Political Values and the Educated Class in Africa* (London: Heinemann, 1978).

30. Russell Hardin helped me to understand this point.

31. Robert Bates emphasized this point to me. But here it may be overstated. A less than revolutionary revisionism in the Yoruba historical tradition could make Nigerian northerners into Yoruba blood brothers. See Robin Law, "The Northern Factor in Yoruba History," in I. A. Akinjogbin and G. O. Ekemode (eds.) *The Proceedings of the Conference on Yoruba Civilization*, University of Ife, 26–31 July 1976.

32. F. G. Lugard, *The Dual Mandate in British Tropical Africa* (London: Frank Cass & Co., 1922).

33. This historical reinterpretation of British colonial rule relies heavily on J. A. Atanda, *The New Oyo Empire* (London: Longmans, 1973). S. O. Babayemi's "The Fall and Rise of Oyo c. 1760–1905: A Study in the Traditional Culture of an African Polity" (Ph.D. diss., Birmingham, 1979) is partly in agreement with, and in part a refutation of, Atanda's argument. Babayemi places the British strategy of providing power to a weak but legitimate Alaafin as preceding Lugard (pp. 268–69). In

this sense, the Atanda thesis could be strengthened. But Babayemi emphasizes the ritual power of new-Oyo and its Alaafin, which was independent of British actions. He doubts whether Ibadan could ever have established a centralized state without borrowing the ritual legitimacy of the Alaafin. Also, Babayemi points to some examples where British power was used to enhance Ibadan's power (p. 255). We will never know if Ibadan could have established its own empire. But the weight of evidence does support the point that Atanda and Babayemi make in common: that British governors promoted the traditional power of a near defunct kingdom in order to enhance British imperial designs.

34. Samuel Johnson (n. 3), p. 574.

35. Ibid., p. 584.

36. Atanda (n. 33), p. 102.

37. Ibid., p. 118.

38. Jeremy White, *Central Administration in Nigeria, 1914–1948* (Dublin: Irish Academic Press, 1981), p. 74.

39. R. L. Buell, *The Native Problem in Africa* (Bureau of International Research, Harvard University, 1928; repr. Hamden, Conn.: Archon, 1965), 1:709.

40. Ibid., pp. 666, 709.

41. Atanda (n. 33), p. 203.

42. Ibid., p. 258. See also Post and Jenkins (n. 17), p. 21.

43. See Buell (n. 39), p. 708, who tends to emphasize the Alaafin's objections to collaboration.

44. See Eades (n. 7), p. 11. For the Ile-Ife case, see Oyeleye Oyediran, "In Search of the Power Structure in a Nigerian Community," *Nigerian Journal of Economic and Social Studies* 14, no. 2 (July 1972): 203. See also Oyediran, "Political Change in a Nigerian Urban Community" (Ph.D. diss., University of Pittsburgh, 1971), p. 232.

45. Asiwaju (n. 25), p. 116.

46. Gbadamosi (n. 1), pp. 161–63.

47. Ibid., pp. 164–66; 215–16, and appendix 3. Razak 'Deṛemi Abubakre, "The Contribution of the Yorubas to Arabic Literature" (Ph.D. diss., University of London, 1980), gives further examples. It was the British, he points out (p. 173) who brought an Arabic printing press to Yorubaland. And he notes from personal experience as a grader for the West African School Certificate Arabic examinations (p. 172) that the students from the coastal areas did better than those from the more northern regions. Since British schools were more prevalent on the coast, the author infers that British imperialism had at least some positive impact on the development of Arabic.

48. E. A. Ayandele, *The Missionary Impact on Modern Nigeria, 1842–1914: A Political and Social Analysis* (New York: Humanities Press, 1967), pp. 150–51.

49. R. A. Adeleye, *Power and Diplomacy in Northern Nigeria, 1804–1906: The Sokoto Caliphate and its Enemies* (London: Longmans, 1971), p. 6.

50. R. K. Home, "Urban Growth and Urban Government: Contradictions in the Colonial Political Economy," in Gavin Williams (ed.), *Nigeria: Economy and Society* (London: Rex Collings, 1976).

51. See Pauline H. Baker, *Urbanization and Political Change: The Politics of*

Lagos 1917–1967 (Berkeley: University of California Press, 1974), part 3; and Abner Cohen, *Custom and Politics in Urban Africa: A Study of Hausa Migrants in Yoruba Towns* (Berkeley: University of California Press, 1969).

52. Peter Lloyd, *Yoruba Land Law* (London: Oxford University Press, 1962), pp. 86–89, 357–60.

53. Richard L. Sklar, *Nigerian Political Parties* (Princeton: Princeton University Press, 1963), pp. 235–38.

54. Nigerian National Archives (Ibadan), Ife Division, 1/1/1930, "Ẹgbẹ Ọmọ Ibilẹ Ife."

55. White (n. 38), chap. 12.

56. See references in chap. 4, note 36. In all sources, I have seen no evidence of political forces in southern Nigeria attempting to align with these northern activists.

57. See Stephen Akintoye, *Revolution and Power Politics in Yorubaland, 1840–1893: Ibadan Expansion and the Rise of the Ekitiparapo* (New York: Humanities Press, 1971), p. 80.

58. This is the argument of Olatunde J. B. Ojo, "The Impact of Personality and Ethnicity on the Nigerian Elections of 1979," *Africa Today* 28, 1st quarter (1981).

59. Peter A. Gourevitch, "The Reemergence of 'Peripheral Nationalisms': Some Comparative Speculations on the Spatial Distribution of Political Leadership and Economic Growth," *Comparative Studies in Society and History* 21, no. 3 (July 1979).

60. See, e.g., W. B. Schwab, "The Growth and Conflicts of Religion in a Modern Yoruba Community," *Zaire* 6, no. 8 (1952): 834. Not Schwab, who already saw the secular aspects of traditional ritual eight years before independence, but other anthropologists, in the Durkheimian tradition, tend to seek the "real" tradition, thereby focusing on people who have been least influenced by "foreign" culture. See, e.g., E. E. Evans-Pritchard's cavalier dismissal of Islam in the early pages of his classic study of *The Nuer* (Oxford: Oxford University Press, 1940). It was not that Islam was inconsequential; in fact, many Nuer considered themselves to be devout Muslims. It is just that Evans-Pritchard saw Islam as not part of the real Nuer tradition. In my observation of the Ọṣun festival (the one reported on by Schwab) in 1977, I was struck by the role of high-ranking bureaucrats, visiting from Lagos for the festival, *reading* the "traditional" praise songs to the king. The prepared texts these bureaucrats read from, and the Mercedes-Benz cars in which they traveled to Oshogbo, are no less part of the tradition than the shrine to Ọṣun.

61. This section relies heavily on John C. Paden, *Religion and Political Culture in Kano* (Berkeley: University of California Press, 1973), pp. 36–40. The four cleavages refer to the situation in the Kano Emirate.

62. C. S. Whitaker, Jr., *The Politics of Tradition: Continuity and Change in Northern Nigeria, 1946–1966* (Princeton: Princeton University Press, 1970), pp. 396–97. See also Paden (n. 61), p. 312. On p. 311 Paden reports that Awolowo attempted to break NPC power in the north by asking help from a Tijanniya leader to bless his party, the Action Group.

63. This discussion of the role of minority tribes is based on Billy Dudley, *An Introduction to Nigerian Government and Politics* (Bloomington: Indiana University Press, 1982), chap. 6. Dudley proposes that "state" has become another important cleavage line, a category I do not explore in this study.

64. Nigerian authorities blame "Lebanese and Iranian mullahs" who have illegally entered Nigeria and turned innocent Nigerian youths into religoius "fanatics." But no one denies the potential explosiveness of religious imagery in northern Nigera. See *West Africa* (6 May 1985), p. 876.

65. In Kano, for example, Fulani clan mosques may still exist, "but have been eclipsed in importance by the Islamic brotherhoods, which, in a sense, replaced them." Paden (n. 61), p. 52.

66. The literature on the Fulani jihad in Nigeria is vast. See Michael Crowder, *A Short History of Nigeria* (New York: Praeger, 1966), for a good introduction and bibliography.

67. Looking at the effects of the British conquest of Kano, Paden (n. 61), p. 56, concludes that they "contributed to the establishment of the Tijaniyya brotherhood in Kano." See also Whitaker (n. 62), pp. 279–82, on the "Sanusi affair," showing how Sokoto outpaced Kano in the period of colonial rule.

68. In "Hegemony and Religious Conflict," in Peter Evans et al., *Bringing the State Back In* (Cambridge: The University Press, 1985), I discuss the politicization of religion in postcolonial India.

69. Jean Surat-Canale, *French Colonialism in Tropical Africa*, trans. Till Gottheiner (New York: Pica Press, 1971), p. 73.

70. See A. I. Asiwaju, *Western Yorubaland under European Rule, 1889–1945*, for an exemplary controlled comparison of British and French colonial policies and their different sociocultural impacts.

71. Dov Ronen, *Dahomey* (Ithaca: Cornell University Press, 1975), pp. 42–43.

72. Information on the background of the Benin elites comes from S. Decalo, *Historical Dictionary of Dahomey* (Metuchen, N.J.: Scarecrow Press, 1976). On the *fonctionnaires* in the legislative bodies, see Maurice-A. Glélé, *Naissance d'un état noire* (Paris: Pinchon & Durand-Azuzias, 1969); pp. 314–15. Glélé emphasizes that "le Dahomey ne connut rien de semblable au parti des chefs du Ghana ou du Nigéria . . . On ne retrouve que les évolués, les fonctionnaires dans les Assemblées Electives, dans les Gouvernements, de 1945 à 1965 . . . Les chefs ne pouvant se constituer en parti politique, servent d'agents electoraux pour les partis, attisant les luttes partisanes et contribuant à saper leur propre autorité" (pp. 314, 305).

73. On these electoral data see Martin Staniland "The Three Party System in Dahomey," *Journal of African History* 14, nos. 2–3 (1973), and Glélé (n. 72), p. 205. Note the omission of the 1959 election, in which the Ketu electoral district was subject to gerrymandering—it was coupled with the Fon city of Adakplame. See Glélé, p. 168. Cf. K. W. J. Post, *The Nigerian Federal Election of 1959* (London: Oxford University Press, 1963), and J. D. Y. Peel, *Ijeshas and Nigerians* (Cambridge: The University Press, 1983), for analyses of internal divisions within Nigerian Yoruba towns. My point, viz., that in Nigeria, unlike Dahomey, ancestral cities have spoken with a corporate voice, still holds.

74. Nigerian National Archives (Ibadan), CMS Papers, Yoruba Mission, Letters from the Secretary, CMS, London, to the Secretary, Yoruba Mission, Lagos, March 1903–August 1905 [CMS Y 1/1/13], correspondence on 1 May 1903; 17 July 1903. See also correspondence with Lugard, at the CMS Archives (Birmingham), [G3 A2/0/1923/10], after Lugard became governor in 1914.

75. See Whitaker (n. 62), chap. 3. On the pressures toward an Islamic perspec-

tive in Ilorin, see R. 'D. Abubakre, "The Contribution of the Yorubas to Arabic Literature" (Ph.D. diss., University of London, SOAS, 1980).

76. See Antonio Gramsci on the politics of *transformismo* in Italy, in *Selections from the Prison Notebooks*, ed. Quintin Hoare and Geoffrey Nowell Smith (New York: International Publishers, 1971), pp. 55ff.

CHAPTER 8

1. By neopositivism I am suggesting that the "positivism" of the Vienna Circle and exemplified by A. J. Ayer's *Language, Truth, and Logic* does not accurately describe or effectively guide social science. The goal of universal nomothetic propositions led positivists to seek to eliminate contextual descriptions from their scientific writings. The fulfillment of this goal, in my judgment, cannot lead to a scientific understanding of social and political life. But I remain an unrepentent Popperian in my commitment to the belief that scientific propositions ought to be stated in such a way that other investigators can in principle bring evidence to bear that might disconfirm those propositions. Popper's methodology is not inconsistent with Wittgenstein's advocacy of a science that provides plausible accounts of phenomena that appear odd given our present theories and guided by our form of life. Michael Scriven, writing in the Wittgensteinian tradition, advocates the formation of "normic" statements in the social sciences. These are indeed subject to disconfirming evidence. See his "Explanation, Predictions, and Laws," in H. Feigl and G. Maxwell (eds.), *Minnesota Studies in the Philosophy of Science*. vol. 3 (Minneapolis: University of Minnesota Press, 1962). Wittgenstein's concern for contextual understanding combined with Popper's for the possibility of disconfirmation lead to an approach to the social sciences that I shall refer to as "neopositivist."

2. Brian Barry's central thesis in *Sociologists, Economists, and Democracy* (London: Collier-Macmillan, 1970) is that independent variables that rely on "internalized, normative constraints" have not been successful in explaining whether democracies are likely to persist; but he admits, although he remains a skeptic about their confirmation, that propositions which use "values" as their independent variable are not "beyond the reach of empirical check" (pp. 48, 95).

3. See Clifford Geertz, "Ideology as a Cultural System," in *The Interpretation of Cultures* (New York: Basic Books, 1973). In the final pages of that stimulating essay, Geertz lists a plethora of factors that overrode a symbolically powerful ideology in Indonesia.

4. Abner Cohen, *Custom and Politics in Urban Africa: A Study of Hausa Migrants in Yoruba Towns* (Berkeley: University of California Press, 1969).

5. Clifford Geertz, "Deep Play: Notes on a Balinese Cockfight," in Geertz (n. 3).

6. David Laitin *Politics, Language, and Thought: The Somali Experience* (Chicago: University of Chicago Press, 1977), chap. 6.

7. I am referring to Karl Marx, *The 18th Brumaire of Louis Napoleon*.

8. Ever since Arthur Bentley's *The Process of Government* (Chicago, 1908), the state, in American political science, became reduced to the vector sum of group interests in society. See also David Truman, *The Governmental Process* (New York: Alfred Knopf, 1962); and David Easton, "The Political System Besieged by the State," *Political Theory* 9, no. 3 (August 1981).

9. See J. P. Nettl, "The State as a Conceptual Variable," *World Politics* 20, no. 1 (1968); see also Theda Skocpol, *States and Social Revolutions* (Cambridge: The University Press, 1979), for a recent attempt to bring the state back in as a variable for political explanation.

10. Geertz, "Religion as a Cultural System," in *The Interpretation of Cultures* (n. 3). The Santayana quote is on p. 87; see also p. 90, where Geertz accepts Santayana's framework.

11. Ibid., pp. 124, 90.

12. See P. C. Lloyd, *Yoruba Land Law* (Oxford: Oxford University Press, 1962). Lloyd writes, "Some people say that the African loves a land dispute; one could argue that a protracted land case awakens and reaffirms family or town loyalties. Yet I did not encounter a single informant who felt that land disputes were thus advantageous . . . They all . . . tend to involve a large number of people, being a major call on both their time and their money" (p. 4). Yorubas indeed have been immersed in countless procedural debates in courts about land ownership, not because they value procedures but because they value their land, and civil courts were reallocating titles.

13. See the comments on standard definitions of political culture in the political science literature in Laitin (n. 6), p. 17.

14. See Clifford Geertz, "Art as a Cultural System," in *Local Knowledge* (New York: Basic Books, 1983), pp. 98–99 where he (incorrectly) assumes that the Yoruba cultural attachment to the "line" is deeply embedded and unchanging. In that passage, Geertz can perhaps be excused for reprinting R. F. Thompson's mistranslation of the Yoruba word for civilization, which means, literally, the "opening up of eyes" (not, as Thompson writes, "The earth has lines upon its face"). But it is shocking that Geertz, who has cited approvingly Wittgenstein's *Philosophical Investigations* in his earlier work, would accept etymological information as sufficient to prove a point about contemporary meaning. In fact, any careful analysis of the Yoruba concept of civilization, such as the one done by J. D. Y. Peel, "*Ọlaju:* A Yoruba Concept of Development," *Journal of Development Studies* 14, no. 2 (January 1978), would demonstrate that Yoruba vocabulary, like the vocabulary of all natural languages, is dynamic and changing. Meaning can only be properly judged by observing the language in use. In this case, relying entirely on etymological information, Geertz presents too static a view of culture.

15. This is the argument of Max Weber in "The Protestant sects and the Spirit of Capitalism," in H. H. Gerth and C. W. Mills (eds.), *From Max Weber: Essays in Sociology* (New York: Oxford University Press, 1946). It is developed brilliantly in Cohen (n. 4).

16. For ideas on how to think about "risk aversion" as a "frame" or perhaps even as a "cultural system," see the suggestive work by Amos Tversky and Daniel Kahneman, "The Framing of Decisions and the Psychology of Choice," *Science* 211 (30 January 1981).

17. Crawford Young, *The Politics of Cultural Pluralism* (Madison: University of Wisconsin Press, 1976); and Nelson Kasfir "Explaining Ethnic Political Participation," *World Politics* 31, no. 3 (April 1979).

18. See Richard Madsen, *Meaning and Power in a Chinese Village* (Berkeley: University of California Press, 1984), for an extended discussion on how strategic action can be interpreted only within specified moral frameworks.

APPENDIX

1. Clifford Geertz, *The Interpretation of Cultures* (New York: Basic Books, 1973), p. 20.
2. David D. Laitin, *Politics, Language, and Thought* (Chicago: University of Chicago Press, 1977), chaps. 6–8; on the idea of "cultural system," see Geertz (n. 1), chaps. 8, "Ideology as a Cultural System," and 4, "Religion as a Cultural System."
3. R. H. Tawney, *Religion and the Rise of Capitalism* (New York: Harcourt, Brace & Co., 1935), initially criticized Weber's approach on these terms.
4. Max Weber, *Economy and Society*, ed. Guenther Roth and Claus Wittich (Berkeley: University of California Press, 1978), vol. 1, p. lxiv, from Roth's Introduction. The quotation is a from a letter of Weber's written in 1914.
5. On the methodology of the comparative method in political science, see Arend Lijphart, "The Comparable-Case Strategy in Comparative Research," *Comparative Political Studies* 8 (July 1975); and Alex George, "Case Studies and Theory Development: The Method of Structured, Focused Comparison," in Paul G. Lauren (ed.), *Diplomacy: New Approaches in History, Theory, and Policy* (New York: Free Press, 1979).
6. Max Weber, "The Social Psychology of the World Religions," in H. H. Gerth and C. W. Mills (eds.), *From Max Weber* (New York: Oxford, 1946), p. 267.
7. John S. Mbiti, *African Religions and Philosophy* (New York: Praeger, 1969), chaps. 3, 9, 15.
8. Midday ceremonies in excruciating heat at the Anglican church may have been performed for bureaucratic reasons (to fit into the bishop's schedule) rather than to enhance their public nature.
9. See Edward A. Alpers, "Towards a History of the Expansion of Islam in East Africa: The Matrilineal Peoples of the Southern Interior" in T. O. Ranger and I. N. Kimambo (eds.), *The Historical Study of African Religions* (Berkeley: University of California Press, 1972), p. 194. While acceptance of the myth is widespread, it is not universal. For work that acknowledges the demands on Muslim converts, see W. Arens, "Islam and Christianity in Sub-Saharan Africa: Ethnographic Reality or Ideology," *Cahiers d'études africaines* 15, no. 3 (1975): 446: and R. Kahane, "Religious Diffusion and Modernization," *Archives européenes de sociologie* 21, no. 1 (1980): 121.
10. Interview, 23 January 1980.
11. See T. G. O. Gbadamosi, *The Growth of Islam among the Yoruba 1841–1908* (Atlantic Highlands, N.J.: Humanities Press, 1978), chap. 7; M. O. A. Abdul, "Islam in Ijebu Ode" (M.A. Thesis, McGill University, 1967), p. 38; Patrick J. Ryan, *Imale: Yoruba Participation in the Muslim Tradition: A Study of Clerical Piety* (Missoula, Mont.: Scholars Press, 1978), p. 255; W. O. A. Nasiru, "The Advent and Development of Islam in Ibadan" (unpublished paper, Ibadan, 1979); E. D. Adelowo, "Islam in Oyo and Its Districts in the Nineteenth Century" (Ph.D. diss., University of Ibadan, (July, 1978), pp. 466, 484–85, 497; Alhaji Dawud O. Shittu Noibi, "The Islamic Formula for the Eradication of Corruption in Society," in I. A. B. Balogun (ed.), *Religious Understanding and Cooperation in Nigeria*

(Ilorin, 1978), p. 300; and interviews among the Muslim elders of Ile-Ife, field notes, February–March, 1980.

12. J. O. Awolalu, "Sacrifice in the Religion of the Yoruba" (Ph.D. diss., University of Ibadan, 1970), pp. 339–44, while agreeing with the principle that the Christians used "bloody force" to eradicate traditional sacrifice while Muslims relied on "evolution," still provided evidence of Muslim pressures to change Yoruba traditions. See also Nasiru (n. 11); Adelowo (n. 11), pp. 408–11; and E. D. Adelowo, "The Muslim Concept of Monotheism vis-à-vis the Christian Concept of Trinity and the Theory of Diffused Monotheism in African Traditional Religion—Studies in Comparative Religion," lecture at the University of Ife, November, 1979.

13. J. F. Ade Ajayi, *Christian Missions in Nigeria, 1871–1891: The Making of a New Elite* (Evanston: Northwestern University Press, 1965), chap. 3. See also the data of J. Peel, *Ijeshas and Nigerians* (Cambridge: The University Press, 1983), p. 166.

14. On Protestantism and magic in England, see Keith Thomas, *Religion and the Decline of Magic* (New York: Scribners, 1971). On the Yorubas committing themselves to gods based on their performance, magical or otherwise, see Karen Barber, "How Man Makes God in West Africa: Yoruba Attitudes towards the Orişa," *Africa* (London) 51, no. 3 (1981). For an example of the use of the magic lantern in Ile-Ife, see the Nigerian National Archives (Ibadan), CMS "Y" Phillips: 1/3/8, Diaries 1899. See entry of 23 May.

15. Interview with Father O'Hay, Ibadan, 9 August 1977. The Hallen interviews are from his Notebook no. 1, 1974.

16. E. A. Ayandele, *The Missionary Impact on Modern Nigeria, 1842–1914: A Political and Social Analysis* (New York: Humanities Press, 1967), chap. 1.

17. J. D. Y. Peel, "Conversion and Tradition in Two African Societies: Ijebu and Buganda," *Past and Present* 77 (November 1977): 132, while accepting the notion of identity investment, gives a slightly different assessment of the trade-offs.

18. Respondents were permitted to list as many changes as they wanted. See chap. 3 for a discussion of the meaning of "civilization" in this context.

19. Peel (n. 13), p. 171. The composition of my sample will be discussed in the section "Field Methods" in this Appendix.

20. Oyo State of Nigeria, *Report on the Survey of Religious Organizations in the Oyo State*, Ministry of Finance and Economic Development, Statistics Division, Ibadan (1977), p. 25. For other estimates, see J. D. Y. Peel, "Religious Change in Yorubaland," *Africa* (London) 37, no. 3 (July 1967): 301; J. K. Parratt, "Religious Change in Yoruba Society: A Test Case," *Journal of Religion in Africa* (Leiden) 2, no. 2 (1969): 113–4; and I. H. Van den Driesen, "Some Observations on the Family Unit, Religion, and the Practice of Polygyny in the Ife Division of Western Nigeria," *Africa* (London) 42, no. 1 (January 1972): 51.

21. Phillips Diaries (n. 14), 21 March 1900, and 19 November 1904. See also CMS Archives (Birmingham) (G3 A2/0/1902/128), Rev. Kayode, "The Report of the Work at Modakeke and Ife, June, 1902"; and M. A. Fubunmi, *Itan Ibere Ęsin Kristi ni Ile-Ifę ati Agbegbe* (Ile-Ife; Kosalabaro Press, 1970), p. 11.

22. Oyo State, *Report* (n. 20), p. 7. The Baptists came in second with 15.8 percent. Next came the Aladura-type Christ Apostolic Church, with 13 percent of the Christians. See also Parratt (n. 20), p. 120.

23. J. D. Y. Peel, *Aladura: A Religious Movement among the Yoruba* (London: Oxford University Press, 1968), chap. 6.

24. Gbadamosi, (n. 11), p. 3.

25. S. A. Adewale, "African Traditional Religious Teachings and Nigerian Unity," in Balogun (n. 11), pp. 245–46.

26. Interview with Alhaji M. A. Omotoso, 23 August 1977, Ibadan.

27. Gbadamosi (n. 11), p. 146.

28. Obedene Otojabere, in the column "The People's Parliament," *Daily Times* (Lagos), 28 July 1979.

29. More technically: our variables should be universal; our indicators particularistic.

Guide to Proper Names

Action Group (AG): The first major Yoruba political party. Many of the Action Groupers, including Chief Awolowo, formed the nucleus of the Yoruba-dominated Unity Party of Nigeria in order to contest elections in Nigeria's Second Republic.

Alaafin: The king of Oyo

Awolowo, Chief Obafemi: A leading Yoruba nationalist figure, and founder of the *Egbe Qmọ Oduduwa*, the society that formed the basis of the Action Group, the dominant political party among the Yorubas in the First Republic. He was twice the presidential standard bearer of the Unity Party of Nigeria in the Second Republic. He is an Ijebu Christian.

Azikiwe, Nnamdi: A leader of the earliest Nigerian nationalist movement, the NCNC. He became the first president of the Nigerian Senate and governor-general of the Nigerian Federation. Azikiwe is not a Yoruba but an Igbo. His party nonetheless had early successes in a number of Yoruba cities.

Bendel: A state in the Nigerian Federation, carved from the old Western Region, which has a population of numerous (non-Yoruba) minority tribes.

Civil War: (a) The nineteenth-century civil war that involved coalitions of Yoruba city kingdoms fighting among themselves after the fall of the Oyo Empire. (b) A three-year civil war following the 1967 attempt of the Eastern Region of Nigeria, at that time dominated by the Igbo people, to secede from the Federation as the independent republic of Biafra; the federal forces were able to defeat the secessionists.

Egba: A Yoruba subgroup that was far too decentralized to be called a single city-kingdom. In the post Oyo Empire period, its center became Abeokuta, but the Egbas never developed a city-kingdom on the model of Oyo.

Fulani: The cattle-herding people who populate much of the West African savannah. A Fulani Muslim, Uthman dan Fodio, conquered much of what is today Northern Nigeria, in an early nineteenth-century jihad. The Nigerian Fulanis have intermixed with the sedentary Hausa peoples, who were the major recipients of the jihad.

Hausa: The people who populate much of the northern states of contemporary Nigeria. Their language is the lingua franca of those northern states.

Ibadan: The refugee center and home of the army that controlled vast areas of Yorubaland during the nineteenth-century Yoruba civil wars. Today it is the largest inland city in West Africa.

Ibo: Anglicized spelling for Igbo.

Ife: Short for Ile-Ife.

Igbo: The non-Yoruba peoples who were the dominant group of the old Eastern Region of Nigeria. They tried to form the secessionist state of Biafra in 1967.

241

From the old Eastern Region, two present-day states—Anambra and Imo—are predominantly Igbo.

Ijebu: A city-kingdom never fully incorporated into the Oyo Empire. Ijebu peoples long resisted common identification with Yoruba culture. Chief Awolowo—an Ijebu man—actively promoted a common Yoruba identity that included the Ijebu.

Ile-Ife: According to Yoruba myth, the founding city of the Yoruba peoples. It has long been considered the religious center of the Yoruba "traditional religion."

Ilorin: The Yoruba city-kingdom that sparked the revolt against Oyo in the nineteenth century. It was then ruled by a Fulani emirate from Northern Nigeria and in colonial times was administered as part of the Northern Region.

Kwara: A state in the Nigerian Federation inhabited by Yorubas and many other peoples from Nigeria's north. Ilorin, a Yoruba city, is its capital.

Lagos: A Yoruba city and the capital of Nigeria. (A new capital city, Abuja, will replace Lagos). Lagos is the commercial center of Nigeria, its chief port, and the capital of Lagos State.

Modakeke: A section of Ile-Ife settled by Oyo refugees amid the civil wars of the nineteenth century. The refugees' descendants still live there.

NCNC: A Nigerian nationalist party, organized by Herbert Macauley and Nnamdi Azikiwe in 1944. Its original name was the National Council of Nigeria and the Cameroons. Later, those initials stood for National Convention of Nigerian Citizens. Originally it was a party intending to recruit an all-Nigerian constituency. After independence, it became the party of the Igbo peoples of the Eastern Region. It did maintain considerable support in Ibadan, Lagos, and a few other Yoruba cities.

Ogun: A Yoruba state in the Nigerian Federation that encompasses the Egba subtribe and the old Ijebu city-kingdom.

Ondo: (a) A Yoruba city-kingdom. (b) One of Nigeria's nineteen states, which includes the old Ondo city-kingdom as well as Ekiti and Owo.

Ọọni: The King of Ile-Ife.

Oyo: (a) The political capital of the Oyo Empire (1600–1836), which had sovereignty over much of what came to be known as Yorubaland. (b) The city about 100 miles south of old-Oyo, to which the Oyo king (Alaafin) and his followers fled upon the fall of the empire. (c) The people all over Yorubaland who identify with the Oyo city-kingdom as their ancestral city. (d) The state in central Yorubaland in the present Nigerian Federation that encompasses new-Oyo, Ibadan, Ile-Ife, and Ogbomosho.

Second Republic: Nigeria's regime from 1979 to December 1983, when it was replaced by a military regime. Nigeria had received independence in 1960. Its first Republic (declared in 1963) lasted until overthrown by a military coup in 1966. The military then held power for thirteen years until replaced by the Second Republic.

UPN: The Yoruba-dominated party of Nigeria's Second Republic. It stands for the Unity Party of Nigeria.

Yorubaland: The geographic zone populated by Yoruba-speaking peoples. Never have all Yoruba-speaking peoples shared membership in a single sovereign state, though the Oyo Empire, at its height in the eighteenth century, consolidated a large number of Yoruba-speaking kingdoms and included few non-Yoruba areas. Today, there are about 15 million Yorubas, who live predominantly in Lagos, Oyo, Ogun, Ondo, and Kwara States of Nigeria, and in the eastern portion of the Benin Republic (formerly Dahomey); Yoruba communities extend as far west as Togo. Unless otherwise specified, the term "Yorubaland" in this text refers to the Yoruba-speaking areas within the present boundaries of Nigeria.

Index

Delta church, 47
Democracy, 77. *See also* Equality
Dual Mandate, The (Lugard), 163

Edos, 8, 111
Education: under British, 154; Christian-Moslem differences in, 126–29; issue of free, 79–80
Education Law, 131
Efiks, 8
Egbas, 115, 117, 131, 145, 156, 179–80; in Abeokuta, and trade, 119–20; under British rule, 153; and Christianity, 42, 43, 46
Ẹgbẹ, 60, 61, 85, 137, 138, 145
Ẹgbẹ Ọmọ Ibilẹ Ifẹ, 124
Ẹgbẹ Ọmọ Oduduwa, 121, 155
Eighteenth Brumaire of Louis Napoleon (Marx), 173
Ekiti, 59, 118, 121, 153, 157
Ekitiparapọ, 116, 157
Ẹla, 49
Enuwa Mosque: observations at, 61–62, 65–66, 71–72, 87, 89; research methodology at, 194–97
Epe, 41, 154
Equality: in Christianity, 30–31, 67–72; in Islam, 29–31, 67–72, 90; and political attitudes, 82–88; sexual, 70–72, 84
Evolués, 164–67
Evolution, of religion, 88–90

Fafunwa, A. B., 127
Fakayode, E. O., 64–65
Family: change in, under Ibadan system, 118; and religious politicization, 136, 140–45; Victorian ideology of, 71
Fani-Kayode, R. A., 64, 124–25
Federal Sharia Court of Appeal (FSCA), 1–6, 8–11, 133
Femia, Joseph, 105
Fisher, H. J., 37
Fon, 165
Fonctionnaires, 164, 166
Foreign Mission Journal, 46
France, 119–20; and Benin, 164–67, 174
Freeman, Thomas Birch, 42
Freetown, Sierra Leone, 39, 42, 53
FSCA. *See* Federal Sharia Court of Appeal

Fulanis, 11, 39, 48, 155, 157; Islam of, 34; in Kwara State, 10; of northern Nigeria, 91, 160–64; and Oyo Empire, 114–15, 130; as tribal group, 6–8
Fuller, F. C., 151

Gaventa, John, 103–4, 150
Gbadamosi, T. G. O., 37, 126, 202–3
Gbagbọ, 139–40
Geertz, Clifford, 97–98, 172–81, 186; on cultural analysis, 185; his *Islam Observed*, 23, 24, 85; on religion, 23–24, 28, 50, 85, 90; social systems theory of, 12–17; his "Thick Description," 14, 98
Germany, Anabaptists in, 91
Ghana, 147
GNPP (Great Nigeria Peoples' Party), 162
Goethe, Johann Wolfgang von, 188
Gongola, 8
Gouns, 165, 167
Gourevitch, Peter, 103
Gowon, Yakabu, 2, 8, 134
Gramsci, Antonio, 19, 92, 104–6, 150, 168, 182–83
Grand Alliance, 121
Great Britain, 121, 123, 145; and civil wars in Yorubaland, 116, 119, 177; and conversions to Christianity, 42–48; and conversions to Islam, 39, 40; indirect rule in northern Nigeria by, 160–61, 182; indirect rule in Yorubaland by, 150–60, 168; and Islamic court system, 1–2, 4; and regions of Nigeria, 8
Grier, S. M., 152
Growth of Islam among the Yoruba, The (Gbadamosi), 202–3

Hallen, Barry, 139–40, 190
Harun, 137–38
Hashim, 31
Hausa-Fulanis. *See* Fulanis; Hausas
Hausas, 11, 129, 155, 158; Cohen study of, 15; Islam of, 38–40, 52–53; in Kwara State, 10; of northern Nigeria, 91, 160–63; and Oyo Empire, 115, 130; retribalization of, in Ibadan, 101; as tribal group, 6–8
Hechter, Michael, 103

Yorubas (*cont.*)
field observations, 55–74; reasons for conversions of, 36–38; religions of, 6–8, 17; and Sharia issue, 5–6, 8–11; socioeconomic divide among, 126–29; traditional religion of, *see* Yoruba traditional religion; two problematics of, stated, 16–17
Yoruba traditional religion: adherence to, 142; and evangelists, 189–90; influence of world religions on, 138–39; perceived as "deep," 203; and religious syncretism, 85; and world religions compared, 34–36

Young, Crawford, 98–99

Zaire, 98–99
Zinsou, Emile, 166
Zolberg, Aristide, 91